Developing Self-Regulating Learners

DEBORAH L. BUTLER
University of British Columbia

LEYTON SCHNELLERT
University of British Columbia

NANCY E. PERRY
University of British Columbia

PEARSON

Toronto

Editorial Director: Claudine O'Donnell
Acquisitions Editor: Kimberley Veevers
Senior Marketing Manager: Michelle Bish
Program Manager: John Polansky
Project Manager: Sarah Gallagher
Manager of Content Development: Suzanne Schaan
Developmental Editor: Johanna Schlaepfer
Production Services: Garima Khosla, iEnergizer Aptara®, Ltd.
Permissions Project Manager: Alison Derry
Photo Permissions Research: Navin Kumar Srinivasan, Integra
Text Permissions Research: Renae Horstman, Integra
Interior and cover Designer: iEnergizer Aptara®, Ltd.
Cover Image: KidStock/Blend Images/Getty Images; Syda Productions/Shutterstock;
    oliveromg/Shutterstock; WavebreakMediaMicro/Fotolia; bikeriderlondon/Shutterstock;
    Lord and Leverett/Pearson Education.
Vice-President, Cross Media and Publishing Services: Gary Bennett

Library and Archives Canada Cataloguing in Publication

Butler, Deborah Lynne, 1958–, author
    Developing self-regulating learners / Deborah Butler, Leyton Schnellert, Nancy Perry.

    Includes index.
    ISBN 978-0-13-390690-5 (paperback)

    1. Learning. 2. Self-control. 3. Study skills. 4. Academic achievement.
I. Schnellert, Leyton, author II. Perry, Nancy E. (Nancy Ellen), 1962–, author III. Title.

LB1060.B877 2015   370.15'23   C2015-906581-X

2   16

ISBN 13: 978-0-13-390690-5

PEARSON

Dedication

To all educators who strive to foster the development of self-regulating learners.

This book would not have come to fruition without the considerable patience, goodwill, and insights of our spouses. Thank you Teresa, Trevor and Phil for your support and wisdom.

Contents

Part 3   Pulling it All Together: The Promise of Supporting Self-Regulated Learning   141

10 Meeting the Needs of Diverse Learners   141

11 Motivating and Engaging Learners   162

Preface

WHY MIGHT YOU READ THIS BOOK?

What might attract you to reading this book? Perhaps you are interested in learning more about highly effective teaching and learning practices, and wonder where *self-regulated learning (SRL)* fits in? Or, perhaps you already know something about self-regulation, but want to learn more, for example, about why *self-regulation* is so essential in *learning*, what SRL looks like in classrooms, or how you can design classroom practices to support the development of *self-regulating learners*? If you have questions of this sort, this book is designed for you! Our goal is to engage educators in considering the nature of SRL and how to support it in classrooms.

If you have not yet thought about why you might read this book, we invite you to take a moment to consider that at the outset (see *Food for Thought* below). What specific questions do you have about SRL? What goals might you have that could be informed by this reading? You will get the most out of a resource like this one if you bridge what you are reading with what you are seeing in practice. To that end, we encourage you to consider how and why reading this book might help you achieve your goals for your own professional learning.

> ## Food for Thought
> ## Your Goals for Reading this Book
>
> 1. What do you already know about self-regulation and self-regulated *learning*?
>
> 2. What do you wonder? What do you already do to foster self-regulated learning in your context?
>
> 3. What do you wonder?

WHY FOCUS ON SELF-REGULATED LEARNING?

In the introduction to his 2013 book, *Calm, Alert, and Learning: Classroom Strategies for Self-Regulation*, Stuart Shanker makes a persuasive case for prioritizing attention to self-regulation. He argues that,

> We are in the midst of a revolution in educational thinking and practice. Scientific advances in a number of fields point to a similar argument—how well students do in school can be determined by how well they are able to self-regulate. Some theorists believe that self-regulation should now be considered a more important indicator of educational performance than IQ (Blair & Diamond, 2008; Duckworth & Seligman, 2005; Shonkoff & Phillips, 2000). (Shanker, 2013, p. ix)

Like Shanker and the other colleagues he cites, we are convinced that fostering self-regulation, and, more specifically, self-regulated *learning*, is an essential aim if we are to support students to succeed in school. We would add that it is also abundantly clear that students have to know *how to learn*, not just while in our school systems, but also through the next 70 to 80 years of their lives (Gerber, 2001). If students are to thrive in our current fast-paced, ever-evolving societies, we cannot rely on teaching them content they can count on for the rest of their lives or careers. Our students need to become lifelong learners who can find, generate, and think critically with ideas that we haven't even thought of today. They must be prepared to seize opportunities and overcome challenges we can't yet even imagine (Dumont, Istance, & Benavides, 2012).

By fostering the development of self-regulating learners, we can empower students to succeed, not just during the school years, but also into their lives long after.

What characterizes successful, lifelong learning? Barry Zimmerman, an American Psychological Association lifetime achievement award winner, argues that lifelong learners are *self-regulating* (Zimmerman, 2002). Self-regulating learners know how to read situations, determine goals, and take deliberate control over action. They persist in the face of obstacles and persevere through difficulty. They engage in iterative cycles of deliberate, strategic problem solving over time to achieve their goals. So, why should we focus on fostering the development of self-regulating learners? Our response is that because in so doing we empower students to succeed, not just during the school years, but also into their lives long after.

ORGANIZATION: UNDERSTANDING AND SUPPORTING SELF-REGULATED LEARNING

We wrote this book to serve as a resource to educators interested in understanding and supporting SRL. The book is organized into three parts that combine to achieve this purpose.

Part One of this book presents "portraits of SRL" designed to help educators define self-regulated learning (Chapter 1), consider why fostering SRL is so important (Chapter 2), and see relationships between SRL, social-emotional learning, and executive functioning (Chapter 3). Then, building from those three opening chapters, we identify goals important in fostering SRL (Chapter 4). You should come away from this first part of the book with a clear vision of goals essential in fostering rich forms of SRL by learners in your context.

Part Two of this book describes and illustrates SRL–promoting practices. We launch this part of the book by describing how educators can establish safe and supportive learning environments necessary for learners to engage in rich forms of learning and SRL (Chapter 5). Then, we offer guidelines educators can follow when building opportunities and supports for SRL into those environments (Chapter 6). Next, we elaborate on how educators can design activities and tasks that create opportunities for rich forms of learning and self-regulation (Chapter 7), build supports into activities that nurture the development of effective forms of SRL (Chapter 8), and structure assessments and feedback to inform and empower learning (Chapter 9). After reading this second part of the book, you should be able to identify important principles and practices you can use to foster the development of *self-regulating learners* in your context.

Part Three deepens the discussion. In this last part of the book, we pull together ideas presented in Parts One and Two to give rich examples of how and why supporting SRL can assist educators in meeting the needs of diverse students (Chapter 10); motivating and empowering learners (Chapter 11); and, ultimately, empowering 21st-century learning (Chapter 12). Our concluding reflection invites you to consider how you might build from the ideas introduced in this book, on your own or collaboratively with others, to support the development of self-regulating learners both within and outside of schools (Epilogue).

THIS BOOK AS A RESOURCE TO PROFESSIONAL LEARNING AND INQUIRY

In our work with preservice and in-service educators, we often use an *inquiry* framework to support their professional learning. We expect that this book will be a valuable resource to any educator wishing to learn more about SRL and how to support it. But we also imagine it as a particularly useful resource for individuals or teams of educators engaged in inquiry with the goal of developing SRL–promoting policies and practices in their particular contexts.

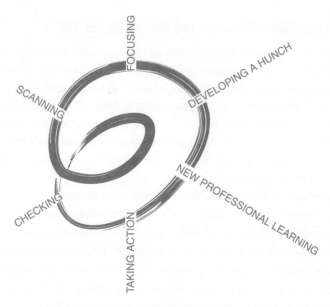

Figure A Spirals of Inquiry

Source: Halbert, J., & Kaser, L. (2013). Spirals of inquiry for equity and quality. British Columbia (BC): BC Principals' and Vice-Principals' Association.

What does *inquiry* look like? Based on their extensive professional development leadership, Judy Halbert and Linda Kaser (2013) recently described *inquiry processes* as unfolding in spirals (see Figure A). In their model, inquiry often begins when educators *scan* their current context to identify pressing questions, challenges, or goals; decide to *focus* attention on a key priority; and *develop a hunch* about what might be happening. Inquiring educators then deliberately engage in *new professional learning* to inform their practice development. They *take action* based on what they are learning, reflectively *check* on what happens, and then refine inquiry questions and processes based on successes and challenges. Research suggests that engaging in iterative cycles of inquiry is a powerful way for educators to structure and sustain their on-going professional learning (see Timperley, 2011).

In our own research on inquiry-based professional learning, we have documented the power of inquiry-based professional development frameworks for both teachers and students (e.g., see Butler & Schnellert, 2012; Butler, Schnellert, & Cartier, 2013; Perry, Brenner, & Fusaro, 2015; Schnellert, 2011; Schnellert & Butler, 2014). We have also shown that an important condition for teachers' learning and practice change is that they have access to rich resources that can inform their engagement in inquiry cycles.

However, as we worked with teachers, we realized we needed *a resource specifically crafted to inform teachers' inquiry about self-regulation in relation to learning.* We wrote this book in order to meet that need. Our hope is that this book will be useful to educators wishing to inquire about SRL, whether they are just developing their identities, knowledge, and competencies within a preservice program or are practicing professionals seeking to learn more about these topics (e.g., on their own, within a graduate-level program, in collaboration with colleagues).

What Kinds of Questions Have Teachers Been Asking?

In Table A, we summarize themes underlying some of the inquiry questions new and experienced teachers have been asking within our professional learning projects. These themes reflect questions being taken up by preservice teachers in a university-based teacher

Table A	Questions Educators Are Asking about SRL

- Is there a difference between self-regulation and self-regulated learning?
- How can we create a safe and supportive early primary classroom that fosters SRL?
- How could changes to the physical learning space in an intermediate classroom support a community of self-regulating learners to engage in deep forms of inquiry?
- How can I support cultural diversity in an SRL–supportive classroom and community?
- How can educators make learning meaningful for Aboriginal students while focusing on SRL?
- If students learn to recognize, use, and evaluate strategies for managing emotions, will their focus and reading improve?
- How can I motivate students to engage in SRL and active learning?
- How can kindergarten teachers support self-regulation through play?
- How can I integrate supports for SRL into inquiry-based or research projects?
- How can I promote self-regulation to support students' organizational abilities?
- If we explicitly teach and model SRL strategies, will students take ownership over learning?
- How can formative assessment help in developing SRL among middle school students?
- How does feedback affect student progress and development of SRL?
- How can co-regulation between peers be an effective strategy for teaching self-regulation?
- How can I work with parents to support SRL by students?

education program, practicing teachers working within collaborative learning teams, and graduate students enrolled in masters-level courses. Whatever the context for their professional learning, these educators have shared an interest in connecting their learning about SRL with practice or policy as relevant to their contexts.

We invite you to imagine whether any of these questions might be meaningful in your work with students. If so, we hope you will take this opportunity to pick up on one or more of these themes. Certainly, as you work through this book, you will be invited to advance your professional learning in relation to questions that are most meaningful in your context.

FEATURES: SUPPORTING YOUR INQUIRY INTO SELF-REGULATED LEARNING

As you read this book, you will notice that we include pedagogical features designed to support your engagement in inquiry processes, should you wish to take up this model of professional learning (see Figure A). Across chapters, whenever we describe strategies and provide concrete examples, inquiry-oriented activities will assist you in considering how to refine practices, take action, check on progress towards goals, and/or imagine next steps for ongoing practice and learning. For example, tools are provided to support you in *scanning* for evidence of SRL in action (Chapter 1), *focusing* on the needs of learners in your context and developing a *hunch* about what might be needed to support them effectively (Chapter 4), and *taking action* and *reflecting* on implications (Chapters 5, 7, 8, and 9).

We also include many pedagogical features designed to support your active learning about SRL and how to support it in your context:

Activities
Activities will support you to work with and apply key themes from each chapter.

SRL Vignettes
We present extended "SRL Vignettes" to help you imagine SRL in action both within and outside of schools. These boxes are designed to help you make connections between theory and practice.

Starting Small

In our Starting Small feature, we offer examples of how other educators have taken first steps in building SRL–promoting practices into their own teaching.

Food for Thought

Our Food for Thought feature will provoke your thinking about key ideas in relation to your own learning, practice, or inquiry.

SRL Planning Tools

Many chapters contain a "SRL Planning Tool," a template designed to help you consider how to integrate SRL–promoting practices into your own work with learners.

Links to Resources

Links to Resources will direct you to accessible sources of additional tools, examples or information.

Other Features

- **Learning Intentions** are listed at the beginning of each chapter to signal what you should be able to do after engaging with the material.
- **Key Terms** are bolded when first introduced and are defined in the Glossary.
- **Margin Notes** are provided to help you in focusing and reflecting on key points.
- **Recommended Resources** are provided at the end of each chapter to identify related readings you can access for further information.

While this book is ideal for supporting educators engaged in inquiry-based professional learning, it is certainly not necessary for you to take that approach to profit from this publication. Whether or not you choose to adopt an inquiry framework, your learning through reading this book will be enhanced if you use it as a resource for learning about something you care about deeply and that you think will make a significant difference for students. Based on overwhelming research evidence coupled with practice-based insights developed in collaboration with teachers, we are convinced that supporting SRL is something worth caring about deeply. SRL is hugely consequential in students' success, not only during the school years, but into adulthood. Through engaging with this book and the various kinds of learning supports embedded within it, we hope that you too will have the opportunity to appreciate and witness the power of SRL as a framework for advancing students' learning in classrooms and beyond.

Links to Resources

Butler, D. L., & Schnellert, L. (2012). Collaborative inquiry in teacher professional development. *Teaching and Teacher Education, 28*, 1206–1220.

Butler, D. L., Schnellert, L., & Cartier, S. C. (2013). Layers of self- and co-regulation: Teachers' co-regulating learning and practice to foster students' self-regulated learning through reading. *Education Research International*. DOI:10.1155/2013/845694

Dumont, H., Istance, D., & Benavides, F. (Eds.) (2012). The nature of learning: Using research to inspire practice. Practitioner Guide from the Innovative Learning Environments Project. OECD: Centre for Educational Research and Innovation.

Gerber, P. J. (2001). Learning disabilities: A life span approach. In D. P. Hallahan & B. K. Keogh (Eds.), *Research and global perspectives in learning disabilities* (pp. 167–180). Mahwah, NJ: Erlbaum.

Halbert, J., & Kaser, L. (2013). *Spirals of inquiry for equity and quality*. British Columbia (BC): BC Principals' and Vice-Principals' Association.

Perry, N. E., Brenner, C. A., & Fusaro, N. (2015). Closing the gap between theory and practice in self-regulated learning: Teacher learning teams as a framework for enhancing self-regulated teaching and learning. In T. J. Cleary (Ed.) *Self-regulated learning interventions with at risk populations: Academic, mental health, and contextual considerations* (pp. 229–250). Washington, DC: American Psychological Association.

Schnellert, L. (2011). Collaborative inquiry: Teacher professional development as situated, responsive co-construction of practice and learning. (Doctoral dissertation). Retrieved from https://circle.ubc.ca/handle/2429/38245.

Schnellert, L., & Butler, D. L. (2014). Collaborative inquiry for teacher development. *Education Canada.* Available at http://www.cea-ace.ca/education-canada/article/collaborative-inquiry.

Shanker, S. (2013). *Calm, alert, and learning: Classroom strategies for self-regulation.* Don Mills, ON: Pearson.

Timperley, H. (2011). *Realizing the power of professional learning.* NY: Open University Press.

Zimmerman, B. J. (2002). Becoming a self-regulated learner: An overview. *Theory into Practice, 41*(2), 64–70.

LEARNING RESOURCES FOR CLASSROOM USE

There might be times when instructors would like to take up this book in their classes. Pearson Canada provides a number of complementary resources to support use of the book for that purpose.

Pearson eText

Pearson eText gives students access to the book whenever and wherever they have access to the Internet. eText pages look exactly like the printed text, offering powerful new functionality for readers and instructors. Users can create notes, highlight text in different colours, create bookmarks, zoom, click hyperlinked words and phrases to view definitions, and view in single-page or two-page view. Pearson eText allows for quick navigation to key parts of the eText using a table of contents and provides full-text search.

Learning Solutions Managers

Pearson's Learning Solutions Managers work with faculty and campus course designers to ensure that Pearson technology products, assessment tools, and online course materials are tailored to meet your specific needs. This highly qualified team is dedicated to helping schools take full advantage of a wide range of educational resources, by assisting in the integration of a variety of instructional materials and media formats. Your local Pearson sales representative can provide you with more details on this service program.

ACKNOWLEDGMENTS

We would like to acknowledge the contributions to our thinking of the many teachers who have shared their expertise with us across the past 20+ years, whose work inspired this book. In addition, we would like to thank the following educators who have agreed over time to share their work with us and other educators interested in SRL:

Briana Adams	Shelley Moore
Denise Briard	Kim Ondrik
Paul Britton	Jennifer Ross
Christy Catton	Brigitte Sebulsky
April Chan	Amy Semple
Lynn Drummond	Darcy Vogel
Dave Dunnigan	Linda Watson
Janelle Feenan	Nicole Widdess
Sheri Gurney	

We would like to acknowledge and thank our colleagues for their contributions, to frameworks we build on, examples we provide, and/or tools we included to support educators' collaborative inquiry into practice. We are particularly grateful to:

Maureen Dockendorf	Linda Kaser
Judy Halbert	Niamh Kelly
Sharon Jeroski	Simon Lisiango

In particular, we would like to thank Linda Kaser and Judy Halbert for their consistent, compelling, and enthusiastic encouragement for us to author this book.

Finally, we would like to thank colleagues who took time to provide thorough and thoughtful reviews of early versions of this book:

Dawn Buzza, Wilfrid Laurier University
Sylvie Cartier, Université de Montréal
Carol Hryniuk-Adamov
Nancy L. Hutchinson, Queen's University
Ben Pare, Burnaby School District
Pamela Richardson, University of British Columbia, Okanagan
Gabrielle Young, Memorial University of Newfoundland

About the Authors

DEBORAH L. BUTLER has many years of teaching experience, particularly in supporting diverse learners in secondary and post-secondary settings. She is currently a Professor in the Faculty of Education at the University of British Columbia (UBC). At UBC, she coordinates the Faculty's innovative inquiry-based programs designed to support educators interested in fostering self-regulated learning (see http://pdce.educ.ubc.ca/srl-inquiry-hub-2015-learning-teams/ and http://ecps.educ.ubc.ca/human-development-learning-and-culture/hdlc-graduate-programs/concentration-in-self-regulated-learning-srl/). In her collaborative research with educational partners, she has studied how to support academic success by students with diverse learning needs in support contexts and inclusive classrooms, how and why supporting self-regulated learning is so key to empowering learners, and how teachers can work together, in communities of inquiry, to construct practices that achieve positive outcomes for students. Since joining UBC in 1994, she has published an edited book and over 40 influential articles and book chapters, presented over 60 refereed papers at national or international conferences, and produced over 100 research reports for educational partners and/or government.

LEYTON SCHNELLERT is a passionate educator who has been a middle and secondary years classroom teacher and learning resource teacher, K–12. He is currently an Assistant Professor in the Faculty of Education at The University of British Columbia–Okanagan (UBC-O). His research attends to how teachers and learners can mindfully embrace student diversity, inclusive education, self- and co-regulation and pedagogical practices that draw from students' funds of knowledge to build participatory, collaborative, and culturally-responsive learning communities. He is the lead for the Pedagogy and Participation research cluster in UBC-O's Institute for Community Engaged Research. His scholarship takes up pedagogy and research methodologies that work from epistemological orientations to living and learning that are relational and community-honouring. He has presented and published his work in local, provincial, national and international forums. He has also co-authored 6 books for educators including *Student Diversity*, *It's All About Thinking* and *Pulling Together*.

NANCY E. PERRY worked as a classroom and resource teacher in school districts in British Columbia, Canada, before obtaining her PhD from the University of Michigan in 1996. Today, she is Professor in the Department of Educational and Counselling Psychology, and Special Education at the University of British Columbia (UBC). There she teaches courses across two program areas: Human Development, Learning, and Culture and Special Education. She is a recipient of UBC's Killam Teaching Prize and holds the Dorothy Lam Chair in Special Education. Her research program, "Seeding Success through Motivation and Self-Regulation in Schools," is profiled on her Web site: http://self-regulationinschool.research.educ.ubc.ca. Currently, she is a section editor for the *Journal of Learning and Instruction* and serves on the editorial boards of the *Educational Psychologist*, *Metacognition and Learning*, and *Teachers College Record*. She is a Past President of the Canadian Association for Educational Psychology and currently is President of Division 15 (Educational Psychology) of the American Psychological Association.

Chapter 1
What Is Self-Regulated Learning?

Christopher Futcher/E+/
Getty Images

INTRODUCTION

This book is designed to serve as a resource for educators interested in learning more about *self-regulated learning* (SRL) and how to support the development of *self-regulating learners*. Toward these ends, Part One of this book engages readers with ideas, examples, and activities to help them construct a rich understanding about SRL and, correspondingly, the goals they need to set if they are to support SRL in their contexts. The present chapter is the first of four that make up this introductory part of the book.

Learning Intentions

By the end of this chapter, you should be able to do the following:

LI 1   Define *self-regulation* and *self-regulated learning* (SRL) and the relationship between them.

LI 2   Identify key dimensions of self-regulation, including *cognition* and *metacognition*, *motivation* and *emotions*, and *strategic action*, as well as how those dimensions are implicated in learning activities.

LI 3   Imagine rich examples of SRL in your own and others' learning experiences.

WHAT DO YOU KNOW ABOUT SELF-REGULATED LEARNING?

To anchor our consideration of SRL, an important first step is for you to articulate what you already know. To support you in that, we encourage you to record your answers to the questions in Activity 1-1. As you work through this book, you will have opportunities to consider how your initial understandings about SRL might be shifting or deepening through what you are reading and observing.

What you'll notice is that the first two questions in Activity 1-1 ask you to identify what you know already about self-regulation and SRL, based on your previous formal learning and professional experience. We recommend that you keep your prior knowledge in mind as you read this book, noting when what you are reading is consonant with or divergent from your initial thinking. We also recommend that you reflect regularly about how what you are reading is advancing your understanding about the questions you are bringing to this book.

The third question in Activity 1-1 asks you to reflect on the photo at the opening of this chapter. Consider whether and how this picture captures your current understanding about self-regulation or SRL. What is consistent with your current thinking? What, if anything, about the picture is surprising or different than what you have been imagining?

A CLASSIC DEFINITION OF SELF-REGULATION

Barry Zimmerman is a world-renowned scholar who has been highly influential in conceptualizing self-regulation and SRL. In 2008, he provided a widely relied-upon definition of **self-regulation** as *the ability to control thoughts and actions to achieve personal goals and respond to environmental demands*. One key idea within this definition is that self-regulating individuals take *deliberate control* over their engagement in daily activities. Another key idea is that self-regulation is *goal directed*. When they self-regulate, individuals deliberately navigate activities so as to achieve their personal goals. The last key idea in this definition is that self-regulation is *contextualized*. When self-regulating, individuals are working to navigate activities as defined within the environments in which they are living and working.

Individuals self-regulate their engagement in all sorts of different activities, not just learning in classrooms. Models of self-regulation are often used to describe how students engage in academic tasks, such as reading a novel; learning from informational texts; writing stories, poems, or essays; solving math problems; and researching in classrooms. But individuals also self-regulate in all sorts of other activities both inside and outside of schools. For example, individuals self-regulate in workplaces whenever they strive to attain goals necessary for success in those contexts. Teachers are self-regulating when they plan a lesson to achieve goals for students. Physicians self-regulate as they try to determine

> **Self-regulation** refers to the ability to control thoughts and actions to achieve personal goals and respond to environmental demands. It is a term that is broadly applicable and can be used to describe an individual's engagement in any sort of activity.

> Activity 1-1
What Do You Already Know about Self-Regulated Learning?

Before you read this chapter, take a moment to answer these questions:

1. What have you heard or read about self-regulation? Can you think of an example of self-regulation in your own experience or context? What do you wonder?

2. How do you think self-regulation applies to *learning*? Can you imagine an example of self-regulated learning

(SRL) in your own experience or context? What do you wonder?

3. Take a look at the photograph at the opening of this chapter. Does this photograph reflect your current understanding of self-regulation or SRL? What aspects of the picture are consistent with or differ from your current understanding?

what is troubling a patient. Individuals are also self-regulating when they drive or shop for groceries or make a plan with friends to go to the movies.

What, then, is the relationship between self-regulation and self-regulated learning (SRL)? In our view, self-regulation is a term that is more broadly applicable and can be used to describe an individual's engagement in any sort of activity. In contrast, **Self-regulated learning (SRL)** occurs in the subset of activities during which individuals are deliberately seeking to learn. In this book, we will focus primarily on how we can foster the development of self-regulating learners.

Self-regulated learning (SRL) occurs is self-regulation in the subset of activities in which individuals are focused on self-regulating *learning*.

DEVELOPING SELF-REGULATING LEARNERS

The title of this book is *Developing Self-Regulating Learners*. We use this language very intentionally to emphasize that self-regulation is a *process*. It is *not* a stable trait that individuals have or don't have or that they carry around with them from context to context. Self-regulation is what individuals do all the time to navigate day-to-day activities, albeit more or less successfully. It follows that fostering effective forms of self-regulation is a means to an end rather than a goal on its own. Our aim is to support the development of self-regulating readers, writers, researchers, or learners. Fortunately, there is much that educators can do to assist *all* students in learning how to engage in effective forms of self-regulation in all sorts of different activities.

A key idea that we will come back to over and over in this book is that individuals can take and feel in control over their learning and success if they deliberately and reflectively self-regulate their engagement in activities. Our job as educators is to assist students in taking deliberate control over their participation in the various kinds of activities they are engaged in both in and outside of school.

Individuals can take and feel in control over their learning and success if they deliberately and reflectively self-regulate their engagement in activities.

Furthermore, it is essential to recognize that self-regulating individuals are active agents in thinking through and managing their engagement (Bandura, 2006). It is they who have to understand and self-regulate their engagement in activities while working alone or with others. Teachers, parents, mentors, or peers can support an individual's development of effective approaches to self-regulation. But supporting self-regulation is *not* the same as regulating others; our role is not to control or manage another person's engagement. Our goal is to help individuals take control over their own engagement, so that they can *be* and *feel* empowered to understand and navigate environments successfully.

SELF-REGULATION ACROSS THE LIFESPAN

Individuals are self-regulating all the time, albeit more or less effectively. Models of self-regulation describe how individuals engage in goal-directed action in all kinds of day-to-day activities. Self-regulation is something that starts in infancy, as young children learn through intentional action. It extends through early childhood, as preschoolers practise taking on different kinds of roles during imaginative play. Older children self-regulate as they learn to navigate the increasingly complex academic tasks set for them in school. In adulthood, we all self-regulate daily as we tackle professional responsibilities or undertake personal pursuits. Thus, our goal as educators is not to develop self-regulation in students per se. Rather, our goal is to support learners to learn how to engage in effective forms of self-regulation within different kinds of activities, including academic work.

Our goal is to support learners to engage in effective forms of self-regulation within different kinds of activities, including academic work.

Imagining Self-Regulated Learning (SRL) in Schools

What does SRL look like in classroom environments? Consider two different students, Brigitte and Stewart, working in Mrs. Nyad's class on the same assignment (see SR Vignette 1-1). Can you identify ways in which each student is self-regulating their learning by making choices to achieve goals within this environment?

More and Less Effective Forms of SRL

Brigitte and Stewart are two students in Mrs. Nyad's Grade 5 classroom. Below are summaries of how each approached a multi-lesson activity for which they had to choose a topic, select and read texts to inform their thinking, write about what they found, and then share their learning with peers. How do their approaches reflect more effective or less effective forms of self-regulation?

Brigitte. As soon as Mrs. Nyad started talking about the assignment, Brigitte panicked and stopped listening to what felt like an overwhelming set of instructions. She worried about how she was going to manage it all. She had no idea what topic to choose or how to decide. Worst was that she realized she had to read. She knew she was going to do miserably and that it was going to take her *forever*. It was so embarrassing when her friends sailed on to the writing part of assignments while she was still struggling with the reading. So, to make sure she could keep up with her friends, she decided to pick a topic she already knew about and a book she knew would be easy. When writing, she copied as much of the language from the book as she could, since that really helped her with explaining and spelling. The only thing she looked forward to was talking about her topic with her classmates. On the day of her presentation, she was excited when she could stand up and tell her peers everything she knew about her topic. Once her presentation was over, she slumped down in her chair, breathing a huge sigh of relief, happy the project was over. She just hoped she wouldn't have to face a similar project too soon.

Stewart. As Mrs. Nyad explained the project to the class, Stewart listened attentively, reading along with the written instructions to ensure he understood the assignment. Even so, once he started working, he realized he didn't understand one point. So, he asked one of his peers about it, a friend of his who he knew would have the answer. He and his friend decided from then on to share ideas as they worked. He was excited that he could choose a topic he wanted to learn more about. He chose a book he knew was difficult because it contained a ton of great information. When he recognized information gaps in that reading, he sought out additional resources. As he read, Stewart organized his notes in categories, based both on samples his teacher provided and ideas he and his friend had generated. Then he organized his presentation around those categories, including the most important and interesting information. Stewart was generally happy with how his presentation went on the day it was his turn to speak. He had been quite anxious when he started to talk, but was pleased that he was able to calm down and focus once he got into it. It had been a good call to organize his information in categories, since that had really helped him stay on track and cover all of the topics he had wanted. Still, he decided that if he had a chance to do another presentation, he would practise more so that he could be less nervous at the beginning.

DIMENSIONS OF SELF-REGULATION

In SR Vignette 1-1 Brigitte and Stewart were working at the same grade level, in the same classroom, on the very same assignment. But how they reacted to and approached the assignment varied across many important dimensions. Models of self-regulation are powerful because they help us to think about the whole person and the many factors that influence how people interpret, react to, and engage in activities. In particular, models of self-regulation explain how an individual's engagement in activities involves these key dimensions: *cognition* and *metacognition*, *motivation* and *emotion*, and *strategic action* (see Figure 1-1). In our description below, we define these dimensions and give examples of how each might be involved in learning activities like the one in Mrs. Nyad's classroom.

Imagining More or Less Effective Forms of SRL in Classrooms

As you read SR Vignette 1-1, what did you notice about Brigitte's and Stewart's approaches that reflect more effective or less effective forms of SRL, at least from their teacher's perspective? What kinds of goals did each student set? Why?

What dimensions of self-regulation did you notice in how they engaged in the activity (e.g., emotions, motivation, and learning processes)?

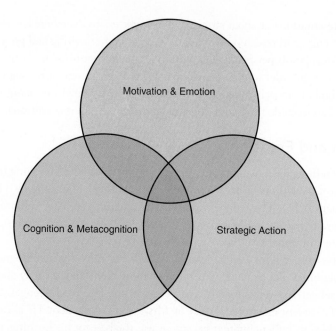

Figure 1-1 Dimensions of Self-Regulation

Source: Reproduced with permission from Butler, Perry, & Schnellert (2015).

Cognition and Metacognition

From an SRL perspective, cognition and metacognition are implicated in most activities. **Cognition** refers to how individuals think when performing activities, such as reading to learn, solving math problems, planning a route to get from A to B, or gathering thoughts for a presentation. Most activities require cognitive processes to achieve task requirements. For example, for Mrs. Nyad's assignment, Brigitte and Stewart engaged in cognitive activities when they read and made meaning from the books they chose, took notes on what they were reading, and prepared a presentation for their peers. But did you notice differences in the cognitive strategies they used to accomplish key task requirements? When taking notes, Brigitte's strategy was to copy points from her reading, while Stewart read for main ideas on particular topics. To structure their class presentations, Stewart organized his ideas in advance around key categories, while Brigitte brainstormed everything she knew about her topic when speaking.

 Metacognition refers to individuals' knowledge about and orchestration of their cognition (Butler, in press; Borkowski, 1992; Brown, 1987; Flavell, 1976, 1987). A key aspect of metacognition is the metacognitive knowledge individuals bring to an activity. **Metacognitive knowledge** is reflected in the understandings individuals bring to activities about the following:

- themselves and their strengths and challenges;
- activities and what they typically require (i.e., what they are being asked to do and what is required to be successful); and
- strategies they might use to accomplish different activities or bridge the gap between what they already can do and what they need to learn.

For example, Brigitte and Stewart brought different kinds of metacognitive knowledge to Mrs. Nyad's assignment. Stewart recognized his strengths as a reader and built from relatively well-developed metacognitive knowledge about research projects and about reading, writing, and presentation strategies. For instance, he knew that if he took notes in categories while reading, it would help him plan for his writing and presentation. Brigitte was acutely aware of her reading struggles, which strongly influenced how she approached the assignment. But she did not have strong metacognitive knowledge about the activity (e.g., what

Cognition refers to how individuals think within activities such as reading a textbook, writing, planning a route to get from A to B, or gathering thoughts for a presentation.

Metacognition refers to individuals' knowledge *about* and *orchestration of* cognition.

Metacognitive knowledge is reflected in the understandings individuals bring to activities about learning and themselves as learners.

makes a good presentation) or about strategies she might use to overcome her reading challenges or how to engage in research, take notes, or organize her writing and presenting.

From a self-regulation perspective, cognition and metacognition are both very important to engagement. In order to deliberately manage their engagement through tasks, individuals need to build from rich and productive metacognitive knowledge about themselves, tasks, and strategies to guide their thinking and learning (i.e., their cognition).

Motivation and Emotion

Many models of self-regulation emphasize the importance of children learning to take more deliberate control over their motivation and emotions (e.g., Boekaerts, 2011; Shanker, 2013; Zimmerman, 2011). These dimensions of self-regulation are very important, because it is certainly hard to participate in activities effectively when one is disinterested, stressed, anxious, frustrated, or unhappy.

Motivation is a broad term used to describe what drives individuals' willingness to invest and engage in activities. For example, when highly motivated, students may choose to take up an activity, set activity-related goals, and persist in the face of challenges. Stewart is a good example of a student motivated to take up Mrs. Nyad's assignment. He chose a topic he cared about, tackled a challenging text because it was the best for his learning, and demonstrated considerable initiative (e.g., choosing to work with a peer, defining categories beyond those suggested by his teacher). When he encountered challenges, he found ways around them. In contrast, Brigitte was motivated enough in Mrs. Nyad's classroom to work on each part of the assignment. But she was more motivated to avoid frustration, keep pace with her classmates, and look competent among peers. Consequently, she chose a topic she already knew a lot about and an easy, familiar text she could read quickly. Her personal goal focused more on getting through the task than on learning through the activity.

Emotion refers to individuals' affective responses when presented with or engaged in an activity. How individuals experience and respond to emotions is central to how they engage in activities. For example, students like Brigitte who struggle with reading may feel demoralized when facing a reading task, and get frustrated quickly. In contrast, Stewart was excited about the opportunity to engage in research and so dove into the project enthusiastically. Furthermore, although Stewart found speaking in front of his peers to be stressful, he was able to settle in once he got rolling with the help of his carefully prepared notes. If individuals do not have knowledge and strategies that enable them to manage their emotions during activities, they are likely to avoid the activity altogether or give up quickly when faced with obstacles.

Strategic Action

Finally, self-regulating individuals engage in cycles of strategic action. **Strategic action** includes (1) interpreting tasks and setting goals, (2) planning, (3) enacting strategies, (4) monitoring, and (5) adjusting. For example, to be maximally effective, self-regulating learners in Mrs. Nyad's classroom would take time to interpret the demands of the activity and set goals aligned with activity expectations. They would then make a plan for how to tackle a task and choose a topic, resources, materials, and strategies best matched to accomplishing their goals. They would enact strategies for reading, writing, and presenting. Throughout the task, they would monitor how they were progressing and make adjustments to goals and strategies as needed. Once finished, they would take a moment to reflect on what did and didn't go well, and think ahead about what they might do differently the next time.

In SR Vignette 1-1, both Brigitte and Stewart were engaged in forms of goal-directed strategic action. For example, Stewart worked hard to interpret activity expectations by listening attentively to instructions, following along with a written description while his teacher was explaining, identifying what he did not understand, and asking a friend for clarification. The goals he set for himself were well aligned with his teacher's hopes and expectations.

Motivation is a broad term used to describe what drives individuals' willingness to invest and engage in activities.

Emotion refers to individuals' affective responses when presented with or engaged in an activity (e.g., stress, excitement, pride, anger, frustration).

Strategic action is iterative and includes: (1) interpreting tasks and setting goals, (2) planning, (3) enacting strategies, (4) monitoring, and (5) adjusting.

When planning, he chose a topic and text that would advance his learning. The strategies he chose and enacted were ones that supported him to grapple with ideas and communicate effectively. While reading his chosen text, he monitored whether he had enough information on important topics. When he recognized gaps, he adjusted his approaches by seeking additional information. After his presentation, he judged that his organizational strategies had helped him convey exactly what he had hoped, but concluded that he might have been less nervous at the outset had he practised just a bit more. Ultimately, his approaches enabled him to successfully achieve the goals envisioned by his teacher.

In contrast, while she was excited about talking with peers about her topic, Brigitte did not focus much on interpreting expectations. Instead, she considered how she could achieve her personal goal to get through the task quickly without being embarrassed. When planning, she chose a topic she already knew about and an easy, familiar reading. She also chose and then enacted strategies designed to get through the assignments quickly and bypass anticipated frustration with reading and spelling. When completing the task, she monitored how quickly she was moving through the activity in relation to peers rather than focusing on what she was learning. After her presentation, she was relieved for having "got through" the assignment. While her approaches were successful in achieving her personal goals, the cost was that she did not take advantage of opportunities to build capacity in challenging areas, engage richly with ideas, and/or learn new skills and strategies for reading, writing, or communicating.

MODELS OF SELF-REGULATION: AN INTEGRATIVE FRAMEWORK

Researchers have been investigating self-regulation in the context of all sorts of different activities for well over two decades (for a helpful overview of this history, see Zimmerman, 2008). They have generated different models of SRL, rooted in varying theoretical perspectives (e.g., cognitive, behavioural, cognitive-behavioural, constructivist, socio-cultural, or socio-constructivist; see Zimmerman & Schunk, 2001). Interested readers might like to learn more about the models of self-regulation developed by Boekaerts (2011), Butler and Winne (1995), Corno (1994), Winne and Hadwin (1998), and Zimmerman (1989, 2002, 2008). In our work, we have certainly been informed by these perspectives. In this book, we also draw directly from the socio-constructivist model of self-regulation developed by Butler and Cartier (Butler & Cartier, 2004; Cartier & Butler, 2004).

Whatever the theoretical stance adopted, most researchers agree that the dimensions outlined above, including cognition and metacognition, motivation and emotion, and strategic action, are integral aspects of self-regulation that intertwine before, during, and after any given activity (e.g., see Zimmerman, 2008). Thus, in this book, we draw from across contemporary models and research to offer one integrative framework that pulls these dimensions of SRL together. While this integrative perspective can be applied to describe engagement in a variety of activities within and outside of school, in the sections to follow we illustrate our main points using the example of students' self-regulating *learning* in classrooms (see Figure 1-2).

In addition to showing how important dimensions of self-regulation interact within an activity, a strength of this integrative framework is that it helps to explain more specifically

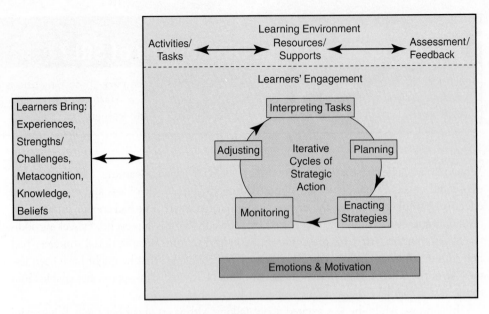

Figure 1-2 An Integrative Model of Self-Regulation.

Source: Reproduced with permission from Butler and Schnellert (2015), based on the work of Butler & Cartier (2004) and Cartier & Butler (2004).

SRL in classrooms is shaped by an interaction between what students bring to contexts and the learning environments in which they are working.

how self-regulation involves *individuals* navigating *contexts*. That is, Figure 1-2 depicts how SRL in classrooms is shaped by an interaction between what learners bring to a context (left side of the figure) and the learning environment in which they are working (top of the figure).

What Individuals Bring to Contexts

Individuals bring to contexts all sorts of experiences, strengths, challenges, metacognition, knowledge, and beliefs that influence their engagement. For example, in some school districts over 100 languages are spoken. Some learners may have started their schooling in a very different cultural context, while others may never even have attended school. How might these prior experiences shape students' learning in North American classrooms? What kinds of metacognitive knowledge might these students have constructed in other educational systems about what schooling is about, about the respective roles and responsibilities of teachers and students in classrooms, or about classroom routines and activities common in North American schools? Can we assume that all of our learners share our perspectives about teaching and learning in classrooms, understand the nature of the activities we assign, or have knowledge about strategies for completing them? If not, what can we do as educators to help students construct understandings about learning in school and their roles as students, and about the activities we give them and strategies for completing them?

Even in supposedly homogenous classrooms, students bring to their learning a constellation of experiences, strengths, challenges, knowledge, and beliefs that are hugely influential in shaping how they self-regulate their engagement in activities. For example, Brigitte brought to Mrs. Nyad's classroom a history of reading challenges, prior knowledge about the topic she chose, very low self-perceptions of competence in reading, and limited metacognitive knowledge about research activities and strategies. These combined to influence the goals she set and the choices she made about how to engage in a complex, multi-step research activity. In contrast, Stewart built from more successful past experiences, his strengths in reading-related processes, and well-developed metacognitive knowledge in ways that led him to set learning-related goals, build on his personal interests, access resources, and engage in richer forms of reading, writing, and learning processes.

Environmental Influences

In Figure 1-2 we also depict how the environments in which individuals are working influence their self-regulating processes. For example, in classrooms, learners' approaches to SRL are influenced by the nature of activities and tasks assigned, the resources and supports provided (e.g., instruction, scaffolding, modelling, texts or other resources, and opportunities to learn with peers), and assessment practices and feedback.

Research suggests that productive forms of SRL can be inspired, supported, or undermined by these kinds of contextual features. For example, multi-step activities that unfold over time, like the research project in Mrs. Nyad's class, create opportunities for SRL because students need to apply their knowledge and skills in making decisions, setting goals, planning, enacting strategies, monitoring learning, and adjusting approaches as needed. Complex, multi-step activities also create more opportunities for teachers to build in supports for students' development of effective forms of SRL. In Part Two of this book, we come back to this integrative framework to identify and illustrate in detail how educators can construct learning environments that support students' development of effective forms of SRL.

For now, it is important to recognize that, as we saw in the case of Brigitte and Stewart, not all learners respond to an environment in the same way. Instead, *how students self-regulate learning is the result of the interaction between the learning environment and what the individual brings to it.* For example, given her past struggles with reading, low self-perceptions, and limited metacognitive knowledge, Brigitte perceived Mrs. Nyad's complex, multi-step activity to be overwhelming. The result was that she set personal goals focused more on finishing and avoiding embarrassment than on learning. In contrast, given what he brought to the classroom, Stewart responded much more enthusiastically to the same activity. The result was that he set learning goals and engaged in more academically effective forms of self-regulation.

Pulling It All Together

By focusing on individuals working in context, the integrative model of SRL presented here helps in relating the different dimensions of self-regulation to one another. At the heart of Figure 1-2 is a learner's engagement in cycles of strategic action, which includes interpreting tasks and setting goals, planning, enacting strategies, monitoring, and adjusting. The framework shows how students' strategic action is shaped by the experiences, knowledge, and beliefs (including metacognitive knowledge) they bring to an environment. The framework also identifies how individuals' cognition is influenced by strategic action cycles. For example, the cognitive strategies Brigitte and Stewart used (e.g., for taking notes) were linked to the personal goals they set and plans they made on how to navigate an assignment. Finally, Figure 1-2 depicts how emotions and motivation are foundational to learning. For example, emotions and motivation influence how individuals set goals, plan, choose strategies, and monitor success. Indeed, Stewart's and Brigitte's ways of working were influenced by emotions such as excitement, stress, and frustration and by their varying motivations (e.g., a focus on learning versus finishing quickly, respectively).

> ## Food for Thought 1-3
> ## Pulling It All Together
>
> Have you seen the dimensions of SRL at work in your context? Have you noticed differences in how learners engage with the same activity? What individual and contextual factors combined to shape these different reactions?

SEEING DIMENSIONS OF SELF-REGULATION IN DAY-TO-DAY ACTIVITIES

Figure 1-2 relates important dimensions of self-regulation in one integrative framework, showing how cognition and metacognition, motivation and emotion, and strategic action are interdependent and rooted in context. How, then, can we apply this model in order to see dimensions of self-regulation in different kinds of activities?

To imagine how dimensions of self-regulation might interact within a day-to-day activity, imagine Mike, a father of two, doing the week's grocery shopping. Mike might self-regulate his engagement in grocery shopping by doing the following:

- considering his strengths and weaknesses as a shopper (e.g., he tends to buy too many unhealthy items if he shops when he is hungry),
- clarifying his goals for this shopping trip (e.g., finishing within 30 minutes, buying just what he needs without forgetting anything essential),
- pre-planning (e.g., eating a snack before shopping, making a shopping list, and choosing the best store for buying all of those items),
- enacting his shopping strategies,
- monitoring how his shopping is going (e.g., whether the store is out of something key, whether he is moving through the store efficiently, whether he is getting frustrated), and
- making adjustments to his goals or strategies if things are not going as planned.

In this example, Mike is taking deliberate control over his engagement in an activity (grocery shopping) within a given context (a particular store). The dimensions of self-regulation (cognition and metacognition, motivation and emotions, strategic action) can be seen functioning together to shape how he approaches the activity.

Earlier, we differentiated between self-regulation and SRL by associating SRL with activities in which individuals are deliberately seeking to advance their *learning*. We complicate that a bit here by noting that we are actually learning all of the time as we engage in activities, whether we are trying to or not. For example, Mike learns every time he goes grocery shopping. He elaborates his thinking about himself as a shopper, about potential shopping pitfalls, and about the best store for different kinds of products. He builds better grocery shopping strategies and brings his developing metacognitive knowledge about shopping forward to further shopping adventures. He also learns about when and why he is likely to get most frustrated as a shopper (e.g., when stores are very busy and crowded) and to avoid shopping in those situations.

That said, Mike's learning and growth are likely to be richer if he is purposeful and reflective in how he approaches his grocery shopping experiences. In other words, there are times when individuals can focus very deliberately on learning through an activity. In these cases, we can see dimensions of SRL in how individuals take control over *learning*. For example, Mike could engage in strategic action by setting a goal to learn to grocery shop more efficiently or economically. He could plan to visit a different store each week or try out what it's like to shop at different times of the day. He could take a minute to reflect on lessons learned after a given grocery shopping experience. As another example, imagine Sofia, who has chosen to take golf lessons so that she can keep up with her friends who are avid golfers. To advance her learning, Sofia might schedule her practice around her work and lessons, manage her frustration as she masters a difficult new skill, sustain her motivation through challenges, and find ways to practise with a purpose. Or imagine how dimensions of self-regulation would be apparent in the activity of Sofia's three-year-old daughter, who is working hard to figure out how to use the telephone to call her grandparents across the country.

Self-regulated learning (SRL) occurs any time individuals take deliberate control over their own learning in the context of an activity. Mrs. Nyad likely hoped that Brigitte and Stewart would take deliberate control over their learning about a topic they cared about as they engaged in research and shared their learning with their peers in her classroom.

IS SELF-REGULATION THE SAME THING AS WORKING ALONE?

A common misconception about self-regulation is that it is focused on how individuals work alone, or independently, to accomplish activities. This is an understandable inference given the term *self*-regulation. Models of self-regulation do focus centrally on how individuals take control over their participation in environments. In fact, models of self-regulation are so powerful because they describe how individuals interpret and navigate environments rather than thinking of them as passive recipients of or responders to circumstances. As such, these models align with a focus on empowering 21st century learners to be active, critical thinkers and drivers of their own learning processes. But models of self-regulation also describe how individuals navigate activities that are rooted in social contexts while working alone and with others.

Models of self-regulation describe how individuals navigate activities that are rooted in social contexts while working alone and with others.

Responding to Socially and Culturally Defined Expectations

There are at least three ways in which models of self-regulation recognize social influences on individuals' learning and performance. First and most broadly, to be successful, individuals need to recognize and respond to socially and culturally defined expectations. Imagine, for example, international students coming to learn in Canada. To be successful, these students need to be aware of and negotiate the expectations of a Canadian cultural context, their new local community, and a particular school. To succeed in a new educational system, they may need to take on new and unfamiliar roles as students in relation to teachers and peers. They may need to recognize and respond to the requirements of new kinds of academic activities or curricula. They may need to adopt new behavioural norms when interacting with peers in the schoolyard.

An important caveat here is that self-regulation is *not* equivalent to complying with expectations. Success can arise when individuals effectively interpret and achieve expectations as defined in a particular context (e.g., the assignment expectations of a particular teacher). But self-regulating individuals may also achieve goals by negotiating new expectations (e.g., asking for an extended deadline for submitting a project) or even leaving an environment (e.g., quitting a job with an unreasonable work schedule). Still, one way or another, self-regulation depends on individuals successfully reading and navigating expectations as defined in socially and culturally rooted environments in a deliberate, strategic way.

Knowing How to Work with Others

A second way in which self-regulation must be social is that successfully navigating environments requires individuals to know *how* to work with others. In the workplace and in schools, individuals are expected to work collaboratively and cooperatively with others to achieve goals. Self-regulating individuals need to build knowledge about themselves and others if they are to participate in social relationships successfully. They also need to learn and apply strategies for collaborating effectively.

Social Influences on Engagement

Finally, models of self-regulation are socially rooted because they explicitly consider how individuals scaffold or shape each other's engagement in activities. Researchers have identified different ways in which social interactions work to shape self-regulating processes within activities (e.g., see Hadwin, Jarvela, & Miller, 2011; Hutchinson, 2013; Perry, 2013; Volet, Vauras, & Salonen, 2009). For example, researchers have described the following ways in which regulation is influenced through social interaction:

Co-regulation involves giving and receiving support that is instrumental to the development of effective forms of self-regulation.

Co-regulation occurs when a person receives support to engage in self-regulation effectively. In classrooms, co-regulation can be multi-directional. Adults can co-regulate children's engagement in effective forms of SRL, peers can co-regulate each other's learning, and children can co-regulate adults (e.g., by providing information that helps teachers refine their practice to better meet their needs).

Socially shared regulation occurs during collaborative activities, when two or more individuals engage together in an activity by co-constructing understandings about tasks and pooling their respective resources to achieve goals.

Socially shared regulation occurs during collaborative activities, when two or more individuals regulate their engagement together through an activity. For example, when engaged in socially shared regulation, individuals typically co-construct understandings about tasks and combine their respective resources to achieve goals.

Socially responsible self-regulation occurs when individuals self-regulate in prosocial and socially competent ways to achieve personal success or foster success in others

Socially responsible self-regulation occurs when individuals self-regulate their engagement in activities in prosocial and socially competent ways to achieve personal success or foster success in others.

In everyday learning and practice, these forms of regulation are often hard to disentangle. For example, when working collaboratively in a workplace, colleagues may move dynamically between self-regulation, co-regulation, socially shared regulation, and socially responsible self-regulation. But, one way or another, our key point here is that individuals' engagement in self-regulation can be heavily influenced by their interactions with others.

Summary: Self-Regulation Is Social

In sum, in this section we have argued that, because models of self-regulation focus on how individuals navigate activities in social environments, they *cannot* just focus on individuals learning independently. Instead, they are particularly useful for describing how individuals learn to engage with others within the communities they must navigate as part of their day-to-day worlds.

> Activity 1-2
What Are You Learning about Self-Regulation and SRL?

After you have read this chapter, we recommend that you record your thinking on the questions below. This will help you to build on the ideas, insights, and questions you are identifying as we move through the rest of this book. To that end, you might consider creating a reflective journal to record your thinking and learning over time, particularly as you engage with activities here and in upcoming chapters.

1. After reading this chapter, how would you define self-regulation? Can you imagine an example of self-regulation in your own experience or context? What do you still wonder?

2. After reading this chapter, how do you now think self-regulation applies to learning? Can you imagine an example of self-regulated learning (SRL) in your own experience or context? What do you still wonder?

3. What are the key dimensions of self-regulation? Can you generate an example of how each of these dimensions might be implicated in SRL in a particular activity in your own experience or context?

4. If you were to scan for SRL in your context, what would you look for? Can you start to imagine goals you might need to take up in order to foster more effective forms of SRL?

5. Given what you have read so far, can you imagine how you could foster the development of self-regulating learners? What are you doing already? What else could you do? What do you wonder?

FOSTERING SRL: CHECKING IN

In this first chapter, we introduced quite a bit of information about self-regulation and SRL. In coming chapters, you will have opportunities to grapple with examples and exercises that will bring these ideas to life and, hopefully, bring additional clarity to your thinking about SRL and how to support it. For now, we encourage you to take a few moments to work through Activity 1-2 to assist you in consolidating your thinking so far.

Recommended Resources

Bandura, A. (2006). Toward a psychology of human agency. *Perspectives on Psychological Science, 1*(2), 164–180.

Boekaerts, M. (2011). Emotions, emotion regulation, and self-regulation of learning. In B. J. Zimmerman & D. H. Schunk (Eds.), *Handbook of self-regulation of learning and performance* (pp. 408–425). New York, NY: Routledge.

Borkowski, J. G. (1992). Metacognitive theory: A framework for teaching literacy, writing and math skills. *Journal of Learning Disabilities, 25*, 254–257.

Brown, A. L. (1987). Metacognition, executive control, self-regulation, and other more mysterious mechanisms. In F. E. Weinert & R. H. Kluwe (Eds.), *Metacognition, motivation, and understanding* (pp. 65–116). Hillsdale, NJ: Erlbaum.

Butler, D. L. (in press). Metacognition and self-regulation in learning. Invited chapter to appear in D. Scott & E. Hargreaves (Eds.), *The SAGE handbook on learning*. Thousand Oaks, CA: Sage.

Butler, D. L., & Cartier, S. C. (2004). *Learning in varying activities: An explanatory framework and a new evaluation tool founded on a model of self-regulated learning*. Paper presented at the annual meetings of the Canadian Society for Studies in Education. Winnipeg, MB.

Butler, D. L., Perry, N. E., & Schnellert, L. (2015). *Developing self-regulating learners*. Presentation at the 2nd annual SRL Summer Institute. Vancouver, BC.

Butler, D. L., & Schnellert, L. (2015). Success for students with learning disabilities: What does self-regulation have to do with it? In T. Cleary (Ed.), *Self-regulated learning interventions with at-risk youth: Enhancing adaptability, performance, and well-being* (pp. 89–111). Washington DC: APA Press.

Butler, D. L., & Winne, P. H. (1995). Feedback and self-regulated learning: A theoretical synthesis. *Review of Educational Research, 65*, 245–281.

Cartier, S. C., & Butler, D. L. (2004, May). Elaboration and validation of the questionnaires and plan for analysis. Paper presented at the annual meetings of the Canadian Society for Studies in Education. Winnipeg, MB.

Corno, L. (1994). Student volition and education: Outcomes, influences, and practices. In D. H. Schunk & B. J. Zimmerman (Eds.), *Self-regulation of learning and performance: Issues and educational applications* (pp. 229–251). Hillsdale, NJ: Erlbaum.

Flavell, J. H. (1976). Metacognitive aspects of problem solving. In L. B. Resnick (Ed.), *The Nature of Intelligence* (pp. 231–235). Hillsdale, NJ: Erlbaum.

Flavell, J. H. (1987). Speculations about the nature and development of metacognition. In F. E. Weinert & R. H. Kluwe (Eds.), *Metacognition, motivation, and understanding* (pp. 21–64). Hillsdale, NJ: Erlbaum.

Hadwin, A. F., Jarvela, S., & Miller, M. (2011). Self-regulated, co-regulated, and socially shared regulation of learning. In B. J. Zimmerman & D. H. Schunk (Eds.), *Handbook of self-regulation of learning and performance* (pp. 65–84). New York, NY: Routledge.

Hutchinson, L. R. (2013). Young children's engagement in self-regulation at school. (Unpublished doctoral dissertation). University of British Columbia, Vancouver. Available at https://circle.ubc.ca/handle/2429/44401.

Perry, N. E. (2013). Classroom processes that support self-regulation in young children [Monograph]. *British Journal of Educational Psychology, Monograph Series II: Psychological Aspects of Education—Current Trends, 10*, 45–68.

Shanker, S. (2013). *Calm, alert, and learning: Classroom strategies for self-regulation.* Don Mills, ON: Pearson.

Volet, S., Vauras, M., & Salonen, P. (2009). Self- and social regulation in learning contexts: An integrative perspective. *Educational Psychologist, 44*(4), 215–22.

Winne, P. H., & Hadwin, A. (1998). Studying as self-regulated learning. In D. Hacker, J. Dunlosky, & A. Graesser (Eds.), *Metacognition in educational theory and practice* (pp. 279–306). Hillsdale, NJ: Erlbaum.

Zimmerman, B. J. (1989). A social cognitive view of self-regulated academic learning. *Journal of Educational Psychology, 81*, 329–339.

Zimmerman, B. J. (2002). Becoming a self-regulated learner: An overview. *Theory Into Practice, 41*(2), 64–70. [Published online in 2010, see http://dx.doi.org/10.1207/s15430421tip4102_2]

Zimmerman, B. J. (2008). Investigating self-regulation and motivation: Historical background, methodological developments and future prospects. *American Educational Research Journal, 45*(1), 166–183.

Zimmerman, B. J. (2011). Motivational sources and outcomes of self-regulated learning and performance. In B. J. Zimmerman, & D. H. Schunk (Eds.), *Handbook of self-regulation of learning and performance* (pp. 49–64). NY, NY: Routledge.

Zimmerman, B. J., & Schunk, D. H. (Eds.) (2001). *Self-regulated learning and academic achievement: Theoretical perspectives* (2nd ed.). Hillsdale, NJ: Erlbaum.

Chapter 2
Why Is Supporting Self-Regulated Learning Important?

Courtesy of Harv Craven and Joni Eros

INTRODUCTION

Part One of this book is designed to help you construct a rich understanding about self-regulated learning (SRL) and the goals we need to set if we want to foster the development of self-regulating learners. In Chapter 1, we defined *self-regulation* and *SRL*. We also identified key dimensions of self-regulation, including *cognition* and *metacognition*, *motivation* and *emotion*, and *strategic action*. In this chapter, we build from the foundational definitions of Chapter 1 to consider why supporting self-regulation and SRL is so essential.

Learning Intentions

After reading this chapter, you should be able to do the following:

LI 1   Describe why self-regulation is so important before, during, and well beyond the school years.

LI 2   Define what it is that individuals need to self-regulate to be successful during activities.

Why Is Supporting Self-Regulation So Important?

Before you read this chapter, we suggest you take a moment to consider what you already know about self-regulation and, more specifically, self-regulated *learning*. Why do you think self-regulation is so important to success, not only during the school years but also in life long after? What aspects of performance might individuals have to "regulate" to be successful in any activity?

ANCHORING OUR DISCUSSION

In Chapter 1, we defined self-regulation and self-regulated learning (SRL) and the relationship between them. To review, according to Zimmerman (2008), individuals are self-regulating when they deliberately control their thoughts and actions to achieve personal goals and respond to environmental demands. Self-regulation unfolds when individuals engage in goal-directed activity by themselves or with others. For example, preschool children self-regulate when they try on different social roles during play (e.g., playing doctor or having a pretend tea party). Adolescents self-regulate when they master a new app for their smart phones. Teachers are self-regulating when they work alone or collaboratively to plan a lesson.

Self-regulated learning is self-regulation that occurs during activities focused intentionally on *learning*. For example, teachers engage in SRL when they form a study group to learn about a particular practice or program. They also self-regulate learning when they deliberately reflect on practice in order to articulate insights gleaned through experience. Brigitte and Stewart are two students described in Chapter 1 who were self-regulating their learning during a research activity in Mrs. Nyad's classroom.

Also in Chapter 1, we identified key dimensions of self-regulation, including cognition and metacognition, emotion and motivation, and strategic action. We provided an integrative model (see Figure 1-1) depicting how those dimensions of self-regulation interact before, during, and after an activity. We also explained how students' engagement is shaped by the interaction between what they bring to learning (e.g., prior knowledge, metacognitive knowledge) and the qualities of the environment in which they are working (e.g., how activities are defined, available resources).

In this chapter, we build from these foundational ideas to describe how and why self-regulation and, more specifically, SRL are essential to successful performance. We also offer additional examples and activities to help bring these ideas to life.

SELF-REGULATION PREDICTS SUCCESS ACROSS THE LIFESPAN

An individual's ability to achieve desired goals is dependent on how they self-regulate performance in all sorts of different activities, from infancy to adulthood, both within and outside of schools.

Why is fostering self-regulation and SRL important? Evidence generated across the past three decades shows that an individual's ability to achieve desired goals is dependent on how they self-regulate performance in all sorts of activities, from infancy into older adulthood, both within and outside of schools (e.g., see Zimmerman & Schunk, 2011).

Predicting Success

Imagine Lucy, a five-year-old girl just starting kindergarten (see Perry, Brenner, & Fusaro, 2015). What do you think is the best predictor of Lucy's success in school? Lucy has very well-developed language skills for a five-year-old. She also has strong emergent literacy skills. For example, she understands how books work, recognizes that letters represent sounds, and can already write her name. She also has good number sense and is developing skills in numeracy (e.g., counting). Are these powerful predictors of Lucy's success in school? Research suggests that they are.

However, research also shows that the *even more powerful* predictors of Lucy's success are her ability to pay attention, follow directions, resist distractions, work well with others, cope with challenges, and adapt to complex environments (Blair & Razza, 2007; Rimm-Kaufman, Curby, Grimm, Nathanson, & Brock, 2009). These are all aspects of performance associated with self-regulation. Self-regulation capacity at school entry predicts early school achievement more powerfully than IQ scores and knowledge of reading and math (Veenman & Spaans, 2005). Successful self-regulation in kindergarten predicts achievement through Grade 6 (Rothbart, Posner, & Kieras, 2006).

Consistent with this research, when you ask teachers to describe the greatest challenges for young children in school, they consistently identify challenges in self-regulation. For example, according to teachers, the children who struggle the most have difficulty paying attention and following directions. They are prone to emotional outbursts when things do not go their way. They have difficultly completing academic tasks, problems with emotion and behaviour control, and challenges in navigating relationships with teachers and peers. Fortunately, there is a great deal that parents and educators can do to foster learners' development of more effective forms of self-regulation, not only when the learners are young children, but throughout the school years and beyond.

> Self-regulation predicts early school achievement more powerfully than IQ scores and knowledge of reading and math.

When Are Self-Regulation and SRL Important?

When are self-regulation and SRL important to success in activities? We identified above how self-regulation and SRL are important for young learners. But the development of self-regulation and SRL also continues over time. Figure 2-1 emphasizes the importance of self-regulation and SRL *across the lifespan.*

In the past, it was often assumed that young children were not capable of the complex cognitive and metacognitive processes needed to engage in deliberate self-regulation or SRL. But research conducted across the past two decades challenges that assumption (e.g., see Perry, 1998; Whitebread et al., 2009). It is now clear that the preschool years are a pivotal time in children's development of effective forms of self-regulation and SRL—even infants as young as six months old turn away from unpleasant stimuli (i.e., a form of environmental control) (see Shaffer & Kipp, 2010). Very young children learn how to self-regulate multiple aspects of their performance as they engage in all sorts of activities in their homes, playgrounds, community centres, libraries, restaurants, sports programs, and preschools. For young children, self-regulation is shaped when they take on pretend roles during imaginative play, practise new skills (e.g., riding a bike or swimming), or complete household tasks alongside their parents or siblings. Children's interactions with others, including parents and teachers, play an important role in their development of more or less effective forms of self-regulation (e.g., see Eisenberg, Cumberland, & Spinrad, 1998).

But if self-regulation and SRL are so critical early on, what does it mean if children are struggling with self-regulation in the preschool or early school years? Parents of young children sometimes ask, "If my child isn't self-regulating effectively now, is it too late to do something about it?" Fortunately, self-regulation and SRL can be learned and improved throughout the school years and into adulthood.

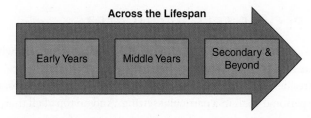

Figure 2-1 When Are Self-Regulation and SRL Important?

Source: Butler and Perry, 2013.

During the school years, students continue to build foundational knowledge and skills related to self-regulation and SRL (e.g., metacognitive knowledge about their own and others' thoughts and emotions). But the added challenge is that, as they progress through school, students must also learn to navigate new expectations in a wide variety of environments. For example, as students transition from elementary to middle and high school, they face increasingly complex academic work in different classrooms, assigned by a variety of teachers, and across many subject areas. Through these transitions, they are also expected to assume greater levels of responsibility for their learning and motivation.

Research clearly demonstrates that learners who develop more effective forms of self-regulation during the school years are more likely to navigate escalating expectations. They better understand and manage, or harness, emotions. They have higher motivation and confidence. They engage in more task-relevant behaviour. They use more productive thinking skills and strategies, and work more productively with others. Ultimately, they achieve more highly (e.g., see Gettinger & Seibert, 2002; Pintrich & Schunk, 2002; Zimmerman, 2002). It is fortunate that educators, parents, and peers can continue to play such influential roles in learners' development of effective forms of self-regulation and SRL through the school years.

But the development of self-regulation does not end after high school. For example, post-secondary settings continue to challenge students to take even more deliberate control over learning. Struggling learners in colleges and universities often evidence significant flaws in their approaches to self-regulation. In contrast, post-secondary learners who self-regulate effectively are more likely to succeed (e.g., Azevedo, Cromley, Winters, Moos, & Greene, 2005; Butler, 1998).

Adaptive forms of self-regulation and SRL are also essential in the workplace—for example, in navigating day-to-day tasks with colleagues, problem-solving challenges, or learning new responsibilities. In many professions, such as teaching, engineering, and medicine, practitioners are expected to self-regulate their continuing professional learning and practice development. But even accomplished professionals can struggle to effectively identify what they do and do not know (e.g., see Eva & Regehr, 2011). Correspondingly, researchers are now studying how we can better support professionals to develop effective forms of self-regulation they can use when learning "on the job" (e.g., Brydges & Butler, 2012; Butler & Schnellert, 2012; Eva & Regehr, 2011). As we age, daily life also poses new challenges that demand the development of new forms of self-regulation; for example, in order to maintain health or manage a chronic illness (e.g., see Bandura, 2005).

In sum, it is now abundantly clear that:

- Self-regulation and SRL are essential to success from infancy through the school years and into adulthood.

- Individuals at different ages need *to learn how to* self-regulate effectively, particularly as they enter new environments, experience challenges, or face new kinds of expectations.

- There is a good deal that parents, educators, peers, and others can do to support an individual's capacity to self-regulate effectively across a wide variety of activities and environments.

WHAT DO PEOPLE SELF-REGULATE?

Self-regulation is complex! It is also multidimensional. It depends on what individuals bring to a context but it is also shaped by features of the contexts where individuals are working. It requires deliberately managing one's engagement through obstacles and challenges to achieve personal goals in a particular setting. And on top of all that, self-regulating individuals must simultaneously attend to multiple aspects of performance if they are to achieve their goals.

What is it that individuals have to self-regulate in order to engage successfully in activities? To address that question, imagine an activity that requires self-regulation. For example, you might visualize a preschool girl in a gymnastics class waiting in line for her turn to summersault on a colourful mat, or a five-year-old boy waiting for his meal when eating out at a restaurant with his family. What might these children have to self-regulate to successfully navigate these activities? Or, imagine a first grader using crayons to illustrate an important event in a story, a fourth grader engaged in silent reading, or a ninth grader just learning to play an instrument in band class. What would these young students need to self-regulate to learn effectively through these activities? Or think of a recent activity that demanded your self-regulation. What was the activity? What did you need "regulate" to navigate that activity successfully?

In SR Vignette 2-1, we give an example of what two self-regulating students might need to be aware of, monitor, and manage things in order to negotiate a classroom-based activity successfully. How might self-regulating in these areas be necessary in the activity you imagined?

> ## SR Vignette 2-1
What Do People Self-Regulate?

Students in a Grade 2 class have just read and discussed a story as a class. Now they must work with a partner to "write" out the three main events (in words and/or pictures). Lydia and Owen have been paired to work together. What would these young students need to think and do to successfully navigate this activity? Research suggests that individuals can be more successful in activities if they strategically self-regulate the following:

The Environment

For example, to self-regulate their work space in their story-mapping activity, Lydia and Owen need to choose a location that allows them to work without distractions, gain easy access to resources, and have ample room to write and draw.

Their Behaviour

Lydia and Owen also need to self-regulate their behaviour so that they can listen carefully to the teacher's instructions, wait patiently for their turn to access materials, work well together, and maintain focus on their project in a busy classroom.

Their Emotions

Lydia and Owen need to monitor their emotions (e.g., frustration, over-excitement) and use good strategies for heading off and/or coping with any emotions that might interfere with their ability to work on the project successfully.

Their Motivation

The two students need to recognize and take ownership of goals matched to their teacher's task (e.g., to draw/write out

the events in the story together); believe in their capacity to achieve those goals if they work hard and use good strategies, including helping one another; and monitor and maintain their motivation to persist at the task in spite of setbacks or challenges.

Their Strategic Action

Lydia and Owen need to interpret task demands (e.g., they can write or draw to outline the main events in the story), plan how they will achieve goals (e.g., materials they might need, strategies they might use to remember the story, write or draw), monitor progress (e.g., if they are finishing on time, if they are including all elements in the story), and refine approaches as needed (e.g., hurry up, get additional materials).

Their Cognition and Learning

As a key part of strategic performance, Lydia and Owen need to engage in active thinking and learning. To that end, they need to choose and use cognitive and learning strategies flexibly and adaptively. A key aspect is that they engage in cycles of strategic action; for example, by choosing good strategies during planning, monitoring how well their learning is going, and adjusting strategies adaptively if needed.

Their Relationships

Lydia and Owen have to negotiate goals and decide how they will achieve them together (e.g., where they will work, whether they will write or draw). To do this, they also need to be able to read each other's reactions and resolve any conflicts.

What Do People Self-Regulate?

In SR Vignette 2-1 we drew on the example of Lydia and Owen working on a story-mapping activity, identifying the multiple aspects of performance that individuals have to self-regulate when engaged in activities. In this exercise, we ask you to imagine these aspects of self-regulation in a concrete example. Start by choosing a specific activity to focus on. You might return to Lydia and Owen's story-mapping activity and think through that example. Or, you might choose an activity that you engage in yourself, or one that you ask learners to complete in your context. In Table 2-1, fill in a description of the activity you have in mind. Then use the remaining rows to identify requirements for self-regulation in that activity. What do learners have to do to successfully navigate the activity? Have you seen strengths and gaps in your own or your students' approaches to self-regulation in the different aspects of performance?

Table 2-1   What Do People Self-Regulate?

Describe the Activity You Have in Mind:	
In your example, explain why and how individuals need to self-regulate their	
Environment	
Behaviour	
Emotions	
Motivation	
Strategic Action	
Cognition/Learning	
Relationships	

Can we assume that Lydia and Owen, or any second grader, know how to self-regulate all of these aspects of their performance while working through this kind of activity? Likely not! Indeed, a key developmental requirement for learners across the lifespan is to continually develop their capacities to navigate multiple aspects of their performance in all sorts of activities both within and outside of schools.

In the early years, children are just starting to understand and learn how to manage their emotions, behaviour, and relationships (Schonert-Reichl & Hymel, 2010; Shanker, 2013; Zins, Weissberg, Wang, & Walberg, 2004). When children have trouble in classrooms (e.g., getting along with classmates, handling frustration, or reading or writing effectively), it is often because they still need to develop knowledge and skills that will enable them to take more deliberate control over their performance in those areas. But again, the development of self-regulating capacities also continues over time. For example, adolescents or even adults may struggle to understand and navigate their emotions or collaborate harmoniously with others.

Fortunately, there is a good deal that educators and parents can do to foster the development of self-regulation in all of these areas, a topic to which we will return. For now, our main point is that to engage successfully in activities, individuals need to be aware of, monitor, and regulate multiple aspects of performance simultaneously by attending to their *environments*, *behaviour*, *emotions*, *motivation*, *strategic action*, *cognition*, and *relationships*.

When children have trouble in classrooms (e.g., getting along with classmates, handling frustration, or reading or writing), it is often because they still need to develop knowledge and skills that will enable them to take more deliberate control over their performance in those areas.

SELF-REGULATING IN CONTEXT

To be successful, individuals have to navigate these various aspects of performance *while engaged* in an activity. For example, it is while reading or writing or grocery shopping that emotions may arise which interfere with engagement. It is when playing with peers in the schoolyard that children may get frustrated and lash out at others. It is during a difficult task that learners may experience threats to motivation. It is when facing academic work that learners need to interpret tasks so as to choose the most applicable cognitive strategies. It is when working in collaborative groups that individuals have to create positive working relationships. To be effectively self-regulating, individuals need to *learn how to* deliberately manage their environments, behaviour, emotions, motivation, strategic action, cognition, and relationships *while they are immersed* in an activity.

There are many excellent approaches we can use to help students develop metacognitive knowledge (e.g., about emotions, about their strengths and limitations as learners) and skills (e.g., strategies for reducing stress or frustration, skills for working with others, strategies for learning) that they can then draw during activities. As we move through this book, we will identify these approaches and how they are useful in supporting self-regulation and SRL. For now, our key point here is that individuals have to learn how to mobilize their knowledge and skills *in context* if they are to self-regulate effectively in the midst of activities.

Individuals have to learn how to mobilize their knowledge and skills in context if they are to self-regulate engagement effectively in the midst of activities.

SELF-REGULATION IN SUCCESSFUL ENGAGEMENT

We have argued that success across the lifespan depends on individuals taking up effective forms of self-regulation in a wide variety of activities and settings. In this section, we consider how self-regulation and SRL are implicated in success a bit more specifically.

From what research and teachers are telling us, starting in early childhood, individuals are expected to pull together multiple dimensions of self-regulation (*cognition* and *metacognition*, *emotion* and *motivation*, and *strategic action*) in order to complete a wide variety of activities. They are also expected to self-regulate multiple aspects of their performance as they negotiate environments. For example, during classroom routines and learning activities, even kindergarten children need to self-regulate *environments* (e.g., chose where to work or play), *behaviour* (e.g., to carry out classroom routines), *emotion* (e.g., cope when things don't go their way), *motivation* (e.g., sustain interest), *strategic action* (e.g., manage time or solve problems), *cognition* (e.g., think actively with ideas), and *relationships* (e.g., interact positively with peers and teachers).

To help you imagine how self-regulation and SRL are foundational to success in and outside of schools, SR Vignette 2-2 describes Geevan's efforts to be a good host to his friends while playing at his house after school. As you read this vignette, can you see the dimensions of SRL at work? Can you identify aspects of performance that Geevan must self-regulate to be successful?

>> Activity 2-2
Self-Regulation in Successful Engagement

As you read SR Vignette 2-2, can you see self-regulation in how Geevan played with his brother and friends? To help you consolidate your learning, we invite you to record your answers to the following questions:

1. How are the different dimensions of SRL evident in this example (i.e., *cognition* and *metacognition*, *emotion* and *motivation*, and *strategic action*)?

2. What aspects of his performance did Geevan need to deliberately control to be successful in that situation (i.e., *environments, behaviour, emotions, motivation, strategic action, cognition, relationships*)?

3. Was Geevan successful in self-regulating his engagement? In what ways? Where did he struggle?

4. What did Geevan's mother do to support him when he was struggling? How did her support help him to self-regulate more successfully?

Self-Regulation in Successful Engagement

Geevan is a seven-year-old boy who was playing one day with his older brother, Liam, and a few other friends at his house after school. Geevan's family had set up a large, colourful playroom in the basement with all sorts of toys and games. But this day the children were attracted to some empty wrapping paper rolls that were destined for recycling. The boys quickly repurposed the sturdy cardboard rolls to serve as swords. After a bit of duelling, Liam suggested they play soldiers and pirates in a pretend high-seas battle. One friend, Cory, jumped on the idea and positioned a "treasure chest" (i.e., a large toy truck) at one end of the room. The children agreed that the soldiers' job would be to protect the treasure. The pirates' job was to steal it.

Geevan was at first excited about playing this game with his friends. But then he got *so* mad when Liam told him to be a soldier. He wanted to be a pirate! He got even madder when his paper-roll sword split at the seams when, out of anger, he wacked it on the table. He could *feel* himself starting to almost *vibrate* with frustration. Just then his mother popped her head into the room and, with a little wave, attracted Geevan's attention. She slowly shook her head from side to side, and then looked at him expectantly. Geevan remembered all of a sudden that he was supposed to be a good host when his friends came over, which included not getting mad, hitting things, or yelling. He sighed and took a deep breath. His mother wondered out loud whether the children might be able to take turns being soldiers or pirates. Geevan jumped on that idea! He suggested to the group that they should all switch roles whenever the treasure was captured. Even Liam agreed.

After that, Geevan really enjoyed playing the game, especially when it was his turn to be a pirate. Geevan knew he was faster than the others, which helped whenever it was his turn to steal the treasure. At first it worked when he pretended to move in one direction, to fake out the soldiers, but then twist around quickly in the other direction to get past them. Unfortunately, his friends caught onto that trick too quickly! After that, it worked better when two pirates distracted the soldiers so that another could sneak behind them. Geevan enjoyed waving his sword and jumping around wildly when it was his job to distract the soldiers. But he definitely preferred it when it was his turn to do the stealing!

What did we observe in Geevan's play? Even in this brief example, it is possible to identify ways in which cognition and metacognition, emotion and motivation, and strategic action were interdependent in how Geevan engaged in the activity. For example, Geevan used strategies for getting around the soldiers (cognition) that were informed by his knowledge that he was relatively speedy and about possible tricks for stealing the treasure (metacognition). He experienced a range of feelings, from excitement to anger to frustration (emotions). While at first his emotions got away from him, he eventually drew on strategies he knew (metacognition), like breathing deeply, to calm down and find another way forward (strategic action). While he was more interested in playing a pirate, he found ways to have fun while taking turns as a soldier (motivation). Throughout the activity, Geevan also had to monitor and self-regulate multiple aspects of his performance. For example, he had to channel his excitement productively (emotions) so that he could focus (behaviour), calm himself down when angry and frustrated (emotions, strategic action), find ways to have fun in different roles (motivation), plan and adapt his strategies for capturing the treasure (strategic action, cognition), and interact cooperatively with his friends and brother (relationships).

Research suggests that success is enhanced when individuals become aware of and take deliberate control of their self-regulated engagement in activities.

Was Geevan conscious of his self-regulation at all times? Did he realize he was taking advantage of his superior speed when choosing strategies for stealing the treasure? Did he imagine himself as engaged in strategic action when "faking out" his friends no longer worked and he had to find another way? Did he understand his emotions when he got so frustrated that he was "vibrating"? Did he know that he was using emotion-control strategies when he took a deep breath and then found another way to solve his problem, or that he was building on his excitement to energize his efforts to steal the treasure? Not necessarily. But research strongly suggests that success is enhanced when individuals become aware of and take deliberate control of these aspects of their performance while engaging in activities. Our task as educators (and parents) is to help children learn how to take up more effective forms of self-regulation during all sorts of activities.

IMAGINING HOW TO FOSTER EFFECTIVE FORMS OF SELF-REGULATION

We have suggested through this chapter that parents, educators, peers, and others play important roles in children's development of effective forms of self-regulation. Thinking ahead to upcoming chapters, can you start to imagine from SR Vignette 2-2 (1) important goals we need to take up if we are to foster self-regulation and SRL and (2) how even young children can be supported to develop more effective forms of self-regulation? For example, where did Geevan experience challenges while playing with his brother and friends? What did Geevan's mother do to help him in developing more effective forms of self-regulation?

Based on the description in SR Vignette 2-2, it seems that Geevan's mother did a bit of pre-work with him to support his development of metacognitive knowledge and skills that he might build from to be more successful while playing with his friends. For example, she spoke with him ahead of time about what it means to be a good host when friends come over. She also worked with him to practise breathing deeply as a strategy for reducing frustration. Then, while he was in the midst of play, she provided him with a discrete and subtle reminder of what they had worked on previously. This cued him to think back to the importance of hosting friends without getting mad, hitting things, or yelling. Furthermore, when she briefly interrupted the children's play, she created space for Geevan to use his deep breathing strategy. Her offhand wondering also helped Geevan seize on a more constructive solution to his problem (i.e., asking his peers to take turns).

You might also notice in this example how, rather than taking control of the situation or trying to regulate his actions, Geevan's mother was helping him to *learn how to* more effectively control himself (i.e. *self*-regulate his engagement). Her goals were to increase Geevan's self-awareness about his own activity and enable him to take deliberate control over his own performance. In coming chapters, we will probe more deeply into strategies educators can use to foster individuals' capacities to take ownership over their approaches to self-regulating and SRL.

FOSTERING SELF-REGULATION AND SRL: CHECKING IN

Our goal in this chapter has been to identify why fostering effective forms of self-regulation and SRL is so important. First, we described how research has consistently linked self-regulation with success in activities, from preschool through to adulthood, both within and outside of schools. Then, we identified the various aspects of performance that individuals need to regulate in order to be successful when engaged in activities. Finally, we illustrated how a seven-year-old boy self-regulated multiple aspects of his performance simultaneously (i.e., environments, behaviour, motivation, emotions, strategic action, cognition, relationships), albeit with a bit of strategic support from his mother, so that he could play successfully with his brother and peers.

As we close this chapter, we invite you to reflect on the information we have put forward in relation to what you knew before reading and engaging with these ideas. What have you learned? What do you still want to know? What important goals do we need to set as educators if we are to foster self-regulation and SRL? Can you start to imagine how we might achieve those goals? What are you already doing that you could build on or refine, based on what you are learning? If you have started a reflective journal, you might record insights you can take forward into upcoming discussions, or sketch out questions concerning things you would like to learn more about as you read further.

Recommended Resources

Azevedo, R., Cromley, J. G., Winters, F. I., Moos, D. C., & Greene, J. A. (2005). Adaptive human scaffolding facilitates adolescents' self-regulated learning with hypermedia. *Instructional Science, 33*, 381–412.

Bandura, A. (2005). The primacy of self-regulation in health promotion. *Applied Psychology: An International Review, 54*(2), 245–254.

Blair, C., & Razza, R. P. (2007). Relating effortful control, executive function, and false belief understanding to emerging math and literacy ability in kindergarten. *Child Development, 78*, 647–663.

Brydges, R., & Butler, D. L. (2012). A reflective analysis of medical education research on self-regulation in learning and practice. *Medical Education, 46*, 71–79.

Butler, D. L. (1998). The Strategic Content Learning approach to promoting self-regulated learning. In B. J. Zimmerman & D. Schunk (Eds.), *Developing self-regulated learning: From teaching to self-reflective practice* (pp. 160–183). New York: Guildford Publications, Inc.

Butler, D. L., & Schnellert, L. (2012). Collaborative inquiry in teacher professional development. *Teaching and Teacher Education, 28*, 1206–1220.

Centre for the Developing Child: http://developingchild.harvard.edu/resources/

Eisenberg, N., Cumberland, A., & Spinrad, T. L. (1998). Parental socialization of emotion. *Psychological Inquiry, 9*, 241–273.

Eva, K. W., & Regehr, G. (2011). Exploring the divergence between self-assessment and self-monitoring. *Advances in Health Sciences Education, 16*, 311–329.

Gettinger, M., & Seibert, J. K. (2002). Contributions of study skills to academic competence. *School Psychology Review, 31*, 350–365.

Kaplan, A. (2008). Clarifying metacognition, self-regulation, and self-regulated learning: What's the purpose? *Educational Psychology Review, 20*, 477–484. Doi: 10.1007/s10648-008-9087-2

Perry, N. E. (1998). Young children's self-regulated learning and contexts that support it. *Journal of Educational Psychology, 90*, 715–729.

Perry, N. E., Brenner, C. A., & Fusaro, N. (2015). Closing the gap between theory and practice in self-regulated learning: Teacher learning teams as a framework for enhancing self-regulated teaching and learning. In T. J. Cleary (Ed.), *Self-regulated learning interventions with at risk populations: Academic, mental health, and contextual considerations* (pp. 229–250). Washington, DC: American Psychological Association.

Pintrich, P. R., & Schunk, D. H. (2002). *Motivation in education: Theory, research, and applications* (2nd ed.). Upper Saddle River, NJ: Prentice Hall.

Rimm-Kaufman, S. E., Curby, T. W., Grimm, K. J., Nathanson, L., & Brock, L. L. (2009). The contribution of children's self-regulation and classroom quality to children's adaptive behaviors in the kindergarten classroom. *Developmental Psychology, 45*(4), 958–972.

Rothbart, M. K., Posner, M. I., & Kieras, J. (2006). Temperament, attention, and the development of self-regulation. In K. McCartney & D. Phillips (Eds.), *Blackwell handbook of early childhood development* (pp.338–357). Malden, MA: Blackwell Publishing Ltd.

Schonert-Reichl, K. A., & Hymel, S. (2010). Educating the heart as well as the mind: Social and emotional learning for school and life success. *Education Canada, 47*(2). Available at http://www.cea-ace.ca.

Shaffer, D. R., & Kipp, K. (2010). *Developmental psychology: Childhood & adolescence* (8th ed.). Belmont, CA: Wadsworth.

Shanker, S. (2013). *Calm, alert, & learning: Classroom strategies for self-regulation*. Don Mills, ON: Pearson.

Veenman, M. V. J., & Spaans, M. A. (2005). Relation between intellectual and metacognitive skills: Age and task differences. *Learning and Individual Differences*, *15*, 159–176. doi:10.1016/j.lindif.2004.12.001.

Whitebread, D., Coltman, P., Pasternak, D. P., Sangster, C., Grau, V., Bingham, …, & Demetriou, D. (2009). The development of two observational tools for assessing metacognition and self-regulated learning in young children. *Metacognition Learning*, *4*, 63–85.

Zimmerman, B. J. (2002). Becoming a self-regulated learner: An overview. *Theory into Practice*, *41(2)*, 64–70.

Zimmerman, B. J. (2008). Investigating self-regulation and motivation: Historical background, methodological developments and future prospects. *American Educational Research Journal*, *45*(1), 166–183.

Zimmerman, B. J., & Schunk, D. H. (Eds.) (2011). *Handbook of self-regulation of learning and performance*. New York: Routledge.

Zins, J., Weissberg, R., Wang, M., & Walberg, H. J. (2004). *Building academic success on social and emotional learning: What does the research say?* New York: Teachers College Press.

Chapter 3

How Is Self-Regulated Learning Related to Social-Emotional Learning and Executive Functioning?

Fuse/Getty Images

INTRODUCTION

Part One of this book is designed to help you identify essential goals we need to achieve if we are to foster the development of *self-regulating learners*. To that end, in this chapter we deepen our discussion about important qualities of self-regulated learning (SRL). We do this by describing connections between SRL and two other educational priorities emerging across North America and globally: *social-emotional learning (SEL)* and *executive functioning*. Our purpose in taking up these topics is two-fold. First, educators often ask us how SRL fits with these two other important priorities, given apparent overlaps. Describing each creates an opportunity for us to make connections. Second, identifying synergies between SRL, SEL, and executive functioning can inform our thinking about important goals necessary in fostering the development of self-regulating learners.

Learning Intentions

After reading this chapter, you should be able to do the following:

LI 1   Define relationships between self-regulated learning, social-emotional learning, and executive functioning.

LI 2   Identify what those relationships suggest about important goals in fostering SRL.

Self-Regulated Learning, Social-Emotional Learning, and Executive Functioning

Before you read this chapter, take a moment to consider what you already know about social-emotional learning and executive functioning. Have you heard these terms before?

Can you identify any connections between what you know about these topics and what you are learning in this book about self-regulation and SRL? What do you wonder?

ANCHORING OUR DISCUSSION

To anchor this chapter's discussion, we recommend that you think back to the big ideas about SRL we have put forward so far. From Chapter 1, it is important to keep in mind the following:

- our definition of *self-regulation* as goal-directed thinking and acting across a wide range of daily activities, and of *SRL* as self-regulation with the deliberate purpose of *learning* through an activity;

- the dimensions of SRL, including *cognition* and *metacognition*, *emotion* and *motivation*, and *strategic action*; and

- how SRL emerges from an interaction between *what individuals bring to contexts* (e.g., experiences, strengths and challenges, metacognitive knowledge, prior content knowledge, beliefs, values, and expectations) and the *environments* in which they are working.

From Chapter 2, it is important to bear in mind the many aspects of performance that individuals need to self-regulate if they are to be successful in an activity. To review, when self-regulating their engagement, individuals might need to attend to their (a) *environment* (e.g., by choosing a quiet place to learn), (b) *emotions* (e.g., by managing stress or harnessing excitement), (c) *motivation* (e.g., by persisting through setbacks), (d) *behaviour* (e.g., by resisting distractions), (e) *strategic action* (e.g., by choosing and using active learning and thinking strategies flexibly and adaptively), (f) *cognition and learning* (e.g., by using good strategies for reading, writing, researching, inquiring, or learning), and (g) *relationships* (e.g., by negotiating roles and responsibilities in a collaborative project).

SELF-REGULATION AND SOCIAL-EMOTIONAL LEARNING

Our framework for describing self-regulation includes attention to how individuals navigate social environments and self-regulate emotions and relationships. So, you might wonder how a focus on self-regulation connects with calls to advance *social-emotional learning* (SEL). What is SEL in relation to what we have been discussing? Why is fostering SEL important? How are self-regulation, SRL, and SEL complementary or connected?

What Is Social-Emotional Learning?

Our colleague, Dr. Kimberley Schonert-Reichl, often begins workshops on SEL by quoting Aristotle. What comes to mind for you when you read the following quotation?

Educating the mind without educating the heart is no education at all.

Several thoughts come to mind for us when we reflect on Aristotle's assertion. One is that influential educators have been emphasizing the importance of SEL for millennia.

Another is that education is about much more than just academics. Consistent with this idea, Greenberg et al. (2003) suggest that a comprehensive education should support children in becoming "knowledgeable, responsible, socially skilled, healthy, caring, and contributing citizens" (p. 466). Finally, Aristotle reminds us that academic success relies on more than cognition. Academic success is also tied to social and emotional competence (Zins, Weissberg, Wang, & Walberg, 2004).

What is **social-emotional competence**? Our description draws on the useful framework provided by the Collaborative for Academic, Social, and Emotional Learning (CASEL; see http://www.casel.org). CASEL defines five core social-emotional competencies:

- *Self-awareness*, about one's emotions, values, strengths, and limitations;
- *Social awareness*, including perspective-taking and showing understanding of and empathy for others;
- *Relationship skills*, including the ability to form positive relationships, work in teams, and deal effectively with conflict;
- *Self-management*, particularly of one's emotions, thoughts, and behaviours; and
- *Responsible decision making*, including making ethical, constructive, and respectful choices to guide personal and social behaviour (see http://www.casel.org/social-and-emotional-learning/core-competencies).

What is **social-emotional learning (SEL)**? SEL encompasses the processes associated with building social-emotional competence.

Why Focus on SEL?

We agree with Aristotle, Zins et al. (2004), and Schonert-Reichl and Hymel (2010) that our goals as educators extend to developing caring, empathetic, socially responsible citizens who know how to build positive relationships. Ideally, individuals bring social-emotional competence into their engagement in all sorts of activities within and outside of schools. Fostering SEL in preschool and school-aged children is certainly an important aim shared by both parents and educators.

In addition to and reminiscent of research on self-regulation as described in Chapter 2, social-emotional competence is clearly linked to *academic* success. For example, Wentzel (1993) found that the prosocial behaviours of Grade 6 and 7 students were a strong predictor of academic outcomes, even after taking into account the effects of academically oriented behaviour, IQ, family structure, and days absent from school. Similarly, in their longitudinal study, Caprara and his colleagues (2000) found that social-emotional competence in Grade 3, as reflected in cooperating, helping, sharing, and consoling, was a better predictor of achievement gains five years later than was Grade 3 academic achievement. In their review of 213 school-based SEL programs from kindergarten through to high school, Durlak and his colleagues (2011) found that supports to SEL were associated not only with gains in social-emotional skills, attitudes, and behaviour, but also with gains in *achievement*.

How Can Educators Support SEL?

According to Schonert-Reichl and Weissberg (2014), fostering social-emotional competence requires that we both (1) create positive learning environments and (2) infuse explicit support for children's development of social and emotional skills into the life of the classroom. Creating positive learning environments establishes caring, supportive, and safe spaces where children can experience and develop social-emotional competencies. At the same time, providing instruction that directly fosters students' development of social-emotional knowledge and skills enables those learners to contribute to the creation of positive spaces

Social-emotional competence reflects competencies needed to successfully navigate social and emotional aspects of activities and environments. These include self-awareness, social awareness, relationship skills, self-management of ones emotions, thoughts, and behaviours, and responsible decision-making.

Social-emotional learning (SEL) encompasses the processes associated with building social-emotional competence.

Excellent, easily accessible resources that educators can draw on to foster learners' development of social-emotional competencies in their contexts are available through the following websites:

- the Collaborative for Academic, Social, and Emotional Learning (CASEL) (http://www.casel.org)
- Harvard's Center for the Developing Child (http://developingchild.harvard.edu/resources/)
- the Children's Resilience Initiative (http://resiliencetrumpsaces.org/providers.cfm?id=5)

- the Technical Assistance Center on Social-Emotional Intervention (http://www.challengingbehavior.org/)
- Vanderbilt University's Center for Social and Emotional Foundational for Early Learning (http://csefel.vanderbilt.edu).

In addition, resources to support students in understanding and managing stress and anxiety can be found at http://www.mindcheck.ca, http://www.anxietybc.ca, and http://youthanxietybc.com/mindfulness-exercises.

for themselves and others. Within SEL–supportive classrooms, all students feel more connected to peers, teachers, and their school. They are also better able to learn.

Many outstanding resources are available to educators interested in more-specific information about how to foster the development of social-emotional competence in their contexts. We strongly recommend articles and book chapters written by Dr. Kimberley Schonert-Reichl and her colleagues (e.g., Schonert-Reichl & Lawlor, 2010; Schonert-Reichl, Smith, Zaidman-Zait, & Hertzman, 2012; Schonert-Reichl & Weissberg, 2014). Also, in Links to Resources 3-1, we identify easily accessible websites through which educators can access research-informed, practical resources for fostering SEL.

Connecting Social-Emotional Learning and Self-Regulated Learning

What connections are you starting to see between SRL and SEL, based on our descriptions so far? While the two are definitely not synonymous, there are clearly important overlaps and intersections between SRL and SEL. For example, both SRL and SEL consider how individuals learn to self-manage *emotions* and *relationships* while engaged in all sorts of activities. Thus, we suggest that frameworks for thinking about SEL and SRL are interconnected.

Furthermore, because of these close connections, research on SEL can certainly help us deepen our understanding of important goals we need to take up if we are to foster the development of self-regulating learners. In particular, an SEL framework can support us in identifying (1) why it is so important to create safe, supportive learning environments for both SEL and SRL; (2) some of what *individuals need to bring to contexts* if they are to engage in effective forms of SRL; and (3) what it looks like for students to self-regulate *emotions* and *relationships* while engaged in learning.

First, what can an SEL framework tell us about the *qualities of environments* that can support learners' development of SEL and SRL? From an SEL perspective, fostering effective learning requires more than just supporting students' knowledge and skill development. It is also essential to create caring, safe, and supportive classrooms. SEL research identifies how safe learning environments create conditions for the development of students' social-emotional competencies. In Chapter 5, we describe how SRL is also supported by setting up a community of learners within safe and supportive classrooms that value all members, celebrate and accommodate individuals' diverse interests and needs, and encourage peer-to-peer co-learning. From an SRL perspective, safe and supportive learning environments liberate students to engage in rich forms of thinking, take risks, and push their learning forward.

Second, an SEL framework can tell us a great deal about *what individuals need to bring to contexts* if they are to self-regulate learning effectively. Building from CASEL's framework for describing social-emotional competencies, it follows that self-regulating students need to develop the following:

- metacognitive knowledge about emotions and relationships,
- prosocial values (e.g., a sense of social responsibility; openness to feeling empathy), and
- SEL–relevant background knowledge and skills (e.g., relationship skills).

Overall, to foster students' successful management of the social-emotional dimensions of SRL, we need to support their development of the metacognition, values, and background knowledge and skills that underlie social-emotional competence.

Finally, by emphasizing the importance of competencies related to self-regulating emotions and relationships, an SEL framework can help us understand *what effective forms of SRL look like in classrooms.* SEL frameworks suggest that SRL unfolds more effectively when individuals can mobilize their knowledge, skills, beliefs, and values in order to:

- be aware of and monitor their own and others' emotions and perspectives, including feeling empathy for others;
- self-manage their emotions, thoughts, and actions in ways that maintain their own and other's positive engagement in learning (see also Boekaerts, 2011; Corno, 1993, 1994); and
- make responsible, ethical, respectful choices and decisions (e.g., see Mayer & Salovey, 1993).

Imagining SEL Competencies at Work in Self-Regulated Learning

To imagine how SEL is involved in effective forms of SRL, it might help to consider what students must do, from a social-emotional perspective, to engage constructively in learning. As a first example, some authors have described how students need to learn how to recognize and control their emotions so that they are "ready to learn." Very high levels of agitation, excitement, or anxiety can interfere with students' ability to concentrate on a task at hand or engage effectively with others. In these cases, supporting learners *to learn how to* monitor and control their emotions can help them settle in and participate more successfully in learning activities (e.g., see Shanker, 2013).

As a second example, Monique Boekaerts (2011) describes how students also need to monitor and control emotions *while immersed in activities.* For example, students who feel threatened in learning environments may experience emotions and "arousal" that lead them to focus more on self-protection (e.g., by avoiding the situation) than on learning. In these cases, students need to know and employ effective *emotion control strategies* during learning activities (e.g., to proactively avoid frustration, to reappraise a situation) if they are to stay engaged or re-engage in learning (see also Corno, 1993; Fried, 2011; Gross, 2013).

As a final example, Izard and her colleagues (Izard, Stark, Trentacosta, & Schultz, 2008) stress that emotion regulation is not just about reducing, amplifying, or sustaining arousal. Instead, they describe how emotional regulation also includes *emotional utilization,* which they define as "the use of techniques and strategies that harness the energy of emotion arousal in constructive thought and action" (p. 156). Imagine a student who is very excited about an impending project. She may be able to harness that energy to motivate and sustain effort through challenging portions of the project. Similarly, imagine how learning and empathy might develop in tandem when students experience rich emotions together while completing a project.

Connecting SEL and SRL

Based on the discussion in this section, what did you learn about SEL and its connection to self-regulation and SRL? Can you identify connections between SEL and effective forms of learning? What do you still wonder? If you were to scan for effective and ineffective forms of self-regulation and SRL in your context, what would you look for, building from this discussion?

Self-Regulated Learning and SEL: Closing Reflections

In this section, we have considered how a focus on SEL can help define goals essential in fostering SRL in classrooms. What do we conclude on that topic? Through our discussion, we have described how drawing on an SEL framework can help by informing understanding about the following:

- the importance of establishing caring, safe learning environments in which students develop social-emotional competencies and feel comfortable engaging in rich forms of learning and SRL;

- important kinds of knowledge, skills, beliefs, and values students need to bring to contexts, and construct through experience, if they are to successfully self-regulate their emotions and relationships while engaged in learning; and

- what it looks like for students to self-regulate emotions and relationships in the service of learning.

Ultimately, fostering students' development of social-emotional competencies can contribute in important ways to them becoming self-regulating learners. Students need to learn how to take deliberate control over their environments, emotions, and ways of working with others if they are to successfully self-regulate their engagement during learning activities. Thus, SEL is an important piece of the overall SRL puzzle. However, as we will see later in this chapter and book, students need to combine attention to social-emotional aspects of learning with other aspects of their performance if they are to self-regulate learning effectively.

SELF-REGULATION, SRL, AND EXECUTIVE FUNCTIONING

Advances in neuroscience and developmental psychology are leading many researchers and educators today to highlight the importance of *executive functions* in successful goal-directed action, including learning in schools. What is executive functioning? Why is fostering executive functioning important? How can a focus on executive functioning inform our understanding about key goals in fostering self-regulation and SRL? These are questions we take up in the second half of this chapter.

What Is Executive Functioning?

Technically speaking, **executive functioning** is an umbrella term used by many researchers and educators to describe the *cognitive control functions* supported by the brain's prefrontal cortex (see Diamond, 2010; Meltzer, 2010). These are the processes we rely on to engage in goal-directed thinking and behaviour. We draw on our executive function processes in particular when we need to move from automatic to more deliberate performance; for example, when we face any kind of novel or challenging situation.

Executive functioning is an umbrella term used by many researchers and educators to describe the "cognitive control functions" supported by the brain's prefrontal cortex. These are the processes we rely on to engage in goal-directed thinking and behaviour.

Table 3-1   Three Types of Executive Functioning Processes

Executive Functioning Processes	Examples
Core Executive Function Processes **Inhibitory Control** requires core processes associated with controlling attention, resisting distractions, and inhibiting irrelevant actions.	Resisting the urge to have a cup of coffee when trying to reduce caffeine consumption. Maintaining attention to reading in a noisy environment.
Working Memory involves core processes associated with holding information in mind and working with that information.	Keeping a multi-step plan in mind while working through a task. Managing multiple aspects of performance (e.g., for learning, group work, and time management). Remembering the rules of a game while playing.
Cognitive Flexibility requires core processes associated with thinking flexibly and adaptively during learning and performance.	Thinking of a new way to approach a task if a first effort fails. Shifting attention between major themes and details while reading, writing or learning.
Complex Executive Function Processes **Complex Executive Functions** are higher-level thinking and learning processes.	Critical thinking, problem solving, creativity, reasoning.
Control Processes **Control Processes** are involved in the top-down control of action.	Prioritizing, goal setting, planning, coordinating thinking and action, self-monitoring.

That said, if you were to read the literature on executive functioning, you might notice substantial variations in the definitions offered by different authors. For example, Lynn Meltzer (2010) identifies the following executive function processes in her practical resource book for teachers: goal setting, planning, prioritizing, organizing, using working memory, shifting attention or thinking flexibly, self-monitoring, and coordinating and deploying skills. Singer and Bashir (1999) describe executive functions as including "inhibiting actions, restraining and delaying responses, attending selectively, setting goals, planning, and organizing, as well as maintaining and shifting" our focus (p. 266).

Still, across varying definitions, researchers have tended to identify three types of executive function processes: (1) *core* processes that enable goal-directed behaviour, including *inhibitory control*, *working memory*, and *cognitive flexibility*; (2) *complex* forms of thinking and learning, such as critical thinking, problem solving, creativity, and reasoning; and (3) *control processes* involved in strategic action, such as prioritizing, goal setting, coordinating thinking and action, and self-monitoring (see Diamond, 2010; Diamond, Barnett, Thomas, & Munro, 2007; Meltzer, 2010; Singer & Bashir, 1999). Table 3-1, provides definitions of these three types of processes along with examples of each.

Imagining Executive Functioning in Classrooms

To help imagine executive functioning at work in a classroom, in SR Vignette 3-1 we describe Darrin Lim, a teacher trying to interpret differences he observed in how his Grade 9 students took up a learning activity. As you read this vignette, see if you can identify how executive functioning might have been implicated in his students' engagement.

Imagining Executive Functioning in Classrooms

Darrin Lim scanned his Grade 9 social studies classroom, watching how his students were engaging in an activity he had assigned for the day. For this activity, his content goals were for students to think deeply about the French Revolution, focusing not just on dates and facts, but also on why it came to pass. What were the experiences of people at that time? What led to the revolution? His process goal was to assist students in pulling out main ideas from reading informational text.

To work toward these two goals, Darrin had designed an activity with three parts. First, for homework the previous day he had asked students to complete a journal chart with two columns. In one column students were to identify one or two main ideas from their readings, using quotations to illustrate their choices; in the other, they were to explain why the ideas they had selected were so important. Part two of the activity was unfolding in class today. As he watched, students were meeting in small groups to compare their journal charts. Their task was to come up with two ideas they agreed were most important and justify those choices. The final step would be for each group to share their ideas in a whole class debrief.

As Darrin scanned his classroom, he wondered why students engaged so differently from each other in activities like this one. Some students navigated the activity seamlessly. They noted instructions and due dates in their daily planners,

completed the readings during the time allotted, and came to class with their homework completed. Their journal charts included thoughtful information in just the right places. As they worked in small groups, they seemed unaffected by the bustle of the classroom. They were busily sharing and comparing their thinking, and negotiating ideas to share with peers. As he had hoped, these students were grappling with big ideas.

But other students were not engaged so productively. Too many hadn't brought their homework to class, either because they didn't complete it or because they had left it at home or in their lockers. Even though they had worked through an example in class, some students were still missing important information in their journal charts or focusing on details rather than main ideas. As he watched, one group of students was having an animated, on-topic discussion. But they seemed to have lost sight of his instructions to come to agreement around key ideas they could share with others. Marianne was half-standing at her desk, waving her arm vigorously to attract the attention of a friend across the room. Fortunately, as Darrin watched, a peer drew Marianne back into her group's discussion by asking to see her journal. Darrin made his way over to a third group, where the students looked stumped. When he asked them how it was going, one student explained that they had shared ideas but didn't find any points in common. So, they weren't sure what to do.

How is executive functioning evident in this classroom? Our interpretation is that many of Darrin's students were drawing on well-developed executive functioning processes to ground their deliberate self-control of goal-directed performance. These were the students who were attending to the task and avoiding distractions (*inhibitory control*), keeping instructions in mind while working (*working memory*), and adjusting approaches as needed (*cognitive flexibility*). They were drawing on more complex executive function processes to grapple with big ideas (*critical thinking, reasoning*). They were relying on *control processes* when setting and working toward goals, coordinating their thinking and action, and self-monitoring progress to make sure they were achieving expectations.

In contrast, other learners were less successful in managing their activity engagement. For example, Marianne struggled to focus attention (*inhibitory control*). Another group of students had trouble keeping the goals of the assignment in mind while sharing their ideas (*working memory*). Another group had trouble adapting when, after sharing ideas, they found no common themes (*cognitive flexibility*). In addition, some students focused more on memory and details than on richer, more complex forms of thinking (*reasoning, critical thinking, problem solving*). Others had difficulty overall with managing their work (*control processes*). Some forgot to do their homework; others forgot to bring their homework to class.

Why Is Executive Functioning Important?

Why is supporting executive functioning so important? Executive functions are required for deliberate self-control over thinking and action in all sorts of activities within and outside of schools. Research has documented that young children's development of executive functioning is strongly related to their success in school and beyond (e.g., Blair & Razza, 2007). In SR Vignette 3-1 we gave an example of how executive functioning could be linked to more or less successful forms of engagement among students at work in Darrin Lim's Grade 9 classroom.

Connecting Executive Functioning to SRL

As you read our description of executive functioning, you might have noticed close connections with our definitions of self-regulation and SRL. For example, the kinds of self-control processes associated with executive functioning map very closely on to our descriptions of strategic action. The result is that researchers and educators often struggle to define relationships between these two perspectives.

Why is it hard to neatly distinguish between these two perspectives? One problem is that researchers focusing on both executive functions and self-regulation have often been trying to explain similar phenomena, just from different frames of reference (e.g., neurological, developmental, educational). This, in part, explains why there are so many overlaps in concepts between the two perspectives. Furthermore, a big part of the problem is that executive functions and self-regulation both provide *multidimensional* frameworks. For example, Lynn Meltzer and Kalyani Krishnan (2007) describe executive function as "an all-encompassing construct" used to describe "the complex cognitive processes that underlie flexible, goal-directed behaviour responses to novel or difficult situations" (p. 79). Within that framework they include aspects of metacognition and self-regulation. Similarly, educational psychologists define self-regulation and SRL in ways that also pull together multiple constructs into a multidimensional framework for understanding teaching and learning. In our own work, we have integrated the key role of executive functioning into a multidimensional framework.

So, how can we move forward in identifying important connections between executive functions and SRL? Given that our goal in this book is to advance understanding of SRL and how to support it, a constructive way forward might be not to try to disentangle executive functioning from SRL, but rather to identify what we can learn about deliberate, goal-directed *learning* from the executive functioning literature. Thus, our way out of this definitional conundrum is to build from research on executive functions to inform understanding of SRL and what it might take to support it.

> Food for Thought 3-3
Connecting Executive Functioning and SRL

Given our descriptions so far, what connections do you see between executive functioning and SRL? How can research on executive functions support our understanding of what effective forms of SRL might look like in classrooms, or in defining goals we might focus on in order to foster learners' development of more effective forms of SRL?

What Can We Learn from Research on Executive Functioning?

What can we learn from research on executive functioning given our quest to foster effective forms of SRL? We suggest that, parallel to our conclusions on SEL, research on executive functioning can also inform our understanding about (1) what *individuals bring to contexts* that might influence learning, and correspondingly, (2) important goals for developing individuals' capacities for goal-directed strategic action.

First, research on executive functioning contributes to our understanding of SRL by highlighting important cognitive processes that students need to draw on to support their deliberate, adaptive, and strategic engagement in learning. For example, to be successful, children need to strengthen core executive functions, including working memory, inhibitory control, and cognitive flexibility. These building blocks are necessary for self-control processes and more complex forms of thinking and learning.

Indeed, you'll likely have noticed that some students struggle with the kinds of core executive function processes described in this chapter (e.g., with maintaining and focusing attention). These students can definitely benefit from explicit supports to build capacities in these areas. But, to engage effectively in SRL, *all learners* can benefit from supports to do the following:

■ build capacities in core executive functions through multiple, rich learning experiences;

■ understand their strengths and challenges (i.e., build metacognitive knowledge about themselves as learners); and

■ develop knowledge about strategies they can use to effectively self-regulate their behaviour so as to stay productively engaged in learning (e.g., for resisting distractions).

Thus a first contribution of research on executive functions is that it defines important kinds of knowledge and skills that children need to construct and rely on during learning, if they are to engage in effective forms of SRL.

Second, research on executive functioning has also uncovered important processes associated with self-control, or the top-down control of action. Research on executive functioning suggests that self-regulating learners need to be able to:

■ mobilize their knowledge and skills, including core executive function processes (e.g., attention control), in order to engage in goal-directed activity;

■ take up *control processes* foundational to *strategic action*; and

■ engage in higher-order thinking (e.g., critical thinking, problem solving creativity, reasoning).

Thus, a second contribution of research on executive functioning is that it provides specific descriptions of the kinds of processes foundational to goal-directed, deliberate performance in the context of all sorts of activities.

How Can Educators Support Executive Functioning?

Developmental research and neuropsychological research combine to suggest that executive functions *need to and can be learned*. Executive functions start emerging in very early childhood, but they also continue to develop through the school years and at least into early adulthood. Thus, when we observe children struggling with aspects of deliberate self-control—for example, over their emotions, motivation, behaviour, or learning—evidence overwhelmingly indicates that they can develop knowledge, skills, and capacities to improve in these areas.

Fortunately, excellent resources are available for educators who want to learn more about how to support executive functioning (e.g., see Barnett et al., 2008; Diamond et al., 2007; Meltzer, 2010). In Links to Resources 3-2, we offer recommendations for educators wishing to learn more about executive functions and how to support them.

Children struggling with aspects of deliberate self-control can develop knowledge, skills, and capacities to improve in these areas.

> ## Links to Resources 3-2
> ## Fostering Executive Functioning

For educators interested in this topic, we recommend Lynn Meltzer's very accessible book, *Promoting Executive Function in The Classroom* (2010). In addition, Harvard's Center for the Developing Child provides very useful resources on executive functioning (see http://www.developingchild.harvard.edu). For example, on the Center's website you will find an outstanding video with a very clear definitions and examples of executive functioning in young children (see http://developingchild.harvard.edu/resources/multimedia/videos/inbrief_series/inbrief_executive_function/). You'll also find advice there for parents and teachers on how they can support the development executive function skills for children from infancy to adolescence.

From Executive Functioning to SRL

It seems then that research on executive functioning can inform our thinking about key pieces of the overall SRL puzzle. Correspondingly, we have observed educators weaving supports for executive functioning into their classrooms, even if they were not necessarily thinking about it those terms at the time, and then building from that in ways that might foster SRL.

For example, in our context, many educators are drawing on the Alert program (see http://www.alertprogram.com/; Shanker, 2013) or Kuypers' Zones of Regulation (see Kuypers, 2011) to support learners in understanding and self-managing their emotions and behaviour. For instance, in Starting Small 3-1, Amy Semple, a participant in one of our professional development initiatives, describes how she was drawing on these programs to support students as a primary special education teacher. Notice how, through the approaches she was using, Amy was helping her students construct meta-cognitive knowledge about how their brains work, about their emotions and needs, and about strategies helpful in taking more deliberate control over their emotions, energy levels, focus, and behaviour. Amy has been building from this foundation to nurture other self-regulating capacities in her students (e.g., for self-regulating their motivation and learning).

Another popular strategy from the Alert program is designed to help students to begin recognizing how they are feeling before or during learning. It asks students to rate their energy and alertness at either of three levels: too low, just right, or too high (see also Shanker, 2013). In our context, we have observed some teachers engage students in using coloured cards to indicate how they are feeling (e.g., red for too anxious or stressed, green for ready to go). Another teacher asks students to place their name card on a board with yellow (too low), green (just right), and red squares (too high) to indicate how they are feeling when they enter the room. This strategy enables her, and her students, to discern at a glance who in their class might need just a bit of support that day and who is feeling good and "ready to go" with their learning. As we illustrate in Figure 3-1, other teachers prefer for students to use a more fluid rating scale to indicate how well or close to the edge they are in terms of how their "engine is running," and then to think of strategies they can use to maintain or adjust their energy levels (Kuypers, 2011; Shanker, 2013).

> ## Starting Small 3-1
> # Building on the Zones of Regulation by Amy Semple

Many of the strategies I have employed over the years have been working. All of my students are very familiar with the Zones of Regulation and the Alert Program. This shares with them what their body looks like and feels like in the green zone (calm and ready to learn), the red zone (highly stimulated—angry or silly) or blue zone (tired or sick). We offer choices as to what strategies can be used if they are within those zones to help them get back into a calmer state. My students are also familiar with deep breathing and using green (positive) thoughts. This was a huge learning curve and should be celebrated.

I have realized, however, that it wasn't enough. There was something that was still missing. I still had questions.

How do I move from my students knowing and being able to talk about the strategies to them actually using them independently? How do I support my students when they are in a classroom in which I am not the teacher (e.g., when they go into their integration classrooms)? How can I help my students become self-regulated learners? How can I help the buddies who come to our classroom put strategies they use in our classroom into use in their own classrooms (when I am not there)? How can I help my students become a part of the school community? I was eager to start gaining more knowledge about all of these questions that I had.

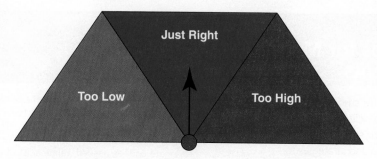

Figure 3-1 Judging "How Your Engine Is Running"

Source: Author made.

Note that these kinds of strategies have been applied to support students with special education needs, such as autism, who often benefit from explicit supports for understanding and managing their own emotions and behaviour. But educators are also now recognizing how *all learners* benefit from these kinds of supports for self-regulation. Research attests clearly to the value of explicitly helping all students learn about the ways their brains and bodies work so that they can strategically self-regulate these aspects of their engagement.

As one final example, SR Vignette 3-2 describes how Dave Dunnigan, an experienced teacher from our local community, helps his Grade 6 and 7 students learn to understand and self-regulate their levels of alertness so that they can remain actively engaged in learning. As you read this vignette, we invite you to consider how his approach has the potential to empower the development of self-regulating learners.

What do you notice across these examples of how teachers were working to help students build more self-regulating approaches to learning? What we notice is that these educators are helping students construct important kinds of knowledge and skills that they will need to draw on to successfully self-regulate their emotions, focus, and behaviour while learning. Their students are building important metacognitive knowledge about the ways their bodies and brains work, about their own and others' emotions, and about strategies they and others can use to manage their engagement. They are also learning to mobilize their knowledge and their emerging skills so that they can become and stay engaged in learning activities. Students are engaging together in effective forms of strategic action during which they are alert to how they are feeling and thinking, choosing and using strategies to help them in achieving their goals, and participating flexibly and adaptively based on how things are unfolding.

Self-Regulated Learning and Executive Functioning: Closing Reflections

We close this section by revisiting one important take-away idea from our discussion on executive functions. That is, we want emphasize again that students do not come to classrooms with fully developed capacities in core executive functions, self-control processes, or complex forms of thinking and learning. Research on executive functioning suggests these are all capacities that develop over time, from infancy through adulthood, and are nurtured through experience. We have provided just a few examples of the many ways in which educators can weave supports for executive functioning into day-to-day activities. In so doing, they also build students' capacities for engaging in active learning and effective forms of SRL.

When educators foster the development of executive functions in their students, they also build students' capacities for engaging in active learning and effective forms of SRL.

Developing Strategies for Maintaining Focus and Alertness with Students

Dave Dunnigan is always working with his students to co-construct strategies they can use to take deliberate control over different aspects of their learning. For example, he and his students explicitly discuss challenges to and strategies for staying focused while learning. Below, you'll find Dave's description of how he built strategies for staying alert with his Grade 6 and 7 students (in a combined class) this past year.

Early on in the school year we take time to share the strategies we use to help us remain focused and alert in class. I share how tactile strategies help me focus—I might hold onto a whiteboard pen and twirl it in my hand as I teach, or bend a paper clip (always a source of amusement to the students). Students are always excited to share their own strategies, which leads to a discussion as to which strategies are effective in the classroom,

and which may be distracting to others or to the teacher. We also identify which strategies help us when we are feeling sad or tired (low energy), which ones help when we are overly excited or energetic (high energy), and which ones are effective in both cases. We then create and, as needed, refine a list of possible strategies students can use to help them remain alert in class. This is an ongoing process; it is common for students to share new strategies and ideas with me and their peers throughout the school year.

In Figure 3-2 you'll find a picture of the strategies Dave and his students developed, which they then posted in their classroom. Students routinely referred to and refined these and other strategies they co-constructed as they moved through the year.

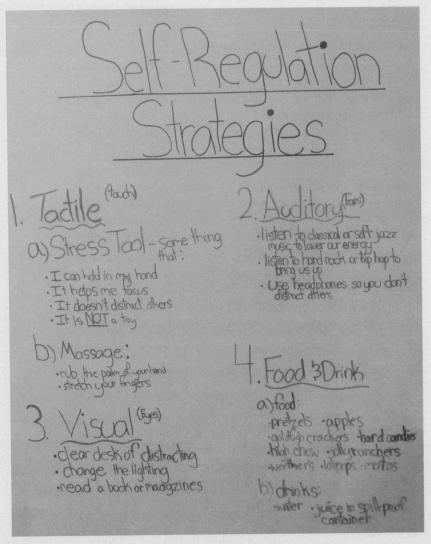

David Dunnigan

Figure 3-2 Strategies for Self-Regulating Alertness

FOSTERING SRL: CHECKING IN

In this chapter, we have described two hot topics in education today that have important synergies with our focus on self-regulation and SRL: *social-emotional learning* and *executive functioning*. Our goals in discussing these topics were to (1) describe how SRL is related to these other educational priorities and (2) support us in identifying important goals in developing *self-regulating learners*. Across the chapter, we examined each topic separately. In this closing section, we invite you to consider two insights generated by considering both topics simultaneously.

First, we have argued that students' engagement in SRL depends in part on the knowledge, skills, beliefs, and values *they are bringing to*, and *building within*, learning environments (see Figure 1-2). SEL and executive functioning frameworks have identified some of the important capacities that learners need to construct if they are to self-regulate learning effectively. For example, SEL frameworks have identified kinds of metacognitive knowledge (e.g., about one's emotions), knowledge and skills (e.g., for navigating relationships), and prosocial values that are important to self-regulating emotions and relationships successfully. Research on executive functioning highlights the importance of students building capacities over time in core, complex, and control executive functioning processes if they are to engage successfully in SRL.

Second, we would note that both SEL and executive functioning frameworks are concerned with how individuals learn to take deliberate control over thoughts and actions while engaged in activities. Like models of SRL, these frameworks suggest that individuals need *to learn how* to engage effectively in cycles of strategic action, including goal setting, planning, coordinating and deploying action, and self-monitoring. For example, research on SEL has uncovered what it takes for learners to self-manage emotions and relationships. Research on executive functions describes how control processes are mediated neurologically, develop over time and through experience, and are implicated in goal-directed action. Educators in our context have been applying these ideas in rich ways to support learners in understanding and self-managing their emotions and behaviour.

What can we conclude from this chapter? We suggest that there are many researchers, working from different perspectives, taking up the important themes represented in the integrative model of self-regulation and SRL we have introduced in this book. We have a good deal to learn from research and practice across disciplines. Together, these fields of research build a strong case for focusing on SRL in formal and informal educational settings, at all grades and ages. Each also helps to define some of the many important goals we need to keep in mind when seeking to foster SRL.

Recommended Resources

Barnett, W. S., Jung, K., Yarosz, D. J., Thomas, J., Hornbeck, A., Stechuk, R., & Burns, S. (2008). Educational effects of the Tools of the Mind curriculum: A randomized trial. *Early Childhood Research Quarterly, 23*, 299–313.

Blair, C., & Razza, R. P. (2007). Relating effortful control, executive function, and false belief understanding to emerging math and literacy ability in kindergarten. *Child Development, 78*, 647–663.

Boekaerts, M. (2011). Emotions, emotion regulation, and self-regulation of learning. In B. J. Zimmerman, & D. H. Schunk (Eds.), *Handbook of self-regulation of learning and performance* (pp. 408–425). New York, NY: Routledge.

Caprara, G. V., Barbaranelli, C., Pastorelli, C., Bandura, A., & Zimbardo, P. G. (2000). Prosocial foundations of children's academic achievement. *Psychological Science, 11*(4), 302–6.

Collaborative for Academic, Social, and Emotional Learning: http://www.casel.org.

Corno, L. (1993). The best-laid plans: Modern conceptions of volition and educational research. *Educational Researcher, 22*(2), 14–22.

Corno, L. (1994). Student volition and education: Outcomes, influences, and practices. In D. H. Schunk & B. J. Zimmerman (Eds.), *Self-regulation of learning and performance: Issues and educational applications* (pp. 229–251). Hillsdale, NJ: Erlbaum.

Diamond, A. (2010). The evidence base for improving school outcomes by addressing the whole child and by addressing skills and attitudes, not just content. *Early Education and Development, 21*(5), 780–793.

Diamond, A., Barnett, W. S., Thomas, J., & Munro, S. (2007). Preschool program improves cognitive control. *Science, 318*, 1387–1388.

Durlak, J. A., Weissberg, R. P., Dymnicki, A. B., Taylor, R. D., & Schellinger, K. B. (2011). The impact of enhancing students' social and emotional learning: A meta-analysis of school-based universal interventions. *Child Development, 82*(1), 405–432.

Fried, L. (2011). Teaching teachers about emotion regulation in the classroom. *Australian Journal of Teacher Education, 36*(3), 117–127.

Greenberg, M. T, Weissberg, R. P., O'Brien, M. U., Zins, J. E., Fredericks, L., Resnik, H., & Elias, M. J. (2003). Enhancing school-based prevention and youth development through coordinated social, emotional, and academic learning. *American Psychologist, 58*(6-7), 466–474. doi: 10.1037/0003-066X.58.6-7.466

Gross, J. J. (2013). Emotion regulation: Taking stock and moving forward. *Emotion, 13*(3), 359–365.

Izard, C., Stark, K., Trentacosta, C., & Schultz, D. (2008). Beyond emotion regulation: Emotion utilization and adaptive functioning. *Child Development Perspectives, 2*(3), 156–163.

Kuypers, L. M. (2011). *The zones of regulation*. San Jose, CA: Social Thinking Publishing.

Mayer, J. & Salovey, P. (1993). The intelligence of emotional intelligence. *Intelligence, 17*, 433–442.

Meltzer, L. (2010) (Ed). *Promoting executive function in the classroom.* NY: The Guilford Press.

Meltzer, L., & Krishnan, K. (2007). Executive function difficulties and learning disabilities: Understandings and misunderstandings. In L. Meltzer (Ed.), *Executive function in education: From theory to practice* (pp. 77–105). New York: Guilford.

Schonert-Reichl, K. A., & Hymel, S. (2010). Educating the heart as well as the mind: Social and emotional learning for school and life success. *Education Canada, 47*(2). Available at http://www.cea-ace.ca.

Schonert-Reichl, K. A., & Lawlor, M. S. (2010). The effects of a mindfulness-based education program on pre- and early adolescents' well-being and social and emotional competence. *Mindfulness, 1*(3), pp. 137–151. doi: 10.1007/s12671-010-0011-8

Schonert-Reichl, K. A., Smith, V., Zaidman-Zait, A., & Hertzman, C. (2012). Promoting children's prosocial behaviors in school: Impact of the "Roots of Empathy" program on the social and emotional competence of school-aged children. *School Mental Health, 4*, 1–21.

Schonert-Reichl, K. A., & Weissberg, R. P. (2014). Social and emotional learning: Children. Chapter to appear in T. P. Gullotta & M. Bloom (Eds.), *The encyclopedia of primary prevention and health promotion* (2nd ed.). New York: Springer Press.

Shanker, S. (2013). *Calm, alert, & learning: Classroom strategies for self-regulation*. Don Mills, On: Pearson.

Singer, B. D., & Bashir, A. S. (1999). What are executive functions and self-regulation and what do they have to do with language-learning disorders? *Language, Speech, and Hearing Services in Schools, 30*, 265–273.

Wentzel, K. R. (1993). Does being good make the grade? Social behavior and academic competence in middle school. *Journal of Educational Psychology, 85*(2), 357–364.

Zins, J., Weissberg, R., Wang, M., & Walberg, H. J. (2004). *Building academic success on social and emotional learning: What does the research say?* New York: Teachers College Press.

Chapter 4

What Goals Should We Focus on to Foster Self-Regulated Learning?

INTRODUCTION

What specific goals do we need to aim for if we are to nurture the development of *self-regulating learners*? Part One of this book was designed to help you answer that question. To that end:

- In Chapter 1 we defined key dimensions of self-regulation (in any kind of activity) and SRL (e.g., when individuals seek to learn deliberately through activities).

- In Chapter 2 we built a case for why fostering SRL is important to students' success in all sorts of activities. We also identified aspects of performance that individuals have to navigate if they are to self-regulate learning effectively (i.e., their *environment*, *emotions*, *motivation*, *behaviour*, *cognition*, *strategic action*, and *relationships*).

- In Chapter 3 we described some of the knowledge, strategies, and skills learners need to develop if they are to engage in effective forms of SRL. We achieved that by identifying connections between SRL, *social-emotional learning*, and *executive functioning*.

To close Part One of this book, in this chapter we pull these prior discussions together to help you see SRL in action in your context and set goals for learners. But, if we are to think seriously about our goals for students, we need to start by taking a big step back to consider the nature of teaching and learning. How is a focus on SRL aligned with visions for education that have been emerging over the past two decades, not only across North America, but also globally?

For example, what does SRL have to do with current calls to empower *21st-century learners*? In this new century, what kinds of capacities are now considered essential to individuals' success, not only while in school but through the next 70 to 80 years of their lives (Gerber, 2001)? What capacities do students need to develop in order to live and work within today's rapidly evolving, multicultural societies?

Also, what does SRL have to do with *self-determination*? The special education literature suggests that individuals with disabilities who have the most positive post-school life outcomes are those who have developed the capacities to be *self-determining*. These learners understand their strengths and needs; can advocate for themselves; and can, and do, make informed decisions about their lives and learning. How can a focus on self-determination help us identify what learners need to take away from their school experiences if they are to be successful into their futures?

In the first half of this chapter, we take up these questions. Doing so will help us keep in mind our goals for students from a bigger picture perspective. The second half of the chapter then focuses specifically on important goals for fostering SRL. As part of that discussion, we offer tools to help you scan for effective and ineffective forms of self-regulation in learning. We close by suggesting steps you can take to bridge from "scanning" for SRL to setting goals for learners.

Learning Intentions

After reading this chapter, you should be able to do the following:

LI 1   Describe goals associated with *21st-century learning* and *self-determination* and what these perspectives add to our understanding of important goals for learners.

LI 2   Scan for and identify effective and ineffective forms of self-regulated learning in practice.

LI 3   Identify important goals you might focus on to foster SRL in your context.

≫ Food for Thought 4-1
Setting Goals for Fostering SRL in Classrooms and Schools

What do you know about 21st-century learning and self-determination? What do these two perspectives on learning suggest about important goals for students? Can you imagine connections between them and our focus on SRL? If you were to scan for effective and ineffective forms of SRL in your context, what would you look for? What are some goals you are already working toward with the potential to foster active forms of learning and SRL? What more do you think you might need to strive for? What do you wonder?

WHAT ARE OUR GOALS FOR STUDENTS?

Later in this chapter we focus specifically on what effective forms of SRL look like in classrooms. We describe how you can scan for SRL and, based on what you see, set goals for students in your context. But before diving into that discussion, it is important to think about the kinds of learning we want students to strive for. What kinds of goals should we be imagining for (or with) students so that, as they are developing as self-regulating learners, they are being supported to engage in powerful, authentic, and rich forms of learning?

If you think about it, to be successful, individuals need to know how to self-regulate effectively in any kind of activity. For example, whether we ask students to memorize

What kinds of goals or activities should we be imagining, so that, as students are developing as self-regulating learners, they are being supported to engage in powerful, authentic, and rich forms of learning?

information or engage in inquiry-based learning, they need to be able to identify the purpose and criteria for success in those activities (i.e., for memorizing or inquiring, respectively). They need to build from their metacognitive knowledge to assess their strengths and needs (e.g., I have trouble memorizing, I don't know much about my inquiry topic). They have to recognize and optimize their emotions, focus, and motivation (e.g., to sustain attention while memorizing or inquiring). They must select, adapt, or even invent strategies for achieving their goals, monitor their progress against their goals, interpret feedback, and adjust their performance accordingly. Self-regulating learners are very adept at interpreting and navigating all sorts of expectations.

We certainly can help students become very proficient at learning and recalling content. But is that enough? When setting goals for students, we need to start by considering what we want the quality of students' engagement and learning to be. Indeed, when we foster SRL, we have an extraordinary opportunity to develop students' capacities to engage in more powerful, active, self-determined, lifelong, and transformative forms of learning. What does that look like? In the first half of the chapter, we respond to that question by considering *why* educators are being asked to foster *21st-century learning* and *self-determination*.

> When we foster SRL, we have an opportunity to develop students' capacities to engage in powerful, active, self-determined, lifelong, and transformative forms of learning.

SRL and 21st-Century Learning

In this day and age, it is very common to hear calls on educators to engage students in 21st-century learning. What is 21st-century learning? Why is it important? How can a focus on SRL contribute to developing 21st-century learners? We take up these questions in this section.

What Is 21st-Century Learning?
Generally speaking, **21st-century learning** is defined as a constellation of knowledge and competencies required to thrive in today's rapidly evolving, information-rich societies. Frameworks for describing 21st-century competencies typically stress how today's learners must grapple with an explosion of new and ever-changing technologies. But most frameworks also associate 21st-century learning with *lifelong learning* and *self-direction*, *critical thinking* and *problem solving*, *communication*, *creativity* and *innovation*, *collaboration*, *social responsibility*, and *leadership*, as well as *technological literacy* (e.g., see http://www.p21.org/about-us/p21-framework).

> **21st-century learning** refers to a constellation of knowledge and competencies required to thrive in today's rapidly-evolving, information-rich societies. These include lifelong learning and self-direction, critical thinking and problem-solving, communication, creativity and innovation, collaboration, social responsibility, and leadership, as well as technological literacy.

Why Is 21st-Century Learning Important?
Why is fostering students' development of capacities in these areas important? Dumont, Istance, and Benavides (2012) provide a powerful description of the fundamental shifts that today's students will face during their lifetimes:

> Students should become self-directed, lifelong learners, especially as they are preparing for jobs that do not yet exist, to use technologies that have not yet been invented, and to solve problems that are not yet even recognized as problems. (p. 8)

In the 21st century, learners need to know how to navigate environments that are transforming at rapid speeds and in unpredictable ways.

It follows that 21st-century learners need to learn not just about content, but also about how to use knowledge flexibly and adaptively. According to Dumont et al. (2012), learners need to develop **adaptive expertise,** which they define as the ability to "apply meaningfully learned knowledge and skills flexibly and creatively in different situations" (p. 3). Learners in the 21st century will succeed if they know how to activate and mobilize knowledge, beliefs, values, and skills flexibly and adaptively in different activities and environments.

> **Adaptive expertise** involves applying knowledge and skills flexibly and adaptively as needed in any given situation.

These competencies are required for individuals to thrive in a changing world. But more than that, our students can and need to play a role in shaping their futures. Who is it that will identify needs we don't yet recognize, invent new technologies we haven't yet imagined, or reframe problems in new and generative ways? To thrive in the 21st century, students must prepare to be innovators and leaders. Fostering 21st-century learning during the school years is necessary for preparing students to be lifelong, self-regulating learners with adaptive expertise who can contribute to shaping the world in which they will live and work.

It might be tempting to conclude that 21st-century competencies are only attainable by our very strongest students. But all individuals will face shifting conditions in workplaces and daily life that demand continual learning and adaptive expertise. The challenge for us as educators is to empower all students to reach their full potential as 21st-century learners.

Connecting SRL and 21st-Century Learning   Descriptions of 21st-century learning suggest that, in order to be successful post-school, students need to know how to take deliberate control over their lives and learning. They need to *learn how to learn*. According to Zimmerman (2002), lifelong learners are self-regulating. He gives the example of self-employed individuals who "must constantly self-refine their skills in order to survive" (p. 66). It follows that models of SRL can help in defining what self-directed, lifelong, adaptive learning *looks like*, and, correspondingly, what it takes to support it. We will build from this idea through the rest of this book.

> To be successful post-school, students need to know how to take deliberate control over their learning. They need to learn how to learn so that they can be lifelong, self-regulating learners.

The 21st century learning framework outlined here reminds us that our aim is to prepare lifelong, self-regulating learners for life after school. Why keep this bigger picture goal in mind? As we move forward, we will start focusing attention more narrowly. For example, we will describe how you can design activities, supports, and assessment frameworks to promote effective forms of SRL (in Chapters 7, 8, and 9, respectively). Keeping the larger picture in mind will remind us that, at the end of the day, all of these puzzle pieces need to fit together to foster students' development as active, deliberate, flexible, adaptive, self-regulating learners.

SRL and Self-Determination

Those of you familiar with research or practice in special education might have noticed the close connections between SRL, 21st-century learning, and self-determination. What is self-determination? Why is it important? How are SRL and self-determination connected? These are questions we take up in this section.

What Is Self-Determination?   When you think of our students who are struggling the most, including those with significant special education needs, can you imagine them as self-aware and autonomous 21st-century learners? If not, you might be surprised to learn that, in the special education literature, researchers have documented the importance of empowering students with disabilities to be *self-determining*. It is becoming increasingly clear that *all students* benefit when they are able to take deliberate control over their lives and learning.

Thus, as we are considering bigger picture goals for students, it will also help to identify the kinds of knowledge, beliefs, skills, and strategies that underlie an individual's capacity to be self-determining. According to Wehmeyer and his colleagues,

> **Self-determination** as a goal defined in the special education literature refers to a combination of skills, knowledge, and beliefs that enable a person to engage in goal-directed, self-regulated behavior. These include capacities to make decisions and solve problems; knowledge skills, and strategies needed to manage one's own performance; self-awareness and self-advocacy; and beliefs in one's capacities to succeed.

> **Self-determination** is a combination of skills, knowledge, and beliefs that enable a person to engage in goal-directed, self-regulated, autonomous behavior. An understanding of one's strengths and limitations together with a belief in oneself as capable and effective are essential to self-determination. When acting on the basis of these skills and attitudes, individuals have greater ability to take control of their lives and assume the role of successful adults. (Field, Martin, Miller, Ward, & Wehmeyer, 1998, p. 2)

Building from this definition, special education researchers have identified many component skills associated with success in life both during and after the school years (see Denney & Daviso, 2012; Wehmeyer, Agran, & Hughes, 1998). Figure 4-1 provides an overview of 12 skills commonly included in descriptions of self-determination.

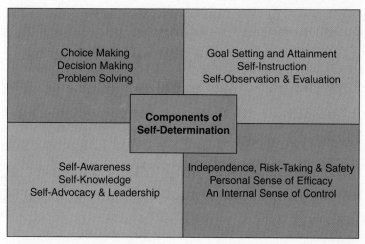

Figure 4-1 Component Skills Necessary for Self-Determined Behaviour

Source: Author created.

Why Is Self-Determination Important?   When we foster self-determination, we empower learners, whatever their unique constellation of strengths and needs, to take control over their own lives and learning. From a self-determination perspective, component skills required to do that include the following (see Figure 4-1): (1) capacities to make decisions and solve problems (i.e., choice making, decision making, and problem solving); (2) knowledge, skills, and strategies needed to manage one's own performance (i.e., goal setting and attainment, self-instruction, self-observation, and evaluation); (3) self-awareness and self-advocacy (i.e., self-awareness, self-knowledge, self-advocacy, and leadership); and (4) beliefs in one's own capacity to succeed (i.e., reflected in independence, risk-taking and safety skills, personal sense of efficacy, and internal sense of control).

Connecting SRL and Self-Determination   As you viewed Figure 4-1, you may have noticed important overlaps between capacities associated with self-determination and the dimensions of self-regulation (i.e., *cognition* and *metacognition, emotion* and *motivation, strategic action*) as we identified them in Chapter 1. For example, like SRL, self-determination relies on individuals' metacognitive knowledge and awareness about their own strengths and needs, as well as on their belief that they can succeed. Both self-determination and SRL also require that individuals know how to engage reflectively in strategic, goal-directed action.

Dr. Barry Zimmerman (2011) highlights another common ground between SRL and self-determination. That is, both emphasize the importance of providing students with opportunities to build their capacities as autonomous learners. Here is how Zimmerman describes this connection:

> A key self-determination concept regarding students' self-regulation is *autonomous self-regulation*, in which students initiate and persist because they can choose learning tasks that are interesting or personally important to them. To enhance autonomous self-regulation, self-determination researchers (Reeve et al., 2008) recommend helping students set their own goals, direct their own behaviour, seek out optimal challenges, pursue their own interest and values, choose their own way to solve problems, to think more flexibly and more actively use more mature coping strategies, and experience more positive feelings about themselves and their learning. (Zimmerman, 2011, p. 52)

Notice here how Zimmerman is pulling advice from the self-determination literature to suggest goals and practices that can foster students' development of *autonomous self-regulation*. Like 21st-century learners, autonomous self-regulators not only know how to identify expectations set for them for others, but they also know how to develop and pursue their own goals, make choices and decisions, think and problem-solve flexibly, and chart their own pathways into the future.

What Are Our Bigger Picture Goals for Students? Closing Reflections

In this first half of this chapter, we have taken a step back to consider our goals for students in light of calls to foster 21st-century learning and self-determination. Our purpose has been to ensure that, as we move into more fine-grained discussions of SRL and how to support it, we retain a vision of our big picture goals for learners.

Our goal must be to support *all of our students* in becoming confident, self-aware, strategic problem finders and solvers who know how to engage in rich forms of thinking and learning, mobilize their knowledge and skills flexibly as they adapt to shifting environments, and take deliberate control over their lives and learning.

Emerging priorities in education today combine to emphasize our responsibility as educators to empower learners who know how to succeed, not only within our classrooms, but in their lives outside of school and into adulthood. Whatever lens we apply (i.e., 21st-century learning, self-determination, SRL), it is abundantly clear that our ultimate goal must be to support *all of our students* in becoming confident, self-aware, strategic problem finders and solvers who know how to engage in rich forms of thinking and learning, mobilize their knowledge and skills flexibly as they adapt to shifting environments, and take deliberate control over their lives and learning.

GOALS IN FOSTERING SELF-REGULATED LEARNING

In the first half of this chapter, we have identified the kinds of learning we want students to strive for if they are to be successful, self-determining, lifelong learners. In Part Two of this book, we will explore how educators can establish learning environments and activities that invite, inspire, and support students to self-regulate their engagement in these rich forms of learning. But before bridging to that, in the second half of this chapter, we encourage you to think more specifically about the goals we need to take up if we are to foster the development of self-regulating learners.

Scanning for Self-Regulated Learning

In the introduction to this book, we suggested that a good way to get going in fostering SRL is to take a moment to "scan" for SRL in your context. According to Judy Halbert and Linda Kaser (2013), when engaged in *inquiry processes*, educators do the following:

- *scan* their current context to identify pressing questions, challenges, or goals;
- decide to *focus* attention on a key priority;
- *develop a hunch* about what might be happening;
- engage deliberately in *new professional learning* to inform their practice development;
- *take action* based on what they are learning; and
- reflectively *check* on what happens and then refine inquiry questions and processes based on successes and challenges.

Akin to building from assessments to inform instruction, when you scan for SRL in your context, you create opportunities to notice what your students are thinking and doing in relation to the conditions you have set up in the learning environment. Based on your observations, you can then identify important goals for your students.

But if you were to scan for SRL in your students' engagement, what would you look for? Because SRL is multi-faceted and complex, it is impossible to create a comprehensive list of everything you might want to observe. So, instead of a list, we link back to the integrative model of SRL from Chapter 1 to offer a conceptual tool that can help you focus your

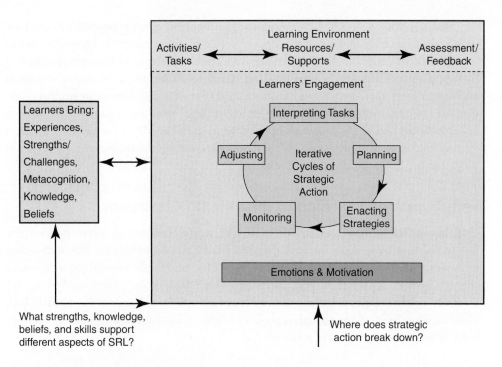

Figure 4-2 A Conceptual Tool to Support Your Scanning for Self-Regulated Learning.

Source: Adapted with permission from Butler and Schnellert (2015), based on the work of Butler and Cartier (2004a); Cartier and Butler (2004).

attention (see Figure 4-2). For example, if you were to engage in the inquiry processes outlined earlier (following Halbert & Kaser, 2013), you could refer to this tool to help you when *scanning* for SRL, deciding where to *focus* your attention, and *developing a hunch* about what is happening to support or undermine the success of learners.

How can this conceptual tool aid you in identifying effective and ineffective forms of SRL in your context? The tool can remind you to look for the following:

- what students *are bringing to contexts* that might influence their approaches to learning (e.g., experiences, strengths/challenges, metacognition, knowledge, beliefs);
- how students' *emotions* and *motivation* might be shaping their engagement; and
- how learners are engaging more or less effectively in *cycles of strategic action* in relation to different aspects of their performance.

If you watch for these things, you will be able to see SRL at work in relation to the environments and practices you are establishing in your context.

Note that, as you scan for SRL, it is particularly important to observe how students are self-regulating the many different aspects of performance that are so important to learning. For example, do your students know how to take deliberate control over their *environment* (e.g., by choosing where to work), *emotions* (e.g., by regulating or utilizing excitement), *motivation* (e.g., in order to fuel and sustain effort), *behaviour* (e.g., by focusing attention), *strategic action* (e.g., by self-assessing progress), *cognition and learning* (e.g., in order to work richly with ideas), and *relationships* (e.g., in order to work well with others or get help)? Ultimately, learners need to consider all of these aspects of their performance if they are to engage effectively in activities. What are your students' strengths and needs in these areas? Correspondingly, what might be important goals for your students?

As you scan for SRL, it is particularly important to observe how students are self-regulating the many different aspects of performance that are so important to effective learning.

Similarly, when scanning for what your students are bringing to contexts, you can look for whether they have developed the kinds of strengths, metacognition, knowledge, skills, strategies, beliefs, and values they will need to effectively self-regulate these many aspects of their performance (i.e., their environments, emotions, motivation, behaviour, cognition and learning, strategic action, and relationships). For example, have your students constructed powerful metacognitive knowledge about their emotions, themselves as learners, or learning strategies? Do your students believe in their capacity to achieve outcomes if they try hard or use good strategies? What kinds of knowledge, strategies, skills, or beliefs do they need to further develop if they are to engage effectively in active learning and SRL?

Self-Regulated Learning in Mrs. Klein's Classroom

To help you imagine how you might scan for SRL in your context, in this section we give you an opportunity to apply the conceptual tool in Figure 4-2 to look for SRL in two case examples. In SR Vignette 4-1 we describe how Elise and Paolo engaged in a "learning through reading" (LTR) activity in Mrs. Klein's Grade 9 classroom. Then, in Activity 4-1 we invite you to describe what you notice about Elise and Paolo's approaches to SRL, and, based on your observations, to suggest goals we might set for them to support their development of more effective forms of learning.

> ## SR Vignette 4-1
> # Scanning for Self-Regulated Learning in Mrs. Klein's Classroom

Elise and Paolo are two students in Mrs. Klein's Grade 9 classroom. Over the past week, Mrs. Klein has asked students to read three short texts, written from varying points of view, on the fall of the Roman Empire. Their task has been to draw from the readings in order to (1) identify factors that led to the Roman Empire's decline, and (2) imagine whether, and if so how, similar factors might lead to the fall of a civilization in today's times. By the end of the week, students are expected to submit written reflections on these topics. On this day, to help them in grappling with these big ideas and preparing to write, Mrs. Klein has asked them to share their ideas with a partner. Below we describe how Elise and Paolo engaged in this activity. From the descriptions, what do you notice about their self-regulated approaches to learning?

Elise. Over the past couple of days, Elise has immersed herself in the assigned readings. She hopes to study history when she goes to university, so this assignment is right up her alley. She also loves reading. In fact, her mother is always complaining that she would read her life away if she had the chance! But she can't help it. She loves getting absorbed in a novel or a story. As she read about the Roman Empire, she imagined herself in another time and place; what life must have been like then! She also recognized many connections with a novel that she'd read about Cleopatra. In class this day, Elise was partnered with Rosa. Initially, Elise was fine with that because Rosa seemed nice. For the first half of the class, she and Rosa had a lovely conversation during which Elise excitedly told Rosa all about Cleopatra. But when Rosa interrupted her rudely mid-sentence, Elise was incensed.

Elise couldn't understand why Rosa wasn't interested in Cleopatra. Her story was so dramatic! So, she decided Rosa wasn't such a great partner after all. Elise knew she'd do fine on this assignment—she always got at least a B. So, after that she mostly worked on her own. Rosa could just figure it all out for herself!

Paolo. Paolo had *not* enjoyed wading through the three readings Mrs. Klein had assigned, but at least it was better than reading the textbook! He could never make it through even a page of that boring book before he caught himself thinking about something else. Paolo felt even more stressed as he faced the written part of this assignment. He just didn't get it. He thought he understood the material while he was reading, but then when he submitted written assignments or took tests, his marks were always lousy. He was game to try hard, in spite of his track record. He hoped this time the results would be different. At least on this day he got to work with Ross, one of his best friends. He and Ross played on the same hockey team, so they often hung out after school. Paolo knew he could ask Ross for help without feeling stupid. As they started talking about Mrs. Klein's questions, Paolo and Ross referred to notes they had taken while doing the readings. Paolo was proud of his notes, which were very detailed. He was sure he had recorded all of the most important dates and facts from each of the readings. He and Ross made plans together about how they could help each other on the next steps of the assignment. Paolo asked Ross what he was going to write about and why.

Scanning for SRL in Mrs. Klein's Classroom

In this activity, we invite you to use Table 4-1 to record what you observed about strengths and challenges in Elise and Paolo's self-regulated approaches when engaged in Mrs. Klein's LTR activity. Based on your observations, what goals might you set to support them in their learning?

Table 4-1 Scanning for SRL in Elise's and Paolo's Engagement

What do you notice about...	Elise (observations? goals?)	Paolo (observations? goals?)
The kinds of knowledge, beliefs, skills, and strategies they were *bringing to learning*?		
The *emotions* and *motivation* they were experiencing and how those were related to their approaches to learning?		
How they were engaged in *strategic action* in relation to different aspects of their performance?		

SRL in Mrs. Klein's Classroom: Our Observations

What did we observe about Elise's and Paolo's engagement in an LTR activity in Mrs. Klein's Grade 9 classroom? Below we describe the result of our scan for each student's SRL, informed by the conceptual tool in Figure 4-2.

Scanning for SRL: Elise   What did Elise *bring to this learning activity*? She seemed to have some well-developed strengths, knowledge, and skills that she could build on to grapple richly with ideas. For example, she was able to concentrate for long periods, immerse herself in new worlds while reading stories, interpret main ideas from informational text, and find connections across what she was reading and learning. She had experience reading historical writing, prior knowledge about the Roman Empire, and a love of history and reading. On the other hand, there were gaps in what Elise brought to this activity. For example, she did not have well-developed metacognitive knowledge about what she was expected to do when reading to learn in her classroom. Also, in order to engage more effectively with peers, she needed to develop better social relationship skills, a prosocial orientation, and self-awareness about her emotions and how to navigate them.

What did we notice about Elise's *motivation* and *emotions* as she engaged in the LTR activity? She studied all three texts with great interest. She linked what she was reading to her favourite novel. She spoke with enthusiasm about Cleopatra with Rosa. She was pursuing her personal passion to learn more about history. But she spent little time thinking about her teachers' questions or expectations. Furthermore, Elise became angry when Rosa did not share her interest in talking about Cleopatra. Instead of negotiating common goals or interests, she chose to stop working with Rosa.

Finally, what did we observe about how Elise was engaged in strategic action in relation to multiple aspects of her performance? Elise was doing a fine job of grappling with big ideas while learning from reading. But she did not seem to be taking deliberate control over her *cognition and learning*. For instance, she did not interpret Mrs. Klein's expectations and use them to guide her performance. If Elise were being strategic, she could have considered her personal passions alongside her teachers' expectations and found a way to achieve both simultaneously. Instead, she did not seem to choose or use strategies that would help her read strategically or prepare for writing (e.g., by reading the texts with questions in mind, taking notes on relevant ideas, or making some kind of organizational tool to support her thinking).

Elise also had trouble self-regulating *relationships* in ways that could have supported her own and Rosa's learning. One problem was that she seemed to lose sight of the purpose of the "pair-share," which was to have peers support each other in thinking about Mrs. Klein's questions and preparing for writing. The result was that she did not self-direct her interactions with Rosa in order to achieve those purposes. When Rosa interrupted her, she struggled to take Rosa's perspective. For example, she couldn't understand why Rosa might want to focus more on the task than on the story of Cleopatra. Finally, when Elise became angry with Rosa, she had trouble self-regulating her *emotions*. Rather than considering how to communicate with Rosa to resolve the conflict, she disconnected from the collaboration. In so doing, she not only lost an opportunity to enrich her own thinking, but she also opted out of the chance she had to engage in *socially responsible self-regulation*; that is, to engage in a way that could support her own and Rosa's learning, as defined in Chapter 1 (see also Perry, 2013).

Scanning for SRL: Paolo   What did Paolo *bring to Mrs. Klein's LTR activity?* Paolo knew he had trouble sustaining attention while reading. He realized that he was getting poor marks on tests and writing assignments. But Paolo had little sense about what to do differently to improve outcomes, other than getting help from Ross. He had limited metacognitive knowledge about strategies he could mobilize to achieve expectations. His metacognitive knowledge about the demands of LTR activities was not a good match to Mrs. Klein's expectations. Mrs. Klein was expecting him to read for and work with big ideas, but Paolo interpreted requirements as listing and learning facts. Paolo did have strong relationship skills, reflected in his sustained friendship with Ross and knowledge about how to work with him effectively as a learning partner.

What did we observe about Paolo's *motivation* and *emotions?* Paolo lacked confidence, but he was willing to try hard in spite of the challenges he was experiencing. He valued academic achievement and wanted to succeed in school. The result was that he persevered through difficulties, with a little help from his friend. He also stayed calm and focused while learning, in spite of the challenges he was experiencing.

Finally, what did we observe about how Paolo engaged in strategic action in relation to multiple aspects of his performance? Paolo was working hard to self-regulate his *cognition and learning*. He started by interpreting his task and setting goals. He recognized that he needed to do the three readings and then prepare a written answer to Mrs. Klein's questions. He was working actively toward those goals. Unfortunately, because Paolo drew on faulty metacognitive knowledge about LTR activities when interpreting expectations, he self-directed all of his subsequent efforts toward learning facts rather than working with ideas. Paolo was strategic in that he was willing to ask for help. He also did a nice job of choosing and using a note-taking strategy to prepare for writing. But the quality of his notes was compromised by his focus on recording factual information. And he didn't know what to do when feedback (e.g., low grades) suggested that his approaches were not working. He was monitoring outcomes but having trouble diagnosing what was going wrong, with the result that he had little idea about why and how he might adapt or adjust his actions to achieve better outcomes.

Paolo recognized he had difficulty in self-regulating his *behaviour*, particularly in maintaining concentration while reading. But he wasn't aware of strategies he could use to maintain his concentration. Instead, in this instance he just associated his relative success with having an opportunity to read shorter texts. In contrast, Paolo seemed to be self-regulating his *motivation* effectively. He valued success in school in spite of his difficulties, which fuelled his persistence. Paolo also seemed to be doing a relatively good job of self-regulating *emotions* (i.e., stress, anxiety). Here, it helped him to know that he could get help from Ross without risking looking "stupid" to others. Finally, Paolo seemed to be doing a solid job of self-regulating *relationships*. He understood the purpose of the pair-share activity. He and Ross made plans together about strategies they could use to advance each other's learning (e.g., sharing notes). They engaged in co-learning together.

From Scanning for SRL to Setting Goals

When thinking about how to foster SRL in their contexts, many educators find it easier to start by narrowing their attention to just one or two students. By doing so, they are able to see the complexity of SRL in action without having to attend to all learners in their class-room simultaneously. Imagine, for example, that you decided to start by focusing attention on just Elise and Paolo. How could you build from scanning to setting goals for their further development as self-regulating learners?

In Activity 4-1 we invited you to imagine goals you might set for Elise and Paolo given your scan of their self-regulated approaches to learning. What did you conclude? Based on our scan, we conclude that Elise would benefit from support in the following areas:

■ constructing metacognitive knowledge about LTR activities and associated strategies, relationship skills, and emotions;

■ adopting prosocial values and fulfilling her social responsibility as a member of a learning community (i.e., to learn with and support peers' learning);

■ finding ways to coordinate her interests and passions with her teachers' expectations; and

■ learning how to engage more effectively in strategic action related to her *cognition and learning, emotions* and *relationships*.

We conclude that Paolo would benefit from support in a number of areas as well, including:

■ constructing metacognitive knowledge about LTR activity requirements and about effective reading, writing, learning, and attention control strategies;

■ taking and feeling in control of his learning and performance, rather than relying for success on having easy texts or getting help from a friend—Paolo needs help to experience success, then attribute improved outcomes to factors within his control, like better understandings about task requirements or use of effective strategies for reading, writing, learning, and concentrating; and

■ engaging more effectively in strategic action in relation to his *cognition and learning*, particularly task interpretation, and then choosing and using cognitive and learning processes better matched to task demands.

Focusing on just one or two students, as we have here for Elise and Paolo, is a great way to get started with fostering SRL in your context. It can help you identify how SRL is required by the kinds of activities you design. It can also reveal how students are thinking about and engaging in the work you give them. You can carry these insights forward as you start scanning for SRL among your full set of students.

In addition, conducting an in-depth scan of students' SRL can be helpful when designing assistance for learners with significant challenges or special education needs (e.g., problems in attention, learning disabilities) (see Butler, 2002; Butler & Schnellert, 2015; Cleary, Callan, & Zimmerman, 2012). For those learners, it can be particularly useful for classroom teachers and special educators to collaborate when scanning for SRL and designing supports for students (see Chapter 10). By creating a rich description of students' approaches to SRL, as we did with Elise and Paolo, you can better identify the source of their challenges, important goals, and constructive plans of action.

Patterns of SRL in Classrooms

Our descriptions of Elise's and Paolo's engagement in learning also remind us that even good students can struggle with SRL for a variety of different reasons. It is important to keep this diversity in mind when deciding how to support learners in K–12 classrooms. That said, as you scan for SRL in your context, you might notice that many students seem to struggle with similar kinds of knowledge or processes. For example, both Elise and Paolo had trouble interpreting the requirements of LTR activities and then focusing their attention effectively to achieve them, albeit for different reasons. Thus, by scanning for SRL *across students* in classrooms, we can often identify goals (such as supporting task interpretation) that could serve to foster effective forms of SRL among many learners simultaneously (see Butler & Cartier, 2004b). As we move through this book, we will build from this point to explain how supports to SRL embedded within classrooms can be very powerful and *efficient* because they can help in addressing the learning needs of a diverse range of students (see Butler, 2002; Perry, 2004). By focusing on SRL, we can create practices that benefit all learners, while still attending in rich ways to individual needs (see Chapter 10).

Patterns of SRL: Extended Example What kinds of patterns in SRL might you observe in classrooms? To provide one example, we summarize findings from a longitudinal research study that investigated how teachers in four secondary schools worked together to foster LTR in subject-area classrooms, such as science or social studies. As did Mrs. Klein's assignment on the fall of the Roman Empire, LTR activities require students to use a rich combination of reading and learning strategies to build meaning from reading and work actively with ideas (see Cartier, 2000).

As part of a district-level initiative, teachers included in this research decided to use two complementary assessment tools to scan for SRL in their classrooms. One tool, the Learning through Reading Questionnaire (LTRQ) (Butler & Cartier, 2004a; Cartier & Butler, 2004), assessed students' perceptions about LTR activities and their engagement in them. The second tool, a performance-based assessment (see Brownlie, Feniak, & Schnellert, 2006), assessed how students were actually engaging with and achieving goals within the LTR activity. Teachers gave, scored, and interpreted assessments in the fall term to develop goals for the coming academic year. They used the same assessment tools in the spring in order to judge how successfully their students were achieving the goals they had set for them.

For research purposes, we explored the assessment data teachers collected to see if we could discern any common patterns in how 646 students were approaching LTR tasks (see Butler, Cartier, Schnellert, Gagnon, & Giammarino, 2011). Results revealed four broad patterns in how students were working through LTR activities (see Figure 4-3). These patterns were multidimensional in that they encompassed students' cognition and metacognition, motivation and emotions, and strategic action. As you can see in Figure 4-3, we also found strong links between these patterns of engagement and students' achievement as measured on the performance-based assessment.

What patterns did we observe? We found that many students (41%) could be described as "actively engaged." They reported positive emotions when given an LTR activity, were confident that they could succeed, and were invested in learning. They engaged deliberately in cycles of strategic action. Their task interpretation was well matched to the goals of the LTR activities, as defined in their teachers' classrooms. They chose and used a rich combination of reading and learning strategies, including ones for working with texts and working with ideas. These students were very willing to seek help when needed. Not surprisingly, these students achieved the highest levels on the performance-based assessment.

Unfortunately, a good number of students (13%) could be described as "disengaged." These students experienced stress or anxiety when faced with an LTR activity. They reported the lowest confidence in their ability to complete key task requirements. Their personal goals were to "finish as quickly as possible" and "read as little as possible."

By scanning for SRL *across students* in classrooms, we can often identify goals that can serve to foster effective forms of SRL among many learners simultaneously.

SRL Dimensions	Actively Engaged (41%)	Passively Efficient (26%)	Actively Inefficient (21%)	Disengaged (13%)
Performance-based Assessment	best	second best	low	worst
Emotions	happy	content	stressed	stressed
Motivation	most confident & invested	confident	low confidence but invested	lowest confidence & investment
Cognition	most strategy choices (text, ideas)	less strategic (i.e., lower use of strategies)	engaged, but text-focused	lowest engagement
Metacognition	best task interpretation	mid-level task interpretation	mid-level task interpretation	lowest task interpretation
Strategic Action	highest strategic action; high help-seeking	mid-level strategic action; low help-seeking	mid-level strategic action; high help-seeking	lowest strategic action; low help-seeking

Figure 4-3 SRL Patterns in Secondary Classrooms: *Learning Through Reading*

Note: Based on findings reported in Butler et al. (2011).

Source: Republished with permission of John Wiley & Sons, Inc, from "Becoming self-regulated readers and writers", *The Reading Teacher*, 56 no.3 permission conveyed through Copyright Clearance Center, Inc

They engaged in the lowest levels of strategic action and cognitive strategies when compared to other students. Still, these students were not likely to ask for help. Not surprisingly, these students received the lowest scores on the performance-based assessment.

Two other patterns were particularly interesting. First, 21 percent of students appeared to be "actively inefficient" (Swanson, 1990). Like Paolo, these students were trying hard and were invested in the activity. They were choosing and using some kind of strategy and were willing to seek help when needed. But, like Paolo, they seemed to lack a clear sense of direction. Their task interpretation was not well aligned with LTR expectations. Correspondingly, their cognitive and learning processes focused more on text features (e.g., finding bold words) than on working with ideas. In short, these students just didn't seem to know how to productively self-regulate their learning activity. As a result, they were highly stressed and lacked confidence in their ability to achieve expectations.

Finally, 26 percent of students seemed to be "passively efficient." These students were content when assigned an LTR activity and confident in their ability to be successful. But, like Elise, these students performed relatively well on performance-based assessments without being deliberately strategic. For example, they were less likely to use cognitive and learning strategies or seek help when needed. Thus, we wondered if these students would know how to self-regulate learning in more challenging situations. For example, Elise's goal was to study history at university, but was she developing the foundational knowledge, skills, strategies, values, and beliefs she was going to need in a post-secondary context, with its increased expectation for independent self-regulation?

What do we conclude from our study of these patterns in engagement? First, our findings provide additional evidence of the relationship between effective forms of SRL and achievement. Students who were engaging actively and deliberately in strategic action cycles scored highest on the performance-based assessment. Second, we identified patterns educators can watch for when scanning for SRL in classrooms. These findings also illustrate how, by scanning for SRL across students, educators are likely to notice clusters of students who share similar needs. Third, these patterns remind us that individual learners can react very differently to the same assignment. Therefore, we need to anticipate the range of challenges different students might experience in the activities we assign (e.g., in task interpretation, in choosing and using strategies, in confidence and motivation) and proactively design supports that ensure all learners can participate as successfully as possible.

Our final observation is that pretty much all of the learners in this study would have benefitted from supports for their development of effective forms of self-regulation. For example, even students who are *actively engaged* need to continue building effective forms of SRL across a variety of activities and subject areas, particularly as expectations shift or amplify across time. *Disengaged* students would clearly benefit from supports for all dimensions of SRL, particularly motivation. *Actively inefficient* students, like Paolo, could use support to better interpret tasks and then channel their self-regulating capacities in more productive directions. They need to experience and observe success so that they can take and feel in control of outcomes. Students who are *passively efficient* also need to learn how to take more deliberate control over learning, particularly if they are going to be successful in more challenging situations.

From Scanning for SRL to Setting Goals: A Final Example

We suggested above that focusing on just one or two students in your classroom is a good way to begin. But you can also narrow your attention by choosing just one or two goals to focus on given the needs of students in your context. For example, in Starting Small 4-1, Brigitte Sebulsky describes her work to foster *growth mindsets* in her Grade 2 classroom.

Mindsets reflect individuals' beliefs about their abilities and whether or not they can grow through experience, effort or persistence.

Fixed mindsets reflect individuals' beliefs that ability is stable, so there isn't much point in trying hard to improve it.

Growth mindsets reflect individuals' beliefs that ability can grow through effort and persistence.

Mindsets are among the beliefs that learners bring to activities that shape their approaches to learning (Dweck, 2006; 2010). Learners with **fixed mindsets** tend to believe that intelligence is determined at birth; you have it or you don't. Students with fixed mindsets are less likely to take risks, ask for help, and persist through difficulties. In contrast, learners with **growth mindsets** tend to believe that ability can grow with effort and persistence. Learners who adopt growth mindsets are more likely to take on challenges and believe that effort can lead to improvement. Building from Dweck's research, combined with what she observed among students in her classroom, Brigitte set *developing growth mindsets* as a priority goal in her work with her students. As you read her description, notice how she assesses "success" in achieving that goal. Take note, too, of the strategies she is using to see SRL, day to day, in her classroom.

≫ Starting Small 4-1
Seeing SRL in Action by Brigitte Sebulsky

Daily observation and formative assessment are two ways that I will know if I have achieved my goals. More importantly, it will be what is happening for my students that I will count as success. For example . . .

- Students are finding quiet places to work or using the dividers when their peers are being distracting. This is happening more frequently. A sign of learning!

- After the growth mindset lessons, the student who I was really worried about is now approaching tasks with an "I will try my best attitude," and from this shift I see that she is now completing more writing assignments. This is truly amazing!

- Students are making their parents come in to see the various stages of our igloo construction and explaining how it is being built, the construction problems we had, and how as a class we solved the problems. I am hearing the connections the students made between the igloo construction and our math units (data collecting and measuring) as they talked to each other, their parents, and other teachers. That's learning!

- Hearing the class say more frequently "I did it" and less frequently "Do I have to?" is definitely a sign of growth.

- One student came back very excited after the weekend and said he "used it," meaning the growth mindset lesson. He proceeded to tell the class how frustrated he was learning a new trick on his skateboard, and that he told himself that he could do it. So he practised some more. When the class asked him how it went, he beamed and said, "I got it!" He learned a new skill at school and applied it at home. How wonderful is that!

These are wonderful signs of learning and growth, and I am right there with the students.

GOALS IN FOSTERING SRL: FINAL REFLECTIONS

Through Part One of this book our goal has been to help you in constructing a rich understanding about self-regulation and SRL. To that end, we have defined SRL in relation to self-regulation, described dimensions of SRL, offered an integrative model to show how those dimensions are implicated within activities, and highlighted multiple aspects of performance which individuals need to self-regulate simultaneously. We have identified connections between SRL, social-emotional learning, executive functioning, 21st-century learning, and self-determination. We have provided examples of self-regulation-in-action in many different kinds of activities, including both day-to-day activities and school-based tasks.

We recognize that the prospect of supporting SRL in classrooms can be intimidating. SRL is complex and multidimensional. And, as you can likely imagine at this point, there is a multitude of goals we might take up if we are to foster the development of self-regulating learners. It is simply not possible to tackle all possible goals at once.

So, where might you begin? So far we have recommended that you start by scanning for SRL in your classroom, and then set goals based on what you have observed. To help you in this, Figure 4-2 provides a conceptual tool you can refer to when *scanning* for SRL, *focusing* your attention, and *developing a hunch* about what is going on with your students (see Halbert & Kaser, 2013). This tool suggests you watch for the following: (1) whether students are bringing to your classroom the kinds of knowledge, skills, strategies, beliefs, and values that underlie active, strategic, and adaptive forms of learning; (2) how students' motivation and emotions are implicated in their performance; and (3) whether students are learning how to engage in strategic action in relation to multiple aspects of performance during activities.

Once you have a sense of your students' needs in these areas, we recommend that you *start small*. It is ideal to reflect on your current practice and build from there. It is also better to start by focusing on just one or two new goals at a time.

As we close this chapter, we offer one additional tool: SRL Planning Tool 4-1. Teachers have used this tool to focus their scanning, record their observations, interpret what they

> Once you have a sense of your students' needs, we recommend that you start small.

SRL PLANNING TOOL 4-1
Scanning for SRL in Classrooms

Name	Grade	Subject(s)	Date
Activity?			

Context: What was your plan for locating SRL in classrooms? What did you do?	Observation. What happened? What did you notice, see, hear? Were there opportunities for SRL? Did students take up the opportunities? Did students initiate SRL?
React and interpret: What did you learn? What did you think and feel about (a) locating SRL in classrooms and (b) supporting SRL in your classroom in the future?	Reflect and Plan: What's next? What are your questions now?

Source: Adapted with permission from Sharon Jeroski, Research Director, Horizon Research & Evaluation. Vancouver, BC.

are seeing, and identify implications. This tool is well aligned with an inquiry-based approach (see Halbert & Kaser, 2013; Schnellert & Butler, 2014). You can use this tool to help you see SRL in your context and set goals based on what you are observing.

In concluding, we encourage you to review the chapters included in Part One of this book to consolidate your thinking about SRL and start thinking about next steps. What have you learned about self-regulation and SRL? Do you feel prepared to scan for SRL in your own and your students' experiences? What goals do you think you might want to take up for your students? What are you already doing that you might build on? What else could you do? We invite you to bring your thoughts and reflections into Part Two of this book, where we will explore principles and practices with great promise to help you in fostering the development of self-regulating learners.

Recommended Resources

Brownlie, F. Feniak, C., & Schnellert, L. (2006). *Student diversity* (2nd ed.). Markham, ON: Pembroke Publishers.

Butler, D. L. (2002). Individualizing instruction in self-regulated learning. *Theory into Practice, 41*(2), 81–92.

Butler, D. L., & Cartier, S. C. (2004a, May). Learning in varying activities: An explanatory framework and a new evaluation tool founded on a model of self-regulated learning. Paper presented at the annual meetings of the Canadian Society for Studies in Education. Winnipeg, MB.

Butler, D. L., & Cartier, S. (2004b). Promoting students' active and productive interpretation of academic work: A key to successful teaching and learning. *Teachers College Record, 106*, 1729–1758.

Butler, D. L., Cartier, S. C., Schnellert, L., Gagnon, F., & Giammarino, M. (2011). Secondary students' self-regulated engagement in reading: Researching self-regulation as situated in context. *Psychological Test and Assessment Modeling, 53*(1), 73–105.

Butler, D. L., & Schnellert, L. (2015). Success for students with learning disabilities: What does self-regulation have to do with it? In T. Cleary (Ed.), *Self-regulated learning interventions with at-risk youth: enhancing adaptability, performance, and well-being* (pp. 89–111). Washington DC: APA Press.

Cartier, S. (2000). Cadre conceptuel d'analyse de la situation d'apprentissage par la lecture et des difficultés éprouvées par les étudiants. *Res academica, 18*(1&2), 91–104.

Cartier, S. C., & Butler, D. L. (2004, May). Elaboration and validation of the questionnaires and plan for analysis. Paper presented at the annual meetings of the Canadian Society for Studies in Education. Winnipeg, MB.

Cleary, T. J., Callan, G. L., & Zimmerman, B. J. (2012). Assessment self-regulation as a cyclical, context-specific phenomenon: Overview and analysis of SRL microanalytic protocols. *Education Research International*, Article ID 428639. doi: 10.1155/2012/428639.

Denney, S. C., & Daviso, A. W. (2012). Self-determination: A critical component of education. *American Secondary Education, 40*(2), 43–51.

Dumont, H., Istance, D., & Benavides, F. (Eds.). (2012). The nature of learning: Using research to inspire practice. *Practitioner guide from the Innovative Learning Environments Project*. OECD: Centre for Educational Research and Innovation.

Dweck, C. (2006). *Mindset: The new psychology of success*. New York: Random House.

Dweck, C. S. (2010). Even geniuses work hard. *Educational Leadership, 68*(1), 16–20.

Field, S., Martin, J., Miller, R., Ward, M., & Wehmeyer, M. (1998). Self-determination for persons with disabilities: A position statement of the Division on Career Development and Transition. *Career Development for Exceptional Individuals, 21*, 113–128.

Gerber, P. J. (2001). Learning disabilities: A life span approach. In D. P. Hallahan & B. K. Keogh (Eds.), *Research and global perspectives in learning disabilities* (pp. 167–180). Mahwah, NJ: Erlbaum.

Halbert, J., & Kaser, L. (2013). *Spirals of inquiry for equity and quality*. BC Principals and Vice-Principals Association.

Perry, N. E. (2004). Using self-regulated learning to accommodate differences amongst students in classrooms. *Exceptionality Education Canada, 14*(2&3), 65–87.

Perry, N. E. (2013). Classroom processes that support self-regulation in young children [Monograph]. *British Journal of Educational Psychology, Monograph Series II: Psychological Aspects of Education—Current Trends*, 10, 45–68.

Reeve, J., Ryan, R., Deci, E. L., & Jang, H. (2008). Understanding and promoting autonomous self-regulation: A self-determination theory perspective. In D. H. Schunk & B. J. Zimmerman (Eds.), *Motivation and self-regulated learning: Theory, research, and applications* (pp. 223–244). New York: Erlbaum.

Schnellert, L., & Butler, D. L. (2014, June). Collaborative inquiry: Empowering teachers in their professional development. *Education Canada, 54*(3). Available at http://www.cea-ace.ca/education-canada/article/collaborative-inquiry

Swanson, H. L. (1990). Instruction derived from the strategy deficit model: Overview of principles and procedures. In T. Scruggs & B. Y. L. Wong (Eds.), *Intervention research in learning disabilities* (pp. 34–65). New York: Springer-Verlag.

Wehmeyer, M. L., Agran, M., & Hughes, C. (1998). *Teaching self-determination to students with disabilities*. Baltimore, MD: Paul H. Brookes.

Zimmerman, B. J. (2002). Becoming a self-regulated learner: An overview. *Theory into Practice, 41*(2), 64–70.

Zimmerman, B. J. (2011). Motivational sources and outcomes of self-regulated learning and performance. In B. J. Zimmerman & D. H. Schunk (Eds.), *Handbook of self-regulation of learning and performance* (pp. 49–64). New York, Routledge.

Chapter 5

Creating Safe and Supportive Learning Environments

Echo/Cultura/Getty Images

INTRODUCTION

Part One of this book established a foundation to build from as we work to support self-regulated learning (SRL) in schools. After engaging with the material in Part One, you should be able to visualize SRL in K–12 classrooms, scan for effective and ineffective forms of SRL, and identify goals necessary for supporting the development of self-regulating learners. Part Two of this book launches a discussion about what educators can do to foster SRL. To begin, this chapter describes how educators can establish safe and supportive learning environments.

What do safe and supportive classrooms look like? Why are they important in fostering SRL? We answer these questions from three points of view. First, we describe the benefits associated with creating a *community of learners* for fostering SRL. Second, we consider how educators can build *positive, non-threatening spaces* within which students feel comfortable taking risks and pushing their learning forward. Finally, we discuss how educators can establish *participation structures* in classrooms that liberate students to focus actively on learning. To pull these ideas together, at the end of the chapter we offer an extended example of how one teacher constructed a safe and supportive learning environment in her classroom.

Establishing Safe and Supportive Learning Environments

Before you read this chapter, we invite you to consider what you already know about these topics. What makes a learning environment "safe and supportive" rather than threatening? Why does creating a safe environment matter in terms of fostering more effective forms of SRL? What strategies could you use to create a safe, supportive space for learners in your context?

Learning Intentions

After reading this chapter, you should be able to do the following:

LI 1 Identify why creating safe and supportive learning environments is important in fostering rich forms of learning and SRL.

LI 2 Explain how you might set up a *community of learners* in which all members are valued and feel comfortable learning with each other.

LI 3 Describe how building *positive, non-threatening spaces for learning* creates conditions for risk-taking and active exploration.

LI 4 Define how *participation structures* can be established to enable active learning and SRL.

ANCHORING OUR DISCUSSION

In Part Two of this book, we explore practices educators can use to foster SRL. To anchor this discussion, it will be helpful to keep in mind what these practices are designed to achieve. For this reason, in this second section of the text, we consistently start each chapter with a brief review of essential goals in developing self-regulating learners.

Why are we so goal focused? Our experience is that teachers are empowered in designing SRL–promoting classroom practices when they have a clear vision of what they are trying to achieve (see Butler, Novak Lauscher, Jarvis-Selinger, & Beckingham, 2004; Butler & Schnellert, 2012). Throughout the rest of this book, we will describe concrete, research-grounded ideas you can try out in your context. But we hope that you will also think beyond what we offer you here. For example, what are you already doing that you could build from? With SRL–fostering goals in mind, are there other kinds of approaches that you can imagine? As you learn from other resources (e.g., in a course or workshop, from a colleague), what ideas can you take up to support you in fostering SRL in your context?

> Our experience is that teachers are empowered in designing SRL–promoting classroom practices when they have a clear vision of what they are trying to achieve.

So, what are the goals we have identified as essential in developing self-regulating learners? In Chapter 4, we identified three general goals essential in nurturing effective forms of SRL (see Figure 4-2). To review, to set SRL–supportive goals within their contexts, educators need to attend to (1) how students are constructing knowledge, skills, strategies, beliefs, and values that underlie active, strategic, and adaptive forms of learning; (2) how students' motivation and emotions are implicated in their performance; and (3) whether students are engaging more or less effectively in cycles of strategic action in relation to different aspects of their performance. As we move into describing the qualities of safe, supportive learning environments, we recommend that you keep these goals in mind. How might the strategies and practices we discuss help in achieving these goals, not only for students who might require more intensive supports, but also for all of the diverse learners included together in today's classrooms?

KEY QUALITIES OF SAFE AND SUPPORTIVE LEARNING ENVIRONMENTS

In this chapter we focus attention on three approaches educators can use to create safe and supportive learning environments: fostering a *community of learners*, creating *positive, non-threatening spaces* for learning, and building *participation structures* with a classroom community.

How can these approaches help to foster the development of self-regulating learners? In safe and supportive learning environments, students are liberated to focus on *learning*. For example, in these contexts, students aren't worried about proving their competence or looking good to others. They realize that they and their peers bring diverse knowledge, skills, strengths, and needs to classrooms and can learn better together. They know what is expected of them in terms of their roles and responsibilities. They understand what is going on throughout the day so that they can quickly and efficiently get down to work. When educators take time to set up safe and supportive environments, they establish a powerful platform for learning.

Fostering a Community of Learners

Communities of learners is created in learning environments when all members are engaged together in working with big ideas; all individuals are valued, recognized, and accepted for their various strengths and challenges, diverse interests and needs are accommodated, and peer-to-peer co-learning is fostered.

One powerful way to establish safe and supportive learning environments is to position all members of a classroom, including teachers, paraprofessionals, and students as members of a **community of learners** (Brown & Campione, 1996). Learning communities respect all individuals as valued members, recognize and accept their various strengths and challenges, accommodate diverse interests and needs, and foster peer-to-peer co-learning. Establishing a community of learners creates an environment in which students feel comfortable taking risks in order to push their thinking and learning forward (see Alton-Lee, 2003a, 2003b; Butler & Schnellert, 2015; Woolfolk, Winne, & Perry, 2015).

How does setting up a learning community establish a space that invites and sustains active learning and SRL? First, learning communities create environments within which all members are, and feel, valued. In her seminal work, Nel Noddings (1992, 1995) identified the importance of creating caring classrooms in order for students to thrive and take responsibility for their environments and learning. In learning communities, all members' strengths, challenges, interests, and differences are recognized and accommodated. Research shows that students engage more positively and productively in environments where they feel teachers and peers understand and care about them (Woolfolk et al., 2015).

For example, in Starting Small 5-1, Briana Adams, a kindergarten teacher in one of our projects, reflects on how she had worked across the year to create a community of learners in her classroom. As she does so, she observes how her efforts created conditions for fostering SRL.

> ## Starting Small 5-1
> ## Creating a Community of Learners by Briana Adams
>
> This fall, I decided that I was going to focus on creating a caring, positive learning environment in my classroom by working hard to create a sense of community. I spent the first month of the year doing community-building activities and explicitly teaching my students about kindness. I cannot even begin to describe the difference it has made. My students are kind and helpful to each other, and it is apparent that they truly care about one another. Upon returning from being away sick for three days last week, I was so happy to read in the note from my TOC (teacher on call, or substitute teacher) that she was extremely impressed with how kind and helpful my students were to each other. The students had also made get well cards for me and all of the other students who had been away sick.
>
> I've noticed that my students are much more willing to take risks and try new things. I have also noticed that I am able to differentiate the lessons and activities in my classroom, or provide choice for students without anyone complaining about why someone else gets to do something different. My students truly understand that everyone needs different things in order to be successful. That understanding and the sense of community in my classroom has made this class a very special group to teach. …
>
> [One article I read] suggests using morning meetings as way to build a sense of community and to teach both social-emotional and academic skills. This is something that I can see being very applicable to my kindergarten classroom. I do a mini morning meeting, where I check in with students to see how they are doing. This allows me to know right away if there are any students who may need more support throughout the day. It also helps my students learn that everyone has different feelings and that our feelings can change from day to day and moment to moment. It also teaches my students to think about how they can support a classmate who is having a rough morning and this further contributes to creating a caring community in my classroom. In my last reflection, I wrote about the positive impact that creating a sense of community has had on my class this year, and I know that beginning to implement SRL in my classroom would not be possible without having first created that safe, caring community.

In Schoenfeld's view (2004), learning communities not only create positive spaces from a relational perspective, they also engage members in grappling with big ideas. As he explains,

> For any big idea, the real question is, what kind(s) of classroom interactions will foster engagement and understanding? It seems clear that the notion of "community of learners" is essential. To function as a real community, the people involved must develop powerful modes of interaction over matters of substance. (p. 251)

In other words, communities of learners deliberately engage in rich forms of thinking together. An influential example of this is the reciprocal teaching approach developed by Palincsar and Brown to support students' development of more strategic approaches to reading (1984, 1988). Other educators have adopted the *Fostering a Community of Learners* (*FCL*) approach to support active learning in subject-area classrooms, including in social studies (see Mintrop, 2004), science (see Rico & Shulman, 2004), and English language arts (see Whitcomb, 2004).

What do these efforts have in common? Schoenfeld (2004) identified four principles underlying the FCL approach, which educators were drawing on to construct specific practices: "activity, reflection, collaboration, and community" (p. 251). He also noticed how FCL approaches are designed so that students become "reasoners and sense makers" in various content domains (p. 237). By following the FCL approach, educators were creating intellectual communities within which ideas were being developed, tested, and shared with others.

More recently, Beishuizen (2009) investigated how creating a learning community might set the stage for fostering SRL. Consistent with Schoenfeld (2004), he identified six essential qualities of a learning community. These communities do the following:

- engage students as partners in knowledge building;
- involve students and teachers in collaborative inquiry;
- address big ideas in a given domain;
- immerse students in the full range of inquiry processes, including collaborating and communicating;
- engage students in reflecting on their work to build self-awareness and critical thinking; and
- create access for students to resources necessary for their work.

Beishuizen then analyzed conditions that are beneficial in supporting SRL in two university-level courses in which a learning community had been established.

How can you establish a community of learners in your context? While more detail is available in the resources we recommend to you throughout this chapter, generally speaking, to establish a learning community, you can do the following:

- Create a caring environment; for example, by showing care and compassion for students and encouraging students to care about and support each other.
- Provide opportunities for students to play and work collaboratively; for example, by engaging them in cooperative games and activities that require them to learn from and with each other.
- Recognize, celebrate, and accommodate diversity; for example, by highlighting and celebrating students' strengths and interests, asking students to share their experiences and histories, and differentiating activities and tasks.
- Offer opportunities for students to grapple in meaningful ways with big ideas; for example, by engaging students in inquiry processes or creating classroom activities that require incisive reasoning with concepts.

To establish a community of learners, construct a caring environment; enable students to play and work collaboratively; recognize, celebrate, and accommodate diversity; and provide opportunities for students to grapple together with big ideas.

Creating Positive, Non-Threatening Spaces for Learning

Establishing communities of learners within which all members feel valued goes a long way toward creating *positive, non-threatening spaces for learning*. But it is also important for educators to use non-threatening teaching and assessment practices. Learning environments can inspire students' investment in growth and learning. Unfortunately, they can also lead to less risk-taking and more self-protecting modes of engagement (Boekaerts, 2011; Wiliam, 2011).

Generally speaking, educators invite more active forms of learning when they emphasize growth, empower students to feel in control over progressively positive outcomes, and position mistakes as opportunities to learn. In contrast, students perceive environments as threatening when errors are made public, the cost of mistakes is high, and quick and high achievement is emphasized. If they perceive environments to be threatening, students are more likely to take easy paths, avoid risk-taking, and make looking smart a priority (see Bandura, 1993; Butler & Schnellert, 2015; Dweck, 2006, 2010; Perry, 2013).

Motivational Messages in Classrooms   Learning environments can send powerful messages to students about academic work, learning, and themselves as learners that contribute to the perceived safety of those environments. For example, in Figure 5-1, we identify some of the messages we might convey in classrooms that can either energize or undermine rich forms of learning and SRL. Keep in mind that what we *say* may not always be what students *hear*.

Figure 5-1 suggests that learners will interpret some of what we say as (a) attributing success to factors within their control, (e.g., effort, using good strategies), (b) encouraging progress and growth (e.g., identifying obstacles and overcoming them), and (c) communicating confidence in them as learners (e.g., "you can do this"). Learners who hear these messages are more likely to perceive the environment as safe and supportive. They are also more likely to develop a growth mindset—that is, a belief that their ability can grow if they work at it (see Dweck, 2006, 2010). These students are more likely to engage in rich forms of learning, take risks, and persist in the face of challenges.

What we might say...	What students might hear...
When a student does well ...	
You are so good at this! How smart you are!	I look smart when I do well. I'd better avoid hard tasks so that I keep doing well and looking smart.
You really studied hard and your improvement shows it!	I do well when I try hard. Maybe I should try even harder next time.
You finished so quickly!	If I don't finish quickly, it means I'm not smart. I should try to do things quickly.
You really stuck with that one until you figured it out!	If I keep trying, I can figure things out. I should keep trying even when I'm struggling.
You got all the answers right!	It's important for me to get everything right. I should try to avoid making mistakes.
You really improved this aspect of your writing between drafts!	It's important for me to try to improve from one time to the next. It's OK to make mistakes because I can fix them.
When a student struggles ...	
That's OK. That test was hard.	The teacher didn't expect me to do well. I can't do well when tasks are hard.
Let's see if we can figure out together what you don't understand.	The teacher thinks I can figure this out and is going to help me understand better.
Don't worry. Johnny did well. Maybe he can show you what he did.	Johnny did so much better than I. I don't mind help. But I can't learn like he does.
Everyone learns in a different way. Let's keep trying to find a way that works for you.	The teacher thinks I can learn. I just need to find a way that works for me.

Figure 5-1 Messages Students Hear in Classrooms

In contrast, regardless of our best intentions, learners can interpret our messages as (a) reflecting low confidence in them as learners (e.g., "I don't expect you to do well on this"), (b) linking success to factors outside of their control (e.g., low ability, a hard test), or (c) encouraging quick, mistake-free performance. Students who hear these messages are more likely to perceive the environment as threatening. They are more likely to develop a fixed mindsets—that is, a belief that they have a certain amount of ability and can't change it (see Dweck 2006, 2010). They are less likely to take on and persist through challenging tasks.

Can We Give Students Work That Is Challenging?
Does creating a non-threatening environment mean that students should be protected from facing challenges? Not at all! In fact, developing effective forms of SRL *requires* that individuals face some challenges while learning. As Rohrkemper and Corno (1988) explain,

> The experience of modifying either tasks or themselves to cope with the stress of class-room demands allows students to learn to respond flexibly and to assume control over their own learning (p. 297).

Students do not need to engage in deliberate forms of SRL when they can tackle routine tasks on automatic pilot. But they *do* need to use effective forms of SRL to navigate new situations, unfamiliar tasks, or difficulties they encounter. It follows that if they don't have opportunities to face challenges then they won't have opportunities to develop strategies for handling them. Of course, we do not want to frustrate students either, for example, by engaging them in activities that are too far beyond their capacity to complete them successfully.

Instead, we need to aim for the "zone of proximal development," identified by Vygotsky (1978), through which individuals can, with support, stretch their thinking and learning.

Thus, creating non-threatening environments does not require offering easy activities. But challenges do need to be presented in ways that are *non-threatening* to students (see Perry, 2013). Some ways to accomplish this are for you to do the following:

- Help students experience and think about learning as something that takes time and effort.

- Build opportunities for students to identify and fix mistakes into activities.

- Encourage students to access support strategically, as needed, from their teacher and peers.

- Create opportunities for students to make choices that allow them to control the level of challenge they are experiencing; for example, by choosing among books on the same topic written at different difficulty levels.

Note that we can construct non-threatening environments to the best of our ability, but we also have to watch for how different learners experience the conditions we establish. Students may perceive activities differently, depending on their histories, strengths, and interests. For example, in Chapter 1 we described two students engaged in a research project in Mrs. Nyad's classroom. One student (Stewart) threw himself into the activity, which he perceived as interesting and important. In contrast, the other student (Brigitte) brought a history of reading and writing difficulties to the activity. She experienced the activity as threatening, because she was worried about being slow and looking incompetent in front of peers. Her response was to survive the task by taking up strategies that reduced her level of anxiety rather than by investing in learning (Boekaerts, 2011). Ultimately, we need to be sensitive to why environments might be perceived as threatening by the individuals working within them.

What about Assessment?   Assessment practices play a very large role in whether or not students perceive learning environments as threatening (Stiggins, 2005). Many students perceive evaluations, particularly high-stakes examinations, to be very stressful. Assessments that highlight social comparisons are also more threatening, especially for learners whose performance is low relative to that of their peers (Wiliam, 2011). Students perceive other forms of assessment as less threatening; for example, when assessments are used formatively to identify both strengths and opportunities for growth (Brookhart, Moss & Long, 2008; Brownlie & Schnellert, 2009). But again, what is important is how individuals experience assessment practices. Even non-threatening assessment practices can cause stress for some students.

How Do Positive, Non-Threatening Learning Environments Support SRL?   When students perceive environments as threatening, they may self-regulate by seeking ways to avoid or exit that situation (Boekaerts, 2011). For example, one student we worked with who struggled with significant learning disabilities characterized herself as a class clown in high school. Tanya's[1] personal mantra through school was, "I'd rather be cool in the hall than a fool in my seat." Correspondingly, she became very adept at finding ways to be thrown out of class. But when she was eventually supported to find strategies that worked for her, and correspondingly, to realize that she could control outcomes and be more successful, she developed the courage to stay in school. Ultimately, she learned to build on her considerable strengths to achieve B's and A's in university-level work.

In contrast to Tanya's initial experience, when students perceive environments to be non-threatening, they are more relaxed and willing to engage with others. They do not

---

[1] Tanya is a pseudonym

have to worry about self-protection. Instead, they are liberated to think about themselves as learners, to try new things, and to make mistakes, which they see as a natural part of learning. They have a sense that, if they have not yet achieved a goal, then they can control outcomes by trying hard and continuing to learn. Overall, they are poised to engage in the iterative cycles of strategic action that are foundational in SRL.

In non-threatening learning environments, students are poised to engage in the iterative cycles of strategic action that are foundational in SRL.

We would note that in non-threatening classroom environments, students are more likely to develop the social-emotional competencies necessary to working productively with others while learning, as described in Chapter 3 (see Schonert-Reichl & Weissberg, 2014). In these environments, students can see how everyone in the community is engaged in growth and improvement. They can learn how to engage positively and prosocially with others to support each other's learning. They can develop knowledge about emotions and relationships that support effective forms of self-regulation. The result is that they are more likely to achieve success academically (see Caprara, Barbaranelli, Pastorelli, Bandura, & Zimbardo, 2000; Durlak, Weissberg, Dymnicki, Taylor, & Schellinger, 2011).

Establishing Participation Structures That Enable Active Learning and SRL

Classrooms are complex environments that include many participants interacting throughout a typical day. To that end, educators typically establish **participation structures** that define expectations and norms of engagement for different kinds of activities. For example, participation structures might define how students should interact and learn with one another, direct their attention, organize their work, request permission to use the washroom, or ask for help. Educators can create powerful learning spaces and support SRL by virtue of how they lead and organize life in a busy classroom (Rimm-Kaufman, Curby, Grimm, Nathanson, & Brock, 2009; Woolfolk et al., 2015). But students need to recognize and navigate participation structures within particular contexts if they are to self-regulate their learning effectively. Thus, in this section, we describe how educators can establish and communicate about participation structures with students.

Participation structures define expectations and norms of engagement for different kinds of activities; for example, how students should interact and learn with one another, direct their attention, organize their work, ask permission to use the washroom, or ask for help.

Why Do Participation Structures Enable Active Learning and SRL?   As we defined it in Chapter 1, self-regulation involves students taking deliberate control over their thoughts and actions to navigate expectations in activities within particular environments (Zimmerman, 2008). But how can students successfully navigate environments if they do not recognize norms of engagement or expectations?

Imagine for a moment the experience of a kindergarten student coming to a school for the first time. Primary educators recognize that these very young learners need to develop new knowledge and skills about how classrooms "work." For example, what are students expected to do when entering the classroom? Is it alright to ask questions during circle time? How are they expected to behave when learning with the whole class versus on their own, or with just one partner? New kindergarteners clearly need explicit support to develop knowledge and skills about expectations if they are to self-regulate performance effectively, given that they are so new to school environments and activities.

Now imagine Grade 8 or 9 students making the transition to a secondary school. Can we assume these students understand how secondary-level learning environments work? What about students who come to school from diverse cultural backgrounds or with different kinds of educational histories? Can we assume these students will interpret classroom environments in the ways teachers expect, or know how to govern their behaviour in these contexts that are new to them? What if there is a mismatch between the intention underlying a student's behaviour (e.g., averting gaze to signal respect) and a teacher's interpretation of it (e.g., that direct eye contact signals attention)?

Empowering Student to Navigate Classroom Environments

What can we do to empower students to understand how classrooms work and what is expected of them? How can we ensure that all of our diverse learners feel welcome in our learning communities, given the kinds of structures and routines we establish within them?

Three General Recommendations What can educators do to help all students learn how to navigate classroom norms successfully? We start this section with three general recommendations:

1. *Explicitly discuss norms and expectations with students at all grade levels.*
   Students are empowered to self-regulate all dimensions of their performance successfully if they have a sense of what they are trying to achieve (Black & Wiliam, 2009).

2. *Build norms and expectations with students.*
   Constructing norms with students can achieve multiple benefits simultaneously, including increases in students' (a) perceptions of ownership and agency; (b) investment in and sense of belonging in a learning community; and (c) metacognitive knowledge about themselves, learning, and relationships (Schnellert et al., 2015).

3. *Remember that learners bring diverse perspectives and experiences to classrooms.*
   Keeping those different perspectives in mind when creating classroom norms can go a long way toward honouring diversity in classrooms. All students benefit from classroom practices that are inclusive of diverse ways of thinking and learning (Alton-Lee, Diggins, Klenner, Vine, & Dalton, 2001; Woolfolk et al., 2015).

Establishing Classroom Routines One way in which educators can organize life in a busy classroom is to develop predictable and routine ways of participating in activities (Weinstein, 2007; Weinstein & Mignano, 2007; Woolfolk et al., 2015). For example, **classroom routines** may define the following:

Classroom routines are predictable, routinized ways for participating in learning environments and activities.

- administrative procedures (e.g., for taking attendance);
- expected actions when students enter a classroom (e.g., where to put coats and bags, what work to have ready, where to sit);
- how a day or class will typically unfold (e.g., structured greetings in the morning, a visual schedule or "shape of the day");
- where and how students should access materials or submit homework;
- how, when, and from whom students can ask for help; or
- how transitions within and between activities will work.

When both teachers and students are clear on classroom routines, then activities in classrooms tend to unfold in predictable, more orderly ways.

For example, in his Grade 6 and 7 classrooms, Dave Dunnigan develops classroom routines with his students at the start of the year. He asks them what kind of "quiet" signal he should use to recapture their attention when they are immersed in activities (e.g., a rattle, a clapper). The students know to listen for that sound while working and so are better able to transition between independent work, group work, class discussions, and other kinds of activities. Dave also negotiates procedures and expectations for moving around the room, going to the washroom, turning in work, and other daily routines.

Similarly, educators can routinize ways of working within different kinds of activities. For example, in seamlessly functioning classrooms, educators may have developed predictable routines for centre time, group work, whole group discussions, or class debates. These routines define how activities will unfold as well as when and how students are expected to act (e.g., group members' roles and responsibilities, whether it is necessary to raise hands to ask questions) (Gibbs, 2006; Schnellert, Datoo, Ediger, & Panas, 2009).

Students who understand classroom routines are more likely to self-regulate performance successfully (Clark, 2012). It follows that if we effectively communicate how different activities work, students can navigate expectations much more successfully. But it is even more powerful to engage students in co-constructing routines, as Dave Dunnigan does with his students. When students are engaged explicitly in co-constructing routines and expectations, they develop important forms of metacognitive knowledge, such as about classrooms and how they function. They are more likely to feel ownership over expectations, refer to them as goals when self-regulating performance, build strategies for achieving them, and develop a sense of control over their ability to be successful.

> Students who understand classroom routines are more likely to self-regulate performance successfully. But it is even more powerful to engage students in co-constructing routines.

Creating Norms and Routines in Ways That Include Diverse Learners

How can we build norms and routines with students in ways that accommodate the diversity we find in today's classrooms? In this section, we offer three suggestions: (1) explicitly discuss and/or co-create norms and routines with students, (2) be alert to students' reactions to the norms and routines we establish, and (3) create norms and routines in ways that are inclusive of diverse learners.

Explicitly Discussing and/or Co-Creating Norms and Routines. When students are engaged in discussing or creating the life of the classroom, they have opportunities to develop common understandings and a shared language for talking about how classrooms work. This empowers *all* learners to navigate expectations successfully, regardless of their prior experiences and particular strengths and needs.

Why is this so important in accommodating diversity? While educators typically have in mind routines and structures they expect students to follow, these often remain unstated. Some students "pick up" the unstated rules quickly, but others don't and thus have trouble self-regulating their actions on that basis. Another challenge for students is that participation structures often vary from classroom to classroom. For example, in one classroom it may be acceptable to call out answers during whole class discussions, while in another classroom students may be expected to raise their hands before speaking. To be successful, students need information about expectations in any given classroom. They also need to *learn how to* identify and adaptively respond to norms, routines, and expectations established for different activities and environments.

Being Alert to Students' Experiences of Different Norms and Routines. Another challenge is that some students may perceive certain norms and routines as particularly threatening. In these cases, even if students know what is being asked of them, they may feel mortified at the prospect of participating as expected. For example, students who struggle with reading fluency may quake if required to take turns reading orally. Students who fear speaking in front of peers may be very uncomfortable if required to give a presentation.

If we are sensitive to learners' potential reactions to routines or expectations, we can either avoid activities, if they are not really necessary, or make sure that we offer supports that help them feel less stressed or anxious in those situations. What kinds of supports might help students participate in challenging routines more confidently? As described earlier, students are more willing to take risks and make mistakes when we build positive, non-threatening environments. We can also establish a community of learners in which students support one another through challenging tasks. For instance, when reading orally, students might offer strategies for each other whenever anyone stumbles (see Perry & Drummond, 2002). We can also support students in building good strategies for accomplishing challenging tasks (e.g., for preparing and presenting). We can discuss with an entire class how some activities are stressful (e.g., that most presenters feel nervous when standing up in front of others), and then brainstorm strategies they can use to get through that (e.g., for handling those first anxious moments). In these ways, we can help learners understand and take on more challenging situations.

Creating Inclusive Norms and Routines.   Alton-Lee and her colleagues (2001) in New Zealand provide a compelling example of how participation structures might be experienced by learners from different cultural backgrounds. In this example, a Maori girl named Huhana had agreed to share her experiences of a recent hospital visit with peers. But when she was asked to speak to rows of students from the front of the class, she looked down and shook her head. Her teacher was insightful enough to recognize that Huhana might be more comfortable speaking to peers if everyone was seated in a circle. By changing the participation structure in this manner, this teacher created an opportunity for Huhana to participate more comfortably, receive support, and demonstrate competence. She also fostered a caring community of learners by respecting and valuing diverse ways of participating.

Building on this example, a powerful way to include learners from diverse cultural backgrounds is to vary the participation structures used in the classroom across activities and time. Then, rather than having to single out a student who is uncomfortable with the "typical" routine, all learners have opportunities to participate in ways that are more comfortable for them, even as they become more familiar and fluent over time with a range of situations (see Schnellert et al., 2015, for more information on using circle structures in the classroom).

Similarly, when class-wide routines and expectations are in place (e.g., a class daily agenda), then specific supports for individuals with special needs can easily be adapted and integrated into those environments without singling out those learners (e.g., a personal calendar for an individual student). Some students with special education needs (e.g., autism) benefit enormously from more structured supports to help them in predicting what is coming up and successfully navigating transitions.

Co-Constructing Roles and Responsibilities   Another way educators can help students learn how to navigate classroom norms is to create a shared vision of everyone's respective roles and responsibilities. We note that most discussions of classroom management today focus, not on pushing for compliance, but rather on fostering students' development of *self*-control (Alton-Lee, 2003a, 2003b; Woolfolk et al., 2015). When engaged in self-control, students manage their own actions in ways that fulfill their *responsibilities* in classrooms and respect the *rights* of others. This perspective on managing classroom life is a good fit with our goal of developing *self*-regulating learners.

Explicitly discussing roles and responsibilities with students can help create a seamlessly functioning classroom. Another powerful approach to fostering students' self-regulation is constructing a list of rights and responsibilities *with students* (see Schnellert, 2013; Woolfolk et al., 2015). Doing so engages students in thinking about both what they can expect of others within classrooms (i.e., their rights) *and* their responsibilities. Defining rights and responsibilities also assists students in developing prosocial values and a sense of civic responsibility (Johnson & Johnson, 1999).

As an example, in SR Vignette 5-1 Dave Dunnigan describes how he engages his students in a visioning process in order to co-create a list of responsibilities and expectations. In Figure 5-2, we reproduce learning intentions he co-constructed with his students this past year in a combined Grade 6/7 classroom.

Visioning Roles and Responsibilities with Students by Dave Dunnigan

At the beginning of the year, the students and I go through a visioning process to create our learning community. I ask students to consider what makes a great classroom? How are the students learning? How is the teacher teaching? How does everyone treat each other and interact with each other? What routines and expectations help us in our learning?

I activate their prior knowledge by asking them to think back to great teachers they have had, and great classroom communities they have been a part of in school. What made them great? What did you most appreciate and enjoy?

The process varies from here; last year children were given small sticky-notes to write their thoughts and ideas, one per note (and who doesn't love sticky-notes?!). In small groups, they then categorized their ideas under headings of their choosing, and we ultimately created a group chart of our intentions for the year. The choice of expressing our ideas as "intentions" is deliberate—students are supported to understand that we might not always live up to our goals, but we will keep trying and supporting each other.

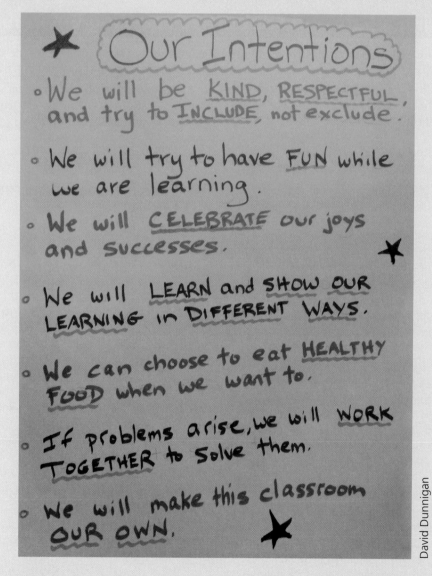

David Dunnigan

Figure 5-2 Learning Intentions Co-Constructed by Dave and His Grade 6/7 Students

CREATING SAFE AND SUPPORTIVE LEARNING ENVIRONMENTS: EXTENDED EXAMPLE

In this chapter, we have described how educators can establish safe and supportive learning environments by fostering a *community of learners*; creating *safe, non-threatening learning environments*; and co-constructing *participation structures* with their students. In these ways, educators can create a powerful foundation for fostering effective forms of SRL.

In SR Vignette 5-2, we offer an extended example of how Kim Ondrik constructed a safe and supportive learning environment in her combined Grade 6/7 classroom. Then, in Activity 5-1, we invite you to record what you observed when reading this vignette. How was Kim creating a safe, supportive learning space in her classroom? What ideas might you build on in your own work with students?

> ## SR Vignette 5-2
> # Constructing a Safe and Supportive Learning Environment

Kim Ondrik's Combined Grade 6/7 Classroom When you walk through the door into Kim's classroom, the first thing you will notice is that you can't locate the teacher's desk. Instead, if you look closely, you will see four or five student desks along with other kinds of workspaces distributed around the room. You will also detect a number of tree stumps, benches, stools, a couch, and two comfy-looking chairs positioned in a circle in a front corner of the room.

You will also notice that Kim's classroom is a very active place. On this day, students are engrossed in project-based learning activities. As you scan the classroom, you see students who are busy working and talking. Some are working alone; others are working in duos or trios. Some are working on computers; others are writing in notebooks. Two girls are sketching a large diagram of the digestive system. Two boys are sitting at a table in the back corner of the room, referring to a description of the *project-based learning process* posted on the wall. They are debating how they will represent their research on ancient Roman politics.

Shay is new in the class. She is sitting with Kim discussing her idea for a project. She is looking back and forth between the project-based learning process on the wall and a *challenge sheet* that Kim had given to the class to outline expectations for this particular project. After working through the project criteria with Shay and addressing two or three of her questions, Kim decides that Shay might benefit from getting support from her peers. She stops and raises her hand. Within 30 seconds the bustling classroom falls silent and all students turn to face Kim. When she sees that she has their attention, Kim speaks to the group: "Class, Shay has some questions about her project. As this is her first project in our class, I think she needs the support of the community." Students working on computers quickly save their work.

Then everyone makes his or her way to the "community" space, joining the circle at the front of the room.

On the wall at the front of the room, above the whiteboard, is a list of rules the class created together at the beginning of the school year:

1. *Community first, individual second.*

2. *Fairness isn't sameness.*

3. *We need to voice problems as they happen. Circle protocol is the way we solve problems.*

4. *We all learn in different ways.*

5. *Learning is a journey.*

6. *We need to show what we know in different ways.*

7. *We need to celebrate!*

As students move to the front of the room, each chooses to sit around the community circle, near the circle, or in the circle. Devon, who is having a tough day, chooses to sit outside the circle. In this classroom, students are responsible for being mindful of their social-emotional state. During the morning community circle time, they check in with their teacher and peers, letting them know how they are feeling and what they need that day. On this day, Devon had let the class community know that he needed some space and time to regroup after a tumultuous morning at home. Pete gives Devon a playful punch on the shoulder as he walks by. Devon smiles for the first time all day, but stays on the periphery.

Once the class has gathered, Bri starts the conversation. This is her second year in the class and she, like the other Grade 7 students, is expected to take a leadership role. She asks, "What do you wonder, Shay?" Shay shrugs and says that she's just not sure what to do. Satnam replies, "I wasn't sure at first either. I always waited to see what everyone else did so I could get it right. But now I know that it's up to me to figure out what I want."

Shay nods. Jackson holds up an 11×17 piece of paper. "I like to get my question and plan down on one sheet. See, here in the middle is my inquiry question and then around it are all the sub-questions I need to answer. Then at the next level, in blue, I have all the places I can get that information. I'm still working on this part. Sometimes I add more of these after I've started my research." Taylor pipes in to say, "That's just Jackson's way. You can do the planning any way you want, but you have to make a plan and get it approved by Mrs. O."

"What goes in my plan?" asks Shay, who is feeling more comfortable. "Well, look up at the project-based learning process on the wall and then look at the challenge sheet for this project," Callie interjects. Looking at the challenge sheet, she notes, "this time we have to include why this project is important to us, at least four sources of information, and show that we have learned something about either the social studies or science outcomes listed here." Shay hadn't noticed that part. She still looks hesitant. "Do you have a question yet?" asks Bri. Shay nods and gives her research journal to Bri. "Nice start!" Bri exclaims, "but it can't be a yes or no answer. It always takes me two or three tries to get a question that Mrs. Ondrik will approve." "Do you want to work together on this? Callie and I are working on showing what makes bogs so great for frogs. If you stick to your topic of saving trees, we can maybe help each other." Mrs. Ondrik looks at Shay. She asks, "What do you think Shay? Would you like to work with the girls to refine your question and maybe do some research together?" The photograph in Figure 5-3 shows students sharing their inquiry strategies in the community circle in Kim's classroom.

Kim Ondrik

Figure 5-3 The Community Circle in Kim's Classroom

How Is Kim Building a Safe and Supportive Learning Environment?

After reading SR Vignette 5-2, we invite you to use Table 5-1 to make a note of what you noticed. How has Kim built a community of learners? How is she using non-threatening practices? What kinds of norms, routines, and roles and responsibilities are evident in her classroom? How might these qualities of her classroom environment have enabled active learning and her students' development as self-regulating learners?

Table 5-1 How Is Kim Building a Safe and Supportive Learning Environment?

How is Kim...	What do you notice?
Creating a community of learners?	
Using non-threatening classroom practices?	
Creating and communicating norms, routines, and roles and responsibilities?	
Accommodating the diverse needs of students in her classroom?	

BUILDING SAFE AND SUPPORTIVE ENVIRONMENTS: FINAL REFLECTIONS

At the end of Chapter 4, as a conclusion to Part One of this book, we provided SRL Planning Tool 4-1 to help you scan for SRL in your context, record your observations, reflect on and interpret what you are seeing, and consider next steps for your learning or practice (see Halbert & Kaser, 2013). You can use SRL Planning Tool 4-1 whenever you want to look for SRL in your context and develop goals for learners.

In this second part of the book, we are moving from setting goals to taking action in support of SRL. As we described in Chapter 4, an effective way to engage in professional learning is to engage in "spirals of inquiry." According to Halbert and Kaser (2013), when engaged in inquiry, educators (a) *scan* their current context to identify pressing questions, challenges, or goals; (b) *focus* attention on a key priority; (c) *develop a hunch* about what might be happening; (d) engage in *new professional learning* to inform their practice development; (e) *take action* based on what they are learning; and, then, (f) *check* on what happens and adjust their approaches based on what they are learning.

As you move through this book, you might be inspired to take action based on what you are learning and then reflect on what happens in relation to the actions you are taking. For example, in this chapter, we started by describing how educators can create safe and supportive learning environments that are optimal for fostering SRL. Perhaps there is something that you've read about in this chapter that you'd like to try. Or, perhaps you have been inspired to build on your current practices in a new way.

To support you in your efforts to build SRL–promoting practices into your work with students, to close this chapter, we offer a second planning tool. This second tool is parallel to SRL Planning Tool 4-1. The difference is that this tool, SRL Planning Tool 5-1, is designed to support *your reflection on action*. Whenever you want to try out an idea, you can use SRL Planning Tool 5-1 to describe your goals, what you tried, what happened, what you learned, and what you might do next to advance your learning or practice. You can bring forward what you are learning through these experiences, including insights and questions, as you continue reading about SRL–promoting practices through the rest of this book.

SRL PLANNING TOOL 5-1
Fostering SRL: Reflecting on Action

Your Name	Grade	Subject(s)	Date

Activity?	

Context: What was your goal? What did you try?	**Observation. What happened?** What did you notice about the students' reaction and learning (e.g., *emotional reaction, engagement; comprehension; metacognition; self-regulation; confidence*)
React and interpret: What did you learn (a) about promoting SRL and (b) about teaching and learning generally?	**Reflect and Plan:** What will you try next?

Source: Adapted with permission from Sharon Jeroski, Research Director, Horizon Research & Evaluation. Vancouver, BC.

Recommended Resources

Alton-Lee, A., Diggins, C., Klenner, L., Vine, E., & Dalton, N. (2001). Teacher management of the learning environment during a social studies discussion in a new-entrant classroom in New Zealand. *The Elementary School Journal, 101,* 549–566.

Alton-Lee, A. (2003a). Executive Summary. From quality teaching for diverse students in schooling: Best evidence synthesis. Wellington, NZ: New Zealand Ministry of Education. Available at http://www.educationcounts.govt.nz/publications/series/2515/5959

Alton-Lee, A. (2003b). Quality teaching for diverse students in schooling: Best evidence synthesis. Wellington, NZ: New Zealand Ministry of Education. Available at http://www.education-counts.govt.nz/__data/assets/pdf_file/0019/7705/BES-quality-teaching-diverse-students.pdf

Bandura, A. (1993). Perceived self-efficacy in cognitive development and functioning. *Educational Psychologist, 28,* 117–148.

Beishuizen, J. (2009). Does a community of learners foster self-regulated learning? *Technology, Pedagogy, and Education, 17*(3), 183–193. doi: 10.1080/14759390802383769

Black, P., & Wiliam, D. (2009). Developing the theory of formative assessment. *Educational Assessment, Evaluation and Accountability, 21*(1), 5–31.

Boekaerts, M. (2011). Emotions, emotion regulation, and self-regulation of learning. In B. J. Zimmerman & D. H. Schunk (Eds.), *Handbook of self-regulation of learning and performance* (pp. 408–425). New York: Routledge.

Brookhart, S., Moss, C., & Long, B. (2008). Formative assessment that empowers. *Educational Leadership 66*(3) 52–57.

Brown, A. L., & Campione, J. C. (1996). Psychological theory and the design of innovative learning environments: On procedures, principles, and systems. In L. Schauble & R. Glaser (Eds.), *Innovation in learning: New environments for education* (pp. 289–325). Mahwah, NJ: Lawrence Erlbaum Associates.

Brownlie, F., Fullerton, C. & Schnellert, L. (2011). *It's all about thinking: Collaborating to support all learners in mathematics and science.* Winnipeg, MN: Portage & Main Publishers.

Brownlie, F., & Schnellert, L. (2009). *It's all about thinking: Collaborating to support all learners in social studies, English, and Humanities*. Winnipeg, MN: Portage & Main Publishers.

Butler, D. L., Novak Lauscher, H. J., Jarvis-Selinger, S., & Beckingham, B. (2004). Collaboration and self-regulation in teachers' professional development. *Teaching and Teacher Education, 20*, 435–455.

Butler, D. L., & Schnellert, L. (2012). Collaborative inquiry in teacher professional development. *Teaching and Teacher Education, 28*, 1206–1220.

Butler, D. L., & Schnellert, L. (2015). Success for students with learning disabilities: What does self-regulation have to do with it? To appear in T. Cleary (Ed.), *Self-regulated learning interventions with at-risk populations: Academic, mental health, and contextual considerations*. Washington DC: APA Press.

Caprara, G. V., Barbaranelli, C., Pastorelli, C., Bandura, A., & Zimbardo, P. G. (2000). Prosocial foundations of children's academic achievement. *Psychological Science, 11*(4), 302–6.

Clark, I. (2012). Formative assessment: Assessment is for self-regulated learning. *Educational Psychology Review, 24*(2), 205–249.

Durlak, J. A., Weissberg, R. P., Dymnicki, A. B., Taylor, R. D., & Schellinger, K. B. (2011). The impact of enhancing students' social and emotional learning: A meta-analysis of school-based universal interventions. *Child Development, 82*(1), 405–432.

Dweck, C. (2006). *Mindset: The new psychology of success*. New York: Random House.

Dweck, C. S. (2010). Even geniuses work hard. *Educational Leadership, 68*(1), 16–20.

Gibbs, J. (2006). *Reaching all by creating tribes learning communities*. Windsor, CA: Center-Source Systems, LLC.

Gould Lundy, K. (2008). Chapter 3: Building Community. In *Teaching fairly in an unfair world* (pp. 32–51). Markham, ON: Pembroke.

Gould Lundy, K., & Swartz, L. (2011). *Creating caring classrooms: How to encourage students to communicate, create, and be compassionate of others*. Markham, ON: Pembroke.

Halbert, J., & Kaser, L. (2013). *Spirals of inquiry for equity and quality*. British Columbia (BC): BC Principals' and Vice-Principals' Association.

Hourcade, J. J., & Bauwens, J. (2002). *Cooperative teaching: Rebuilding and sharing the schoolhouse*. Austin, TX: ProEd Inc.

Johnson, D. W., & Johnson, R. T. (1999). The three Cs of school and classroom management. In H. J. Freiberg (Ed.), *Beyond behaviorism: Changing the classroom management paradigm* (pp. 119–144). Boston, MA: Allyn & Bacon.

Kagan, S. (2009). *Kagan cooperative learning* (2nd Ed). San Clemente, CA: Kagan Publishing.

Mintrop, H. (2004). Fostering constructivist communities of learners in the amalgamated multi-discipline of social studies. *Journal of Curriculum Studies, 36*(2), 141–158.

Noddings, N. (1992). *The challenge to care in schools: An alternative approach to education*. New York: Teachers College Press.

Noddings, N. (1995). Teaching themes of care. *Phi Delta Kappan, 76*, 675–679.

Palincsar, A. S., & Brown, A. L. (1984). Reciprocal teaching of comprehension-fostering and comprehension monitoring activities. *Cognition and Instruction, 1*, 117–175.

Palincsar, A. S., & Brown, A. L. (1988). Teaching and practicing thinking skills to promote comprehension in the context of group problem solving. *RASE, 9*(1), 53–59.

Perry, N. E. (2013). Classroom processes that support self-regulation in young children [Monograph]. *British Journal of Educational Psychology, Monograph Series II: Psychological Aspects of Education—Current Trends, 10*, 45–68.

Perry, N. E., & Drummond, L. (2002). Becoming self-regulated readers and writers. *The Reading Teacher, 56*, 298–310.

Rico, S. A., & Shulman, J. H. (2004). Invertebrates and organ systems: Science instruction and "fostering a community of learners." *Journal of Curriculum Studies, 36*(2), 159–181.

Rimm-Kaufman, S. E., Curby, T. W., Grimm, K. J., Nathanson, L., & Brock, L. L. (2009). Contribution of children's self-regulation and classroom quality to children's adaptive behaviors in the Kindergarten Classroom. *Journal of Educational Psychology, 45*(4), 958–972.

Rohrkemper, M., & Corno, L. (1988). Success and failure on classroom tasks: Adaptive learning and classroom teaching. *Elementary School Journal, 88*, 297–312.

Schnellert, L. (2013, Aug). Engaging learners through community and inquiry in the middle years. Presentation to British Columbia School District No. 43. Coquitlam, BC.

Schnellert, L., Datoo, M., Ediger, K., & Panas, J. (2009). *Pulling together: Integrating inquiry, assessment and instruction in English language arts*. Markham, ON: Pembroke.

Schnellert, L., Watson, L., & Widdess, N. (2015). *It's all about thinking: Building pathways for all learners in the middle years*. Winnipeg, MN: Portage & Main Publishers.

Schoenfeld, A. H. (2004). Multiple learning communities: Students, teachers, instructional designers, and researchers. *Journal of Curriculum Studies*, *36*(2), 237–255.

Schonert-Reichl, K. A., & Weissberg, R. P. (2014). Social and emotional learning: Children. Chapter to appear in T. P. Gullotta & M. Bloom (Eds.), *The encyclopedia of primary prevention and health promotion* (2nd Ed.). New York: Springer Press.

Stiggins, R. (2005). From formative assessment to assessment for learning: A path to success in standards-based schools. *Phi Delta Kappan, 87* (4), 324–328.

Vygotsky, L. S. (1978). *Mind in Society*. Cambridge, MA: Harvard University Press.

Weinstein, C. S. (2007). *Middle and secondary classroom management: Lessons from research and practice* (3rd ed.). New York: McGraw-Hill.

Weinstein, C. S., & Mignano, A. (2007). *Elementary classroom management: Lessons from research and practice* (4th ed.). New York: McGraw-Hill.

Whitcomb, J. A. (2004). Dilemmas of design and predicaments of practice: Adapting the 'fostering a community of learners' model in secondary school English language arts classrooms. *Journal of Curriculum Studies, 36*(2), 183–206.

Wiliam, D. (2011). Providing feedback that moves learning forward. In *Embedded formative assessment* (pp. 107–132). Bloomington, IN: Solution Tree Press.

Woolfolk, A. E., Winne, P. H., & Perry, N. E. (2015). Chapter 12: Creating learning environments. In *Educational Psychology* (Canadian 6th Ed.). Prentice Hall/Allyn and Bacon Canada.

Zimmerman, B. J. (2008). Investigating self-regulation and motivation: Historical background, methodological developments and future prospects. *American Educational Research Journal*, *45*(1), 166–183.

Chapter 6
Guidelines for Designing SRL-Promoting Practices

Ariel Skelley/Blend Images/
Getty Images

INTRODUCTION

Part Two of this book describes what educators can do to foster the development of self-regulating learners. We began in Chapter 5 by describing how educators can establish safe, supportive learning environments that create optimal conditions for active learning and SRL. In upcoming chapters, we explain how educators can design *activities*, *supports*, and *assessment frameworks* to foster SRL. In this chapter, we set the stage for those more-focused discussions by defining four key guidelines to keep in mind when designing SRL–promoting practices. Taken together, these guidelines combine to describe how educators can pair *opportunities* for SRL with *supports* for students to learn how to self-regulate learning effectively.

Learning Intentions

After reading this chapter, you should be able to do the following:

LI 1   Describe four key guidelines you can draw on to design SRL–promoting practices, along with concrete approaches that educators have been using to bring those guidelines to life.

LI 2   Explain why it is so important to pair *opportunities* for SRL with *supports* for students to learn how to self-regulate their learning effectively.

LI 3   Imagine how you could draw on the guidelines presented here to construct SRL–promoting practices in your context.

GUIDELINES FOR FOSTERING SELF-REGULATED LEARNING

As we identify SRL–promoting practices through this and upcoming chapters, it is important to keep in mind the goals we are trying to achieve. To review—broadly speaking, when setting goals for students, educators need to attend to (1) how students are constructing knowledge, skills, strategies, values, and beliefs that underlie active, strategic learning; (2) how students' motivation and emotions are supporting or undermining their performance; and (3) whether students are learning how to engage deliberately and reflectively in cycles of strategic action in relation to multiple aspects of performance.

How can we achieve these goals? In Chapter 5 we introduced strategies educators can use to build safe, supportive learning environments in which all students are positioned as valued members of a learning community, understand how classrooms work, feel comfortable taking risks, and work alone and together to push everyone's learning forward. When students live and learn in these kinds of supportive spaces, they are poised to engage in rich forms of active learning and SRL.

Once this stage is set, how can we build SRL–promoting practices into these safe and supportive environments? Table 6-1 outlines four key guidelines that you can draw on to help you foster the development of SRL by students in your context. In upcoming sections, we describe each of these guidelines in turn. We also give concrete examples of how educators have been taking up those guidelines in their practice.

Creating Opportunities for Self-Regulated Learning

Our first guideline suggests that to achieve our goals for students we need to create *opportunities* for students to engage in rich forms of SRL (Cartier, 2000; Perry, 1998, 2013). Students cannot learn to self-regulate their learning if they do not have opportunities to do so. There are many approaches educators can use to create these kinds of opportunities. For example, educators can create opportunities for SRL by (1) designing activities and tasks so that they require active learning and SRL, (2) creating opportunities for students to experience and control challenges, (3) ensuring students have opportunities to engage in full cycles of strategic action, and (4) sustaining attention to process goals over time (see Table 6-1).

Table 6-1 Four Guidelines for Fostering Self-Regulated Learning

To Foster SRL, Educators Can...	Educators Are Doing That by...
Create opportunities for self-regulated learning	• Designing activities and tasks that require active learning and SRL • Creating opportunities for students to experience and control challenges • Ensuring students have opportunities to engage in full cycles of strategic action • Sustaining attention to process goals over time
Foster autonomy	• Providing opportunities for choice and decision-making • Encouraging students to take ownership over their learning and performance • Bridging from guiding learning to fostering independence • Engaging students in shaping classroom practices
Weave supports for SRL into activities	• Identifying and promoting SRL as a means to an end (vs. an end in itself) • Integrating supports for SRL processes into the curriculum • Focusing instruction explicitly on learning and thinking processes • Assisting students to *learn how to* make good choices and decisions
Support learners' flexible use of knowledge, skills, strategies, and beliefs	• Supporting students' development of rich forms of knowledge, skills, strategies, values, and beliefs • Supporting students to build on those to engage in adaptive and flexible forms of thinking

Designing Activities and Tasks That Require Active Learning and SRL

First, educators can create opportunities for SRL within the activities they design for students. How might activities differ in terms of the kinds of requirements they establish for students' engagement in SRL? To consider that question, in Activity 6-1 we invite you to consider two different activities, both constructed to foster students' attainment of goals, taken from British Columbia's Grade 2 Life Sciences curriculum (British Columbia Ministry of Education, 2005; see https://www.bced.gov.bc.ca/irp/pdfs/sciences/2005scik7_2.pdf).

> Activity 6-1
> # Designing Activities and Tasks That Require SRL

Consider the following two activities that might be assigned by a Grade 2 teacher in order to foster students' understanding about animal growth and changes. What opportunities for SRL do you see in these examples? How would they create opportunities for a teacher to nurture students' development of SRL?

Activity One: Learning about Penguins

In this activity, students are asked to work on a two-page handout on penguins. The first page includes a short text describing the life cycles of penguins. On the second page, students have space to write one or two sentences about what they learned about penguins through the reading. There is also space for them to draw a picture. To launch the activity, the teacher reads the text aloud with the class, giving students an opportunity to ask questions. While reading and during the discussion, the teacher shows students many colourful pictures of penguin parents and babies in their natural habitat. Then, students are given 20 minutes to work on writing their sentences and/or drawing. They are encouraged to ask the teacher if they have any questions.

Activity Two: Conducting an Inquiry Project on Penguins

In this activity, students need to work in a group with two peers to do research on penguins. The overall goal is for the class to decide whether or not penguins should be designated as a protected species. Each trio is charged with preparing a presentation to share with the class two weeks down the road. Groups are given a choice among three big topics to consider in relation to the class goal: (1) life cycles of penguins, (2) penguins' characteristics and how these help in adapting to conditions in their environment, or (3) penguins' behaviours (e.g., infant rearing, migration). Groups are given some time each day to work on their projects. Midway through, they share their progress with another group to get feedback. Students can draw from a variety of resources (e.g., books, videos) to inform their work. In their reports, students are asked to describe facts they learned from their research. Furthermore, to support decision-making about whether or not penguins should be a protected species, they also need to make inferences, draw conclusions, and justify their thinking.

Students need to self-regulate learning effectively to succeed in either  activities described in Activity 6-1. Correspondingly, teachers could suppo effective engagement in SRL in either context. For example, in the fi (Learning about Penguins), students would do better if they took time to teachers' expectations, consider their personal goals, select strategies they complete the activity (for reading, writing, or drawing), try out their appro itor outcomes, and adjust their performance as needed. They also might assistance with identifying strategies they could use for reading, listening t er's reading and explanation, writing (a sentence or two), and drawing. need support to learn how to manage their resources and time so as to c activity within the time allotted.

But this relatively short-term activity does not really invite a high level of strategic engagement. In fact, students could likely complete the activity successfully without pausing to think too hard about their learning goals, planning for how to tackle the task, or monitoring how their work was progressing. In simpler tasks, students often jump into work without strategically managing their learning. The unfortunate outcome is that students may learn to take up ways of working that are more "mindless" than mindful.

In contrast, the second activity (Conducting an Inquiry Project on Penguins) arguably offers a richer context for the development of SRL. In this kind of activity, students need to work deliberately toward a class goal, choose a topic together, select from among resources to advance their thinking, and manage their efforts across a two-week period. They are expected to use productive strategies to engage in active forms of learning. They will likely experience and need to negotiate challenges to their learning, emotions, behaviour, and motivation. They will also have to know how to work well with others and to adjust their actions and plans as a part of group work. In these respects, this second activity creates rich opportunities for teachers to nurture students' developing capacities as self-regulating learners.

In particular, notice how students undertaking this second activity are required to engage more deliberately in full cycles of strategic performance. For example, they have to recognize, interpret, and keep in mind the class goal while negotiating a group topic, and plan their time and resources to sequence their work over time. They have to present their initial thinking, get feedback, and make revisions accordingly. While it is not realistic to build this level of strategic engagement into every activity that students encounter, we suggest that to fully develop students' capacities for SRL, they have to have opportunities to engage regularly, deliberately, and thoughtfully in self-regulating processes.

Creating Opportunities for Students to Experience and Control Challenges

A second way in which classrooms can offer students opportunities for SRL is to ensure they experience challenges. Consider the following frequently cited quotation:

> Anyone who has never made a mistake has never tried anything new.
> —**Albert Einstein**

In this quotation, Einstein reminds us that mistakes are a normal part of learning. If students do not have opportunities to make mistakes, they may come to think that learning should be easy or that it does not require effort. In contrast, any of us who have tried to master a new or difficult skill know that learning takes time, fortitude, and persistence. Thus, if we are to foster SRL, we need to ensure that students have opportunities to experience challenges and overcome them. If we scaffold learning to the point where learners are always easily successful, they cannot learn how to self-regulate in the face of difficulties, which is when SRL is most necessary. Also, they may not have opportunities to develop the capacity to respond adaptively, a quality that is at the heart of SRL (see Perry, Phillips, & Hutchinson, 2006; Rohrkemper & Corno, 1988).

That being said, our goal is certainly *not* to frustrate learners or to give them activities that extend beyond their capacities to be successful. The challenges students experience should stretch their learning within their **zones of proximal development** (i.e., the space between what they can accomplish on their own and what they can do with guidance or support; Vygotsky, 1978). Furthermore to nurture students' sense of competence and control over learning, we can offer them opportunities to control the level of challenge they experience, particularly as their knowledge and skills are developing. For example, emerging writers in kindergarten might be offered a choice between drawing and "kid's writing," with invented spellings, when recording their ideas.

But intriguing research on "productive failure" (e.g., Locke & Latham, 2006) also suggests that "giving students challenging goals encourages greater effort and persistence than providing moderate, 'do-your-best' goals or no goals at all" (Goodwin & Miller, 2013). Experiencing some challenge can be motivating. Furthermore, students need to recognize and experience their growth, from early learning through to more mature understanding, in order to appreciate that learning can be hard and take time. They need to experience difficulties if they are to learn how to diagnose problems, identify solutions, and refine approaches. They need to realize that they can successfully navigate challenges if they are to build confidence in their ability to face and overcome life's obstacles. Note that students are more likely to extend themselves and develop in these ways if we establish safe and supportive learning environments (as described in Chapter 5).

Ensuring Students Have Opportunities to Engage in Full Cycles of Strategic Action

A third way in which activities establish opportunities for SRL is by ensuring that students have opportunities to engage in *full cycles* of strategic action (see Butler, 2002). How can students learn to interpret tasks and set goals if activities do not require them to do so? How can they learn how to plan if activities do not ask them to choose or coordinate resources? How can they learn to use strategies adaptively and flexibly if they do not have opportunities to select, adjust, or even invent strategies to achieve their goals? How can they learn to monitor and refine their approaches if they only do tasks once or have few opportunities to self-assess their progress and try something different?

Furthermore, to fully develop students' capacities for SRL, they need opportunities to engage in full cycles of strategic action related *to all aspects of SRL*. For example, in the Inquiry Project on Penguins activity, students had opportunities to work through strategic cycles when self-regulating their *cognition and learning* (e.g., to draw inferences and make reasoned judgments). They also had opportunities to self-regulate their *relationships* with others. They needed to recognize goals for learning with others, define their relative roles and responsibilities, choose and use strategies for working with peers, monitor group progress, and troubleshoot interpersonal challenges.

How can educators engage students in cycles of strategic action? As one example, in Starting Small 6-1, Jennifer Ross describes how she created supports for her young learners' engagement in full cycles of self-regulated listening in her French immersion kindergarten classroom. Jenn had launched an inquiry project by "scanning" for problems her children were experiencing (see Halbert & Kaser, 2013). When she observed

Zones of proximal development refer to the space between what students can accomplish on their own and what they can do with guidance or support.

To develop effective forms of SRL, students need opportunities to learn how to engage in strategic action cycles related to all aspects of performance.

that her students were having difficulty self-regulating their behaviour strategically during important classroom routines (e.g., listening at the carpet; getting ready to go outside), she decided to start by building in supports for their engagement in strategic action cycles. Note that the practices she developed were inspired by work she had heard about by another teacher, Kelsey Keller, who had been trying to find ways to talk about SRL with her students in "kid friendly" terms (see Perry, Brenner, & Fusaro, 2015). As you read Jenn's description, what do you notice about how she was creating opportunities for SRL in her classroom?

> Starting Small 6-1
Engaging Learners in Full Cycles of Strategic Action.

SRL NEXT! Next steps
By Jennifer Ross

After the environment feels "safe," and they know what a "strategy" is, I introduced three questions to the children.

Modelling three questions:

I started with listening at the carpet (as through scanning, it is the most difficult for some children). We went over three questions in detail: What is my job? What do I need to do my job? Why do I need to do this job? Next, I modelled what

self-regulated listening looks like, as well as had the children model. Now, I go through signs I made with them before any listening activity is to occur.

In Figure 6-1 we reproduce two of the signs Jenn created with students related to self-regulated listening. To generate the first, she and her students answered the question, What is my job? (Quelle est la tâche?) She and her students outlined the steps (les étapes) required in both words and pictures. For the second poster, she and her students considered how to do their job (Comment faire la tâche?). They identified the tools they would need (Quel outils?), and where and with whom they would need to work (Où? Avec qui?).

Figure 6-1 Signs Jennifer Developed with Students to Help Them Understand What Self-Regulated "Listening" Looks Like.

Figure 6-2 Tools Jennifer Developed to Help Students Self-Assess Their Listening

Self-assessment/metacognition:

After they were comfortable with using these three questions to guide their listening, I had the children answer two further questions: How do I know I did a good job, and did I do my job correctly? Then, they engaged in self-assessment by using a simple three-point scale (which I use for assessing a lot of things). I started simply; I decided I was going to have them rate their behaviour using strips after many different types of carpet time activities (see Figure 6-2).

> Jenn created booklets including duplicate pages with the "strips" rating scale shown in Figure 6-2. After different activities, she asked students to rate their listening or other behaviours. She then debriefed with them to help them plan how they might move up the scale, if need be.

Sustaining Attention to Process Goals over Time   Another way to create opportunities for student development of effective forms of SRL is to sustain attention to process goals over time (i.e., goals focused on enhancing students' learning processes). Developing effective forms of SRL is a long-term venture. Students need to build capacity for SRL in many different kinds of activities, particularly as they face escalating expectations across grade levels and environments. It follows that supporting SRL cannot be accomplished in a single lesson. We need to systematically develop students' capacities for SRL over time.

In support of this guideline, in a recent study we examined the qualities of teachers' instructional practices that were most supportive of SRL (see Butler, Schnellert, & Cartier, 2013). In this project, secondary teachers were working together to support self-regulated learning through reading (LTR) in subject-area classrooms (e.g., social studies, science). As part of the research, we traced how teachers were building from assessments of their students' SRL to set goals for their students and then refine their practices to achieve them (see Chapter 4). At the end of the year, we looked for connections between the goals teachers set, the practices they enacted, and the gains they observed for students. What did we find? We identified four qualities of instruction associated with students developing more effective forms of SRL. One of these was that, in SRL-promoting classrooms, teachers sustained attention to process goals over time.

For example, in one classroom, Linda Watson wanted her students to get better at setting learning goals and monitoring their progress toward them. To achieve that goal, she integrated supports for SRL into her social studies unit. At the start of each class, each student set a learning goal for him or herself and shared it with a peer. Then, at the end of class, the students reflected on whether, and how well, they had met their goal for the day. By sustaining attention to this process goal (i.e., fostering students' goal-setting and monitoring) over several classes, Linda was more successful in nurturing the development of this aspect of SRL in her students.

Fostering Autonomy

Our second guideline suggests that, to foster effective forms of SRL, we need to create opportunities for students to exercise *autonomy*. Here again, students cannot learn to take responsibility for learning and self-direct their action if they do not have opportunities to do so. When given opportunities to exercise autonomy, students can take ownership over their learning. They can learn how to develop strategies and goals for themselves. They are also more likely to take risks and persevere during new and challenging tasks (Anderman & Anderman, 2010; Perry, 1998, 2004, 2013; Perry & Drummond, 2003; Perry, Phillips, & Hutchinson, 2006; Perry, Vandekamp, Mercer, & Nordby, 2002; Reeve, 2006).

There are many approaches educators can use to build opportunities for autonomy into environments and activities. Here, we highlight four powerful approaches: (1) providing opportunities for choice and decision-making, (2) encouraging students to take ownership over their learning and performance, (3) bridging from guiding learning to fostering independence, and (4) engaging students in shaping classroom practices (see Table 6-1).

Providing Opportunities for Choice and Decision-Making

One way to foster autonomy is by asking students to make choices and decisions (Anderman & Anderman, 2010; Perry, 2013; Perry & Drummond, 2003). When making choices or decisions, learners have opportunities to take deliberate control over learning. For example, when choosing a topic for a research project, students have opportunities to steer their learning in ways that match their strengths and interests. When given choices, students also have an opportunity to control the level of challenge they experience. For example, students can adjust how difficult a research project is for them if they are given opportunities to choose from among texts at different levels based on their developing capacities as readers.

What kinds of choices might educators offer to students? Educators can provide students with choices on what to learn (e.g., topics, order), materials to use (e.g., resources for a research project), where to work, who to work with, how to learn (e.g., strategies), or how to demonstrate learning. Perry (2013) cautions, however, that not all choices are "equal." Choices only encourage SRL when they require students to make meaningful decisions about learning. For example, choices are powerful when they ask students to consider the demands of tasks, reflect on their learning strengths and weaknesses, decide on learning approaches, and take responsibility for learning.

Choices only encourage SRL when they require students to make meaningful decisions about learning.

Encouraging Students to Take Ownership over Learning and Performance

A second way to foster autonomy is to position students as owners of learning. Educators, of course, still need to play a key role in advancing students' learning need to create activities, provide access to information, offer resources and sup design effective forms of assessment and feedback. At the same time, educate communicate to students that they, themselves, are ultimately responsible for learning goals established within the learning community. Even when we model students to learn effective strategies (e.g., for writing or inquiring, for collabor with others), students need to perceive themselves as responsible for self-regul performance. They need to see themselves as choosing and using the strategie learning to achieve a goal, with our support to do so. Ultimately they need to le

-simplified report card
-student self-assessment
-unit self assessment

build from the instruction and resources we make available to them in order to advance their knowledge and skills.

Bridging from Guiding Learning to Fostering Independence   A third approach we recommend for fostering autonomy is to carefully bridge from guiding learning to encouraging independence. Students certainly benefit when we provide structured, systematic, and explicit supports for their development of important kinds of knowledge and skills. But if we are to foster autonomy and SRL, we also need to sequence activities in ways that transition from guiding students' engagement toward their taking control over their own learning (see Butler, 2002). We can't guide them once they leave our classrooms, and we can't teach them strategies for everything. Ultimately, students need to learn how to choose, adapt, or even invent strategies that work best for them in the context of many different kinds of activities both within and outside of schools.

Engaging Students in Shaping Classroom Practices   Another way to foster autonomy is to engage students in shaping classroom practices. For example, as we described in Chapter 5, many benefits accrue when educators involve students in co-constructing classroom routines or expectations. Students feel a greater sense of belonging in the classroom when they participate in creating the classroom community and defining expectations. We also foster autonomy when students participate in defining learning goals for activities. As we described in Chapter 4, 21st-century learners will be asked to *identify* problems, not only to solve them.

As a final example, we foster autonomy when we include students in the assessment process. When we involve students in co-constructing performance criteria, self-assessment, or generating feedback for peers, we position them as responsible for supporting their own and others' learning. When students are involved in assessment processes, they also have opportunities to develop productive metacognitive knowledge about activities, learning, and themselves as learners (see Brownlie & Schnellert, 2009).

> ## Activity 6-2
> # Fostering Autonomy

Figure 6-3 provides case study illustrations of how educators at different grade levels have woven these kinds of approaches into their work in classrooms. Even in these brief examples, what do you notice about how Lori Davis, Paul Britton, and Kim Ondrik were working to foster students' autonomy in their contexts? We suggest you draw lines in Table 6-2 between each teacher's name and the kinds of autonomy-promoting practices being enacted in his or her classroom. As you do this, take a moment to reflect on how the teacher is fostering autonomy in that particular situation.

Table 6-2   Autonomy-Promoting Practices in Case Examples

Teacher	Practices
Lori Davis	Providing opportunities for choice and decision-making
	Encouraging students to take ownership over their learning and performance
Paul Britton	
	Building from guiding learning to fostering independence
Kim Ondrik	Engaging students in shaping classroom practices

In Lori Davis' Grade 4 classroom, students study ecology. As they are learning about aspects of ecosystems, they have to make a case for whether or not we need more laws to protect living things. The final task is to write a letter to the local newspaper suggesting if and how laws should stay the same or change to maintain or sustain the local ecosystem. Students must draw on content knowledge about ecosystems, as well as ideas from mini-lessons about letter writing, to help them determine what to focus on, how the ecosystem works, human impact on the system, and what would make it thrive. The teacher offers resources, but more importantly, acts as a resource while students work.

In Paul Britton's Grade 8 science classroom, students must design mini-submarines that they take to a lake and test. Students have to create designs based on principles that they are learning. Students must make many choices and decisions throughout the design process, through several cycles of planning, enacting, reflecting, and adapting.

Fostering Autonomy

Kim Ondrik engages her Grade 6/7 students in project-based learning. Students have to develop their own inquires, working within shared criteria for project development (developing a focus and inquiry question, carrying out research, documenting what they are learning, creating a representation of their learning, and presenting their learning). Students must decide how to draw resources (e.g., from prior mini-lessons) into their inquires to further their learning.

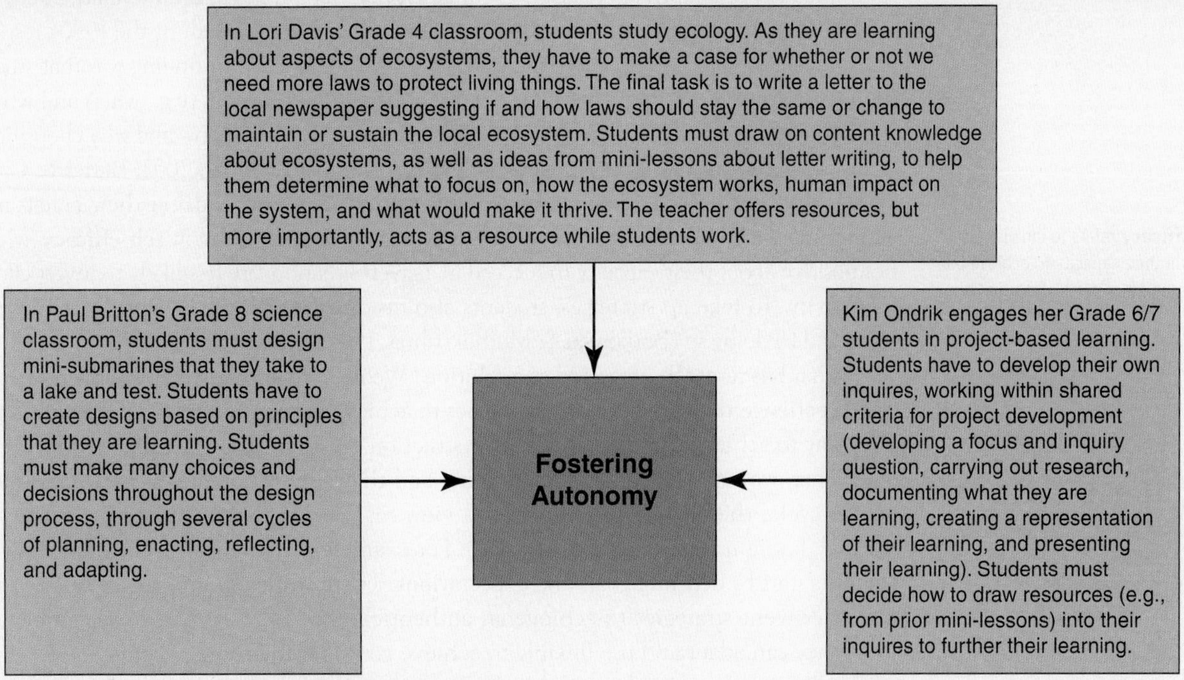

Figure 6-3 Fostering Autonomy: Case Examples

Weaving Supports for Self-Regulated Learning into Activities

The two guidelines discussed so far have emphasized the importance of creating opportunities for students to engage in SRL and exercise autonomy, if they are going to learn how to take deliberate control over learning (see Table 6-1). But providing opportunities for SRL is not enough. It is also critical for educators to weave *supports* for SRL into environments and activities (Perry, 2013). These supports need to be carefully sequenced and structured to scaffold students' development of effective forms of SRL.

> Providing opportunities for SRL is not sufficient for developing self-regulating learners. It is also critical for educators to weave supports for SRL into environments and activities.

There are many powerful approaches educators can use to build supports for SRL into activities. These include (1) identifying and promoting SRL as a means to an end, rather than regarding it as an end in itself, (2) integrating supports for SRL processes into the curriculum, (3) focusing instruction explicitly on learning and thinking processes, and (4) assisting students to *learn how to* make good choices and decisions (see Table 6-1).

Identifying and Promoting SRL as a Means to an End   A powerful way to weave support for SRL into activities is to ensure that students recognize that SRL is a means to achieving important goals, not an end in itself. The goal is not to teach them *about* SRL per se, even if having that kind of declarative knowledge can be useful. Instead, our ultimate goal is to foster the development of *self-regulating* learners. Self-regulation is a process that learners need to take up if they are to learn effectively. Why is this distinction so important? Research across the last several decades has made that abundantly clear.

For example, have you ever noticed that, even after mastering strategies, for example for building meaning from text, taking notes, or organizing writing, some students still fail to use those strategies later unless they are explicitly reminded to do so? In the 1980s, early research on "strategy instruction" clearly showed that students benefited from learning strategies in all sorts of tasks and domains (e.g., reading, writing, mathematics). Unfortunately, findings also showed that students rarely took ownership over instructed strategies or used them spontaneously or adaptively (Butler, 1998, 2015; Perry et al., 2015; Zimmerman, 2008).

What prevents students from taking up strategies they have learned? By the 1990s, researchers were making progress in answering that question. One important finding was that students do not use strategies if they don't have a good sense of their purpose (e.g., when and why the strategy might be effective). In these cases, learners need help to see how and why choosing and using strategies can help them in achieving important goals (Butler, 2002; Butler & Cartier, 2004). Another finding was that students' use of strategies depends on their beliefs about learning and about themselves as learners. For example, students with low **self-efficacy**, who are not positive about their capacity to succeed in a given situation, are less likely to invest effort in an activity. To take up strategies, students also need to "see" and believe they can be more successful by doing so (Borkowski & Muthukrishna, 1992; Zimmerman, 2008).

What has research suggested as a solution? We need to ensure that students understand and experience the value of using strategies to achieve authentic goals. Fortunately, a powerful way to achieve that is to integrate instruction on strategies with supports for SRL.

When we support students in choosing and then using strategies as part of a strategic action cycle, they have opportunities to view SRL processes, not as a curriculum to be learned, but *as an effective way of working*. For example, when engaged in strategic action, students start by defining goals and expectations. Then, while planning, they select, adjust, or even invent strategies to achieve an authentic purpose. They start to see strategies as tools they can adapt and use flexibly to achieve goals. Furthermore, when students experience a direct connection between applying a strategy and improved outcomes, they start to take, and feel, a stronger sense of control over learning (e.g., see Butler, 1998, 2002; Butler & Cartier, 2004; Harris & Graham, 1996; Pressley et al., 1992).

Integrating Supports for SRL Processes into the Curriculum

Another way to weave supports for SRL into day-to-day activities is to integrate supports for SRL processes into the curriculum. As we emphasized above, SRL is not a curriculum to be learned apart from content-area learning. Instead, SRL is the *process* through which learners need to engage with content if they are to learn. It follows that it is not possible to teach SRL one day and then move on to something else the next. Instead, educators need to integrate supports for SRL into the day-to-day life of the classroom. Ultimately, the goal is for SRL to become the way in which learners engage in all sorts of activities both within and outside of school (Butler et al., 2013).

How can we build SRL supports into day-to-day activities? As one example, consider how Sheri Gurney, a Grade 7 teacher, integrated support for SRL within her curriculum to enhance her students' problem solving in math. As students worked through problem sets, Sheri supported them in learning how to interpret math problems by encouraging them to ask themselves the following questions: (1) What do I know for sure? What's happening in this problem? (2) What will the answer tell me? What am I trying to find out? (3) Are there any special conditions and rules that I need to know, or do I need background knowledge?

Sheri's students worked through these questions and problems together in a numeracy circle (see Schnellert, Watson, & Widdess, 2014 for more information). Within that context, students shared their proofs, compared their approaches, reflected on what was and wasn't working, and decided what actions to keep or change before tackling the next problem. Within interactive discussions with Sheri and peers, students engaged in rich forms of learning and problem solving by grappling with big ideas. They constructed productive forms of knowledge and beliefs (e.g., about math content, about problem-solving processes, about SRL). As they worked through math activities strategically and collaboratively, they developed capacities to self-regulate their learning in math.

Self-efficacy refers to individuals' beliefs in their capacity to achieve particular goals in a particular situation.

When students choose and then use strategies as part of a strategic action cycle, they start to view SRL processes, not as a curriculum to be learned, but *as an effective way of working*.

SRL is the process through which learners need to engage with the curriculum if they are to learn. The goal is for SRL to become the way in which learners engage in learning.

Focusing Instruction Explicitly on Thinking and Learning Processes

Another way to weave support for SRL into activities is to focus attention explicitly on thinking and learning processes. For example, earlier we described a study we conducted with secondary-level teachers working to foster self-regulated learning through reading in their content-area classrooms. In one year of that project, we investigated links between goals teachers had set, their classroom practices, and end-of-year outcomes for students (see Butler et al., 2013). As part of our findings, we identified four qualities of practices that were most highly associated with students' development of SRL. As described earlier, one of these was that SRL was supported when teachers sustained attention on process goals over time. We also found that SRL gains for students were greater when teachers focused explicitly on cognitive and learning processes. This finding is consistent with a large body of past research showing the importance and value of explicitly teaching students about processes they need to use in order to navigate academic work effectively.

As an example, in Starting Small 6-2, Janelle Feenan describes how she supported her students through an inquiry-based project in her combined Grade 2/3 classroom. As you read this example, can you identify how Janelle was explicitly focusing on learning processes throughout this activity?

Assisting Students to Learn How to *Make Good Choices and Decisions*

Another powerful way to weave support for SRL into the life of the classroom is to couple opportunities for students to make decisions or choices with *supports* for them in learning how to do so effectively. We empower students when they start to recognize and apply criteria for making good choices and decisions. For example, within a project-based learning activity, educators might explicitly and deliberately support students to make thoughtful choices about the following:

- who to work with (e.g., based on who has knowledge or skills that would contribute to a project and complement their strengths and stretches);

- where to work (e.g., by considering the best place to focus or find necessary resources);

- what resources and materials to use (e.g., based on the kind of information needed or how much challenge they want to experience as their skills develop); and

- how to represent learning (e.g., by considering the purpose of the presentation and the most effective way to communicate with others).

≫ Starting Small 6-2
Focusing Explicitly on Learning Processes by Janelle Feenan

My students are going to prepare three inquiry–writing projects over the course of the year. We have already finished the first one, and although it is inquiry based, I modelled every step with the students so that they knew what the process should look like. Each report looks exactly the same for this initial project, except for the title page, but that is okay because the aim is for the students to learn the process of inquiry and where to find resources. The title page actually ended up being a good example of the students' understanding about grizzly bears, because the illustrations showed what they had learned about habitat and diet. We edited our writing together, and completed the projects at the same time.

For the second project, the students are responsible for finding information on their own, although I, of course, will be available to help them. They will work toward becoming more independent writers, but some work will still be "scaffolded" and modelled by the classroom teacher. I have made up learning targets to help the children, which we review before each session with the iPads. Each statement begins with "I can…" and focuses on the goals we want to accomplish. I don't leave them up all the time, but when we are having a prolonged work period, I refer the children to the targets so that they are aware of the expectations. I have also made learning targets for each subject we study, and so far I have been impressed with the students' ability to be independent learners when they use them. I am inspired to look into how I can use the targets more effectively for a wider range of purposes.

For the final report, students will be expected to utilize all the skills they have learned, to collect information, organize, edit, and finally publish their work. Throughout this process, I will be paying close attention to how the children "interpret expectations, set personal goals, plan, enact cognitive and learning processes, monitor progress, and adjust as needed" (Butler, Schnellert, & Perry, this volume).

In Starting Small 6-3, we provide an example of how Briana Adams, a participant in one of our professional development programs, supported her kindergarten students to make good choices. As you read this example, consider the kinds of choices Briana built into this activity. Also, notice the growth she observed in her students' choice-making over time.

Helping students learn how to make good choices achieves multiple benefits all at once. For example, providing choices is a powerful way to help us accommodate diversity in our classrooms, since students can control the level of challenge they experience. In this way, they help us in "personalizing" the pace and quality of their learning.

Furthermore, this approach can help us achieve many of the goals essential in fostering SRL *simultaneously*. For instance, when identifying and applying decision-making criteria, students construct metacognitive knowledge about activities and how to tackle them. When supported in making good choices, including controlling the level of challenge based on their comfort and progress, they build a sense of control over learning.

Finally, as they deliberately and reflectively make choices, students *learn how to* self-regulate multiple aspects of their performance in the service of learning. For example, when students learn how to make good choices within a project-based learning activity, they are learning how to self-regulate their *relationships* (e.g., when choosing partners and negotiating learning with peers), *environments* (when choosing where to work), *strategic action* (when planning resources or choosing representation strategies), and *cognition* and *learning* (when enacting strategies for making inferences and reasoning).

Weaving Supports for SRL into Activities: Closing Reflection   We conclude this section by emphasizing the importance of building supports for students' development of SRL into activities and tasks. In education today, teachers are being called on to engage students in rich, authentic forms of learning (e.g., 21st-century, inquiry-based, project-based, and service learning). Correspondingly, educators are designing learning activities that create rich opportunities for students' development of SRL. But, if those opportunities are not partnered with supports for students *to learn how to* navigate these demanding kinds of learning activities, the result can be disastrous. While some learners may thrive, others will not achieve to their full capacity. Some students may suffer blows to their self-confidence that *undermine* further investment in active learning. By building supports for SRL into classroom environments, teachers can scaffold

>> Starting Small 6-3
Supporting Choice Making by Briana Adams

Since beginning this program, I have tried to provide lots of opportunities for choice in activities so that my students can access an activity in many different ways. This allows my students to choose a way to access the activity that they know will provide them with the best opportunity for a successful outcome. For example, when doing journals with my kindergarten students, we are focusing on drawing detailed pictures. However, I have also started encouraging my students to write a word or two describing their picture.

Writing can be a very stressful and overwhelming activity for young students. Therefore, I provide my students with lots of different ways in which they can engage in the writing part of journals. My students can choose to glue in a pre-typed phrase based on the subject of the journal entry and then only focus on drawing. They can also glue the typed phrase into their journal and then copy it underneath, or they can copy the phrase off of the board. Finally, the students can choose to use invented spelling to write their own words or sentence describing their picture.

What I have noticed is that all of my students feel as if they can be successful when working in their journals and this leads to more active engagement. I have also noticed that my students really do make choices that are developmentally appropriate for their own level of comfort and ability. We have been doing journals for a few months now, and it has been interesting to watch how the students' choices have changed over time. At the beginning, almost half the class chose to glue the pre-typed phrase into their journals. Now, almost the whole class either copies the phrase off the board, with about half the class choosing to use invented spelling to write their own sentence. The students have progressed through different levels of difficulty; however, it has been at a rate at which they are comfortable, and a sense of control has helped maintain their motivation.

Can you imagine how you might weave supports for students' development of SRL into the context in which you are working? What are you doing already? What more do you wonder?

student success (see Trauth-Nare & Buck, 2001) and facilitate students' development of effective forms of SRL within a wide range of activities.

Supporting Learners' Construction and Flexible Use of Knowledge, Skills, Strategies, Values, and Beliefs

In order to foster SRL, we need to create rich opportunities for students to first construct and then draw flexibly upon the knowledge, skills, strategies, values, and beliefs supportive of SRL. Thus, our last guideline for promoting SRL is to deliberately nurture students' active construction of meaning through their learning experiences.

Supporting Students to Construct Knowledge, Skills, Strategies, Values, and Beliefs
What kinds of meaning do students need to construct through their learning experiences? Students certainly need to construct content knowledge they can then build on as they solve problems or advance their learning. But, more than that, they also need to construct metacognitive knowledge (e.g., about academic tasks and useful strategies for completing them, about learning and themselves as learners, about their own and others' emotions and how to navigate them). While they need to build procedural skills relevant in different kinds of subject-area learning (e.g., in how to use lab equipment in science, steps in solving particular kinds of math problems), they also need to build skills and strategies that they can draw on to interpret expectations, plan their time, organize their writing, maintain attention, and navigate conflicts. To kindle and inspire investment in their learning, they also need to construct important kinds of values and beliefs. For example, they need to value success in learning and helping others to succeed. They need to develop growth mindsets (i.e., a belief in their ability to grow) and positive self-efficacy (i.e., a belief that they can succeed in the activity in front of them; Bandura, 1989).

Any time we engage students in reflecting on their learning and learning processes, we not only set the stage for them to start taking more deliberate control over learning, we also create opportunities to stimulate their active construction of the knowledge, skills, strategies, values, and beliefs associated with more effective forms of SRL. For example, earlier we described how Sheri Gurney was engaging her students in interactive discussions within numeracy circles. Notice how, in just that one activity, her students had opportunities to co-construct knowledge about math concepts, metacognitive knowledge about problem-solving processes and themselves as learners, and growth mindsets, and all of this through their engagement in tracing, talking about, and supporting each other's growth and learning.

> Any time we engage students in reflecting on their learning and learning processes, we create opportunities to stimulate their active construction of the knowledge, skills, strategies, values, and beliefs associated with more effective forms of SRL.

Supporting Students to Engage in Adaptive, Flexible Forms of Thinking
In Chapter 4 we argued 21st-century learners need not just to learn content but also to know how to *use knowledge flexibly and adaptively*. According to Dumont, Istance, and Benavides (2012) learners need to develop *adaptive expertise*, which they define as the ability to "apply meaningfully-learned knowledge and skills flexibly and creatively in different situations" (p. 3). Learners in the 21st-century will be successful if they know how to activate and mobilize knowledge, beliefs, values, and skills flexibly and adaptively in different activities and environments.

How can educators foster learners' capacities to engage in adaptive, flexible forms of thinking and learning? First, as we described in Chapter 5, when we create *communities of learning* we invite students to grapple together with big ideas. Within learning communities, we can help students develop the critical thinking, incisive reasoning, problem solving, and inquiry-based processes expected of today's 21st-century learners (Brown & Campione, 1987; Schoenfeld, 2004).

Guided learning occurs when teachers are primarily responsible for defining learning goals, processes, and assessment practices.

Action learning occurs when students have a hand in deciding goals, planning, and activity organization in partnership with teachers.

Experiential learning affords students the most freedom to set goals and approach learning activities in light of their interests and motivation.

As students learn to engage in strategic action cycles, they develop the capacity to generate and mobilize knowledge and skills creatively, adaptively, and flexibly.

Another approach is to create a balance between *guided*, *action*, and *experiential* forms of learning in classrooms (see Dumont et al., 2012). In **guided learning**, teachers are primarily responsible for defining how strategic action cycles might unfold. That is, they tend to decide on learning goals, strategies students will engage in, and assessment practices. When guiding learning, educators play an important role in students' development of SRL and adaptive expertise through how they scaffold support for students' strategic action. In contrast, in **action learning** students have a hand in deciding goals, planning, and organizing activities. **Experiential learning** affords even more freedom for students to set goals and approach learning activities in light of their interests and motivation. When engaged in *action* or *experiential* activities, students have increased opportunities to learn how to interpret issues, set achievable goals, make and enact plans, mobilize knowledge, and then adapt goals, plans, and actions. As students learn to engage in these kinds of strategic action cycles, they develop the capacity to generate and mobilize knowledge and skills creatively, adaptively, and flexibly.

Why foster adaptive expertise? Ultimately, our goals are for students to develop the capacity to meet and address new challenges both on their own and with others. To do this, it is not sufficient for us to lead them through activities in ways that ensure they will be successful. They also need to draw on the skills and knowledge they have acquired to interpret situations, frame how they might approach a problem, and engage in critical and creative thinking. From a motivational perspective, we note that, as they acquire adaptive expertise, students can also retain a sense of competence and control in what would normally be anxiety-inducing and destabilizing situations. By fostering adaptive expertise, we support students in learning how to build from what they know to interpret and address new challenges in iterative cycles of strategic action and exploration.

GUIDELINES FOR DEVELOPING SRL: NEXT STEPS

In coming chapters we describe more specifically how educators can build from the guidelines described here to create SRL–promoting *activities*, *supports*, and *assessment frameworks* (in Chapters 7, 8, and 9, respectively). But before moving forward, we invite you to consolidate your thinking about the four guidelines, introduced in this chapter, on which you can lean when designing SRL–promoting practices. To help you in doing that, we suggest you grapple with the questions we pose in Activity 6-3.

≫ Activity 6-3
Drawing on Our Four Guidelines to Construct Classroom Practices

In this activity, we invite you to scan the examples we have provided in this chapter to identify how various educators were building the four guidelines introduced in this chapter into their practice. We also encourage you to reflect on your own practice in light of these guidelines. What are you already doing in your context? What might you like to try?

To Foster SRL, Educators Can...	How Were the Educators in Our Examples Bringing These to Life?	What Are You Doing Now? What Could You Try?
Create opportunities for SRL		
Foster autonomy		
Weave supports for SRL into activities		
Support learners' construction and flexible use of knowledge, skills, strategies, values, and beliefs		

In Activity 6-3, we invited you to describe what you are taking away from our discussion of guidelines for designing SRL–promoting practices. Were you inspired by any of the examples you read about here? Have you identified practices you are already using that are a good match to the ideas we presented? Is there anything you might want to try in your context?

To extend your thinking further, we encourage you to take advantage of the Planning Tools we provided in Chapters 4 and 5. For example, you might draw on SRL Planning Tool 4-1 to scan for students' engagement in SRL in relation to the practices you currently have in place, and identify next steps based on what you observe. Or, if you are inspired to take action based on any of the ideas in this chapter, you can use SRL Planning Tool 5-1 to reflect on your goals, what you try, what happens, and implications for your learning or practice. Whether or not you choose to take up these more formalized kinds of inquiry processes (see Halbert & Kaser, 2013), we suggest you take a moment to consolidate your thinking about the guidelines we have outlined in this chapter. We will come back to these big ideas as we move to more specific descriptions of SRL–promoting practices.

Recommended Resources

Anderman, E. M., & Anderman, L. H. (2010). Motivational classrooms for all learners. In *Classroom motivation* (pp. 186–205). Upper Saddle River, N J: Pearson.

Bandura, A. (1989). Human agency in social cognitive theory. *American Psychologist, 44*(9), 1175–1184.

Borkowski, J. G., & Muthukrishna, N. (1992). Moving metacognition into the classroom: "Working models" and effective strategy teaching. In M. Pressley, K. R. Harris, & J. T. Guthrie (Eds.), *Promoting academic competence and literacy in school* (pp. 477–501). Toronto: Academic Press.

British Columbia Ministry of Education. (2005). *Science Grade 2: From Integrated Resource Package 2005.* Available at: https://www.bced.gov.bc.ca/irp/pdfs/sciences/2005scik7_2.pdf

Brown, A. L., & Campione, J. C. (1996). Psychological theory and the design of innovative learning environments: On procedures, principles, and systems. In L. Schauble & R. Glaser (Eds.), *Innovation in learning: New environments for education* (pp. 289–325). Mahwah, NJ: Lawrence Erlbaum Associates.

Brownlie, F., & Schnellert, L. (2009). *It's all about thinking: Collaborating to support all learners in social studies, English, and Humanities.* Winnipeg, MN: Portage & Main.

Butler, D. L. (1998). Metacognition and learning disabilities. In B. Y. L. Wong (Ed.), *Learning about Learning Disabilities* (2nd ed.) (pp. 277–307). Toronto: Academic Press.

Butler, D. L. (2002). Individualizing instruction in self-regulated learning. *Theory into Practice, 41*(2), 81–92.

Butler, D. L. (2015). Metacognition and self-regulation in learning. In D. Scott & E. Hargreaves (Eds.), *The SAGE Handbook on Learning* (pp. 291–309). London: Sage.

Butler, D. L., & Cartier, S. (2004). Promoting students' active and productive interpretation of academic work: A key to successful teaching and learning. *Teachers College Record, 106,* 1729–1758.

Butler, D. L., Schnellert, L., & Cartier, S. C. (2013). Layers of self- and co-regulation: Teachers' co-regulating learning and practice to foster students' self-regulated learning through reading. *Education Research International,* vol. 2013, Article ID 845694, 19 pages. doi:10.1155/2013/845694.

Cartier, S. (2000). Cadre conceptuel d'analyse de la situation d'apprentissage par la lecture et des difficultés éprouvées par les étudiants. *Res academica, 18*(1 & 2), 91–104.

Dumont, H., Istance, D., & Benavides, F. (Eds.) (2012). The nature of learning: Using research to inspire practice. *Practitioner guide from the innovative learning environments project.* OECD: Centre for Educational Research and Innovation.

Goodwin, B., & Miller, K. (2013). Research says grit plus talent equals student success. *Educational Leadership 71*(1), 74–76.

Halbert, J., & Kaser, L. (2013). *Spirals of inquiry for equity and quality.* British Columbia (BC): BC Principals' and Vice-Principals' Association.

Harris, K. R., & Graham, S. (1996). *Making the writing process work: Strategies for composition and self-regulation.* Cambridge, MA: Brookline.

Locke, E. A., & Latham, G. P. (2006). New directions in goal setting theory. *Current Directions in Psychological Science, 15,* 265–268.

Perry, N. E. (1998). Young children's self-regulated learning and contexts that support it. *Journal of Educational Psychology, 90,* 715–729.

Perry, N. E. (2004). Using self-regulated learning to accommodate differences amongst students in classrooms. *Exceptionality Education Canada, 14*(2&3), 65–87.

Perry, N. E. (2013). Classroom processes that support self-regulation in young children. *British Journal of Educational Psychology, Monograph Series II: Psychological Aspects of Education—Current Trends, 10,* 45–68.

Perry, N. E., Brenner, C. A., & Fusaro, N. (2015). Closing the gap between theory and practice in self-regulated learning: Teacher learning teams as a framework for enhancing self-regulated teaching and learning. In T. J. Cleary (Ed.) *Self-regulated learning interventions with at risk populations: Academic, mental health, and contextual considerations* (pp. 229–250). Washington, DC: American Psychological Association.

Perry, N. E., & Drummond, L. (2003). Becoming self-regulated readers and writers. *The Reading Teacher, 56,* 298–310.

Perry, N. E., Phillips, L., & Hutchinson, L. (2006). Mentoring student teachers to support self-regulated learning. *Elementary School Journal,* 106, 237–254.

Perry, N. E., VandeKamp, K. O., Mercer, L. K., & Nordby, C. J. (2002). Investigating teacher-student interactions that foster self-regulated learning. *Educational Psychologist, 37,* 5–15.

Perry, N. E., Phillips, L., & Hutchinson, L. (2006). Mentoring student teachers to support self-regulated learning. *The Elementary School Journal, 106*(3), 237–254.

Pressley, M., El-Dinary, P. B., Gaskins, I. W., Schuder, T., Bergman, J. L., Almasi, J., et al. (1992). Beyond direct explanation: Transactional instruction of reading comprehension strategies. *The Elementary School Journal, 92,* 513–555.

Reeve, J. (2006). Teachers as facilitators: What autonomy-supportive teachers do and why their students benefit. *Elementary School Journal, 106,* 225–236.

Rohrkemper, M., & Corno, L. (1988). Success and failure on classroom tasks: Adaptive learning and classroom teaching. *Elementary School Journal,* 88, 297–312.

Schnellert, L., Watson, L., & Widdess, N. (2014). *It's all about thinking: Building pathways for all learners in the middle years.* Winnipeg, MN: Portage & Main.

Schoenfeld, A. H. (2004). Multiple learning communities: Students, teachers, instructional designers, and researchers. *Journal of Curriculum Studies, 36*(2), 237–255.

Trauth-Nare, A., & Buck, G. (2001). Assessment "for" learning: Using formative assessment in problem- and project-based learning. *Science Teacher, 78*(1), 34–39.

Vygotsky, L.S. (1978). *Mind in Society.* Cambridge, MA: Harvard University Press.

Zimmerman, B. J. (2008). Investigating self-regulation and motivation: Historical background, methodological developments, and future prospects. *American Educational Research Journal, 45,* 166–183.

Chapter 7

Designing Activities to Foster Self-Regulated Learning

Westend61/Getty Images

INTRODUCTION

In Part One of this book, we identified instructional goals essential in fostering the development of self-regulating learners. In Part Two, our attention has shifted to describing guidelines and practices educators can build from to achieve those goals. We started in Chapter 5 by explaining how educators can create safe and supportive learning environments in which all students feel comfortable stretching their learning. In Chapter 6, we offered four guidelines for designing practices supportive of SRL. In this chapter, we start building from those guidelines, in this case to suggest how educators can design SRL–promoting *activities*.

Designing SRL–Promoting Activities

How do you think activities could be structured so that they create opportunities for active learning and SRL? What kinds of activities might *not* afford as many opportunities? Why should educators also be sure to weave support for SRL into activities? What are you doing along these lines in your practice now? What do you wonder?

Learning Intentions

After reading this chapter, you should be able to do the following:

LI 1   Describe why activities play such an important role in fostering SRL.

LI 2   Imagine how you can design activities that create opportunities to foster active learning and SRL.

ANCHORING OUR DISCUSSION

In this chapter we discuss how educators can design activities to foster active learning and students' development of effective forms of SRL. Therefore, to anchor our discussion, we need to keep our goals in mind. What are those goals? As we established in Chapter 4, when setting goals for students, educators need to attend to (1) how students are constructing knowledge, skills, strategies, beliefs, and values that provide a foundation for active learning and SRL; (2) how students' motivation and emotions are supporting, or undermining, their performance; and (3) whether students are learning how to engage deliberately and reflectively in cycles of strategic action in relation to multiple aspects of performance.

Furthermore, in Chapter 6, we introduced four guidelines for designing SRL–promoting practices (see Table 6-1). You can think of these as "guiding lights" to keep in mind when building practices with promise to foster SRL. To review, these guidelines are to (1) create opportunities for SRL; (2) foster autonomy; (3) weave supports for SRL into activities; and (4) support students' flexible use of knowledge, skills, strategies, values, and beliefs.

Building on these guidelines, this chapter describes how educators can structure activities to create opportunities for students to develop effective forms of SRL. However, as we will stress throughout this chapter, an important caveat is that no single activity can stand alone in fostering SRL. First, it may not be possible to focus on all aspects of SRL at the same time. Second, supporting students' development of effective forms of SRL is a lifelong project. Within and across grades, subject areas, and classrooms, students need systematic support to build effective forms of SRL in the context of increasingly complex activities. Thus, as this chapter unfolds, we invite you to imagine how you might design and sequence activities over time to achieve the full range of goals essential in developing self-regulating learners.

A FOCUS ON ACTIVITIES

Defining Activities and Tasks

What is the relationship between *activities* and *tasks*? Different educators and researchers use these terms in different ways, but generally speaking, what activities and tasks have in common is that they set up *events* that unfold in classrooms and schools that *require action* from learners. Both activities and tasks can require rich forms of SRL. In this book, rather than trying to make fine distinctions between activities and tasks, we will use the term **activity** to refer to any coherent set of experiences assembled by educators to support students' learning.

Activities can vary along a number of dimensions. They can be short or long term. For example, a research activity might unfold over weeks; reading one book for that project might unfold over days. Activities can include single or multiple components. For example, a

Activities are coherent sets of experiences assembled by educators to support students' learning. They require action on the part of learners.

research activity might include reading, writing, discussing, and presenting, while reading a book as part of that research might include reading for meaning and taking notes. Activities can focus on a single learning outcome or incorporate multiple goals. For example, a research activity might be designed to foster content-area learning, scientific reasoning, and effective forms of collaboration among peers. Activities can be the same for all learners or allow for differentiation based on students' interests, strengths, or needs; for example, by providing choices in a research project about topics, texts, how to work, or how to represent learning.

Activities likely differ in other important ways not included in these examples. But our point is that educators make quite a number of decisions when setting up activities. In this chapter, we focus attention on how to make those decisions in ways that can create rich opportunities for students to learn how to engage effectively in active learning and SRL.

Why Focus on Activities?

The activities educators introduce are central in fostering the development of self-regulating learners. It is within activities that curricula are brought to life and learning unfolds. It is through activities that students construct knowledge, skills, strategies, values, and beliefs that are essential to active learning and SRL. Within learning activities students experience different levels and kinds of motivation and emotion that they need to understand and navigate if they are to participate successfully. It is within activities that students learn how to engage in deliberate, reflective cycles of strategic action, as well as how to self-regulate all aspects of their performance. Thus, when educators plan lessons and structure activities, they have the opportunity to coordinate their practices in ways that foster students' development as self-regulating learners. They can do so by weaving into activities both *opportunities* and *supports* for active forms of learning and SRL.

CREATING OPPORTUNITIES FOR ACTIVE LEARNING AND SRL

How might activities be designed to create opportunities for the development of SRL? To consider that question, we invite you to review the brief descriptions of learning activities in Figure 7-1. How might activities create opportunities for rich forms of SRL?

Imagine a kindergarten/Grade I classroom in which, across a series of lessons, students read *The Three Little Pigs* (twice), sequence events in the story, write sentences to describe each event, consider the social and moral dimensions of the story, and then choose and write an alternative ending (Perry, Nordby, & VandeKamp, 2003).

Imagine a Grade 2/3 classroom in which students are asked to complete a research project on an animal of their choice. They are asked to do research on their animal by selecting and reading resources, and to write, edit, and "publish" expository text (using the computer; working together) (Perry & Drummond, 2002).

Examples of Activities That Create Opportunities for SRL

Imagine students in Grade 9 English assessing a wide range of strategies for reading and understanding different genres of text. Their task is to try each strategy, first with narrative texts, then poetry, then short stories. Then they need to evaluate the pros and cons of each strategy in relation to texts and tasks, and judge whether the strategy helped them with their learning (Perry, Brenner, & Fusaro, in press).

Imagine a Grade 12 biology unit on the cardiovascular system that asks students to represent their learning in an artistic product. Students are encouraged to thinking broadly in terms of art, photography, computer imaging, video, fashion or textile, dance or drama, etc. The final products are displayed for a week and assessed by peers as well as teachers (Kelly, 2013).

Figure 7-1 Activities That Create Opportunities for Self-Regulated Learning.

Activities That Create Opportunities for SRL

Consider the example activities in Figure 7-1. How might these activities create opportunities for students to develop more effective forms of SRL? What essential goals for students could be achieved through those activities? From your own experience, can you imagine an activity that created opportunities for fostering SRL?

It might take a bit of imagination to identify the potential for supporting SRL from these the very brief activity descriptions in Figure 7-1. So, in this section we elaborate on one of these to highlight opportunities for fostering SRL we see in that example. For this purpose, consider the research project Lynn Drummond assigned to students in her combined Grade 2/3 classroom (for a detailed description, see Perry & Drummond, 2002).

We should emphasize up front that Lynn engaged students in this activity near the end of the school year. At the start of the year, Lynn recognized that her young students would need support to develop their knowledge and skills if they were going to take on a research project more independently. As she explained, "It takes a long time. We've got to start with small steps" (Perry & Drummond, 2002, p. 305). So, across the year, Lynn wove opportunities and supports for SRL *into a sequence of activities* that integrated goals from science (i.e., learning about animal growth and changes, developing research skills) and English language arts (i.e., reading, writing) curricula.

As we summarize in Figure 7-2, at the start of the school year (September to October) Lynn focused on building a learning community within her classroom and developed frameworks with students for research and writing. Then, through November and December, the whole class worked through a first research project together, on chipmunks, with a high degree of support from Lynn. During this project, Lynn guided them through each step. From January to March, the students completed another shared project, this time on penguins, again with Lynn's guidance, but also with opportunities to do more on their own. By the end of the year (May to June), the students were able to take on the research project described in Figure 7-1 more independently. While they often worked on their own, as members of a learning community they also had opportunities to seek support from and share their learning with Lynn and their peers.

Building Opportunities for SRL into Activities

The above description likely leaves you with questions about *how* Lynn supported students' development of SRL through this activity sequence. What kinds of supports did she weave

Sept–Oct	Nov–Dec	Jan–Mar	May–Jun
Creating a community of learners.	Research Project 1	Research Project 2	Research Project 3
	Topic: Chipmunks	Topic: Penguins	Topic: Students' choice
Developing frameworks for researching and writing about animals.	All activities are carried out as a class and guided by Lynn.	Lynn guides activities but encourages students to do more fact-finding, organizing, and writing on their own.	Students work independently on all aspects of their research and writing. They report back to Lynn and the group, who supply support when/where needed.

Figure 7-2 Building in Opportunities for SRL across Activities.

Source: Republished with permission of John Wiley & Sons, Inc, from Becoming self-regulated readers and writers", The Reading Teacher, 56 no.3 permission conveyed through Copyright Clearance Center, Inc.

into these activities to foster SRL? You can find a very detailed description of Lynn's work with students in an article she published with Nancy Perry (see Perry & Drummond, 2002). Furthermore, in Chapter 8, we take up that question specifically. But before jumping ahead to that question, we invite you to take a step back to think about how Lynn designed activities that created *opportunities* to foster students' development of SRL. What SRL–fostering opportunities do you see in this example?

What we notice is that Lynn created rich opportunities to achieve many goals essential in fostering SRL. For example, through these activities students had opportunities to build rich forms of knowledge, skills, strategies, values, and beliefs that serve as a foundation for their active engagement in learning and SRL. Not only did they achieve curricular goals for learning in science and English language arts, but Lynn also incorporated opportunities for them to develop productive forms of metacognitive knowledge (e.g., about research activities, themselves as researchers) and beliefs (e.g., about how learning grows over time across a sequence of tasks).

Furthermore, within the context of these activities, students had opportunities to engage in complete cycles of strategic action, at first with a good deal of support but then progressively more independently. Through a sequence of activities, they were asked to define goals (e.g., to learn about an animal); plan how to advance their learning (e.g., by selecting resources); enact and coordinate multiple reading, learning, and writing processes; share their learning and receive feedback; and adjust their approaches within and across tasks. Thus, across the year, Lynn created opportunities to support students' development of more effective forms of *strategic action* across a sequence of research activities.

Finally, students had opportunities to learn how to self-regulate different aspects of their performance to support their learning. For example, they had opportunities to learn how to engage in strategic action across the sequence of research projects (e.g., by making choices about goals and resources to use). They had many opportunities to learn how to self-regulate their cognition and learning (e.g., while engaging in meaningful forms of research, reading, and writing processes). They also had opportunities to learn how to negotiate relationships with Lynn and peers when collaborating, seeking help, and sharing their learning.

Activities That Are Complex by Design

Nancy Perry has provided a useful framework for describing the qualities of activities that integrate opportunities and supports for students' development of SRL (see Perry, 1998, 2013; Perry, Brenner, & Fusaro, in press; Perry & Drummond, 2002; Perry, Nordby, & VandeKamp, 2003). She refers to SRL–promoting activities as "complex by design." **Complex activities** are *not* meant to be complicated or confusing to learners. Instead, activities that are complex by design extend over time and include enough depth and variety to enable students to engage in rich forms of SRL.

Complex Activities extend over time and include enough depth and variety to enable students to engage in rich forms of SRL.

Building from Perry's work, we suggest that opportunities for fostering SRL are created by activities with the following qualities (see Figure 7-3):

- *Complex activities have multiple instructional goals:* In her animal research activities, Lynn integrated student goals for learning content (about animals), developing research and literacy processes (fact finding, categorizing, drawing, writing, editing, and publishing), and social-emotional learning (how to give feedback to and receive feedback from others respectfully).

Complex activities are not meant to be complicated or confusing to learners. Instead, activities that are complex by design extend over time and include enough depth and variety to enable students to engage in rich forms of SRL.

- *Complex activities focus on large chunks of meaning:* Complex activities engage students with big ideas (see also Schnellert, Datoo, Ediger, Panas, 2009; Schoenfeld, 2004). For example, Lynn's students had opportunities to grapple with big ideas about animals (e.g., appearance, habitat, food, enemies, babies) and share their learning with others.

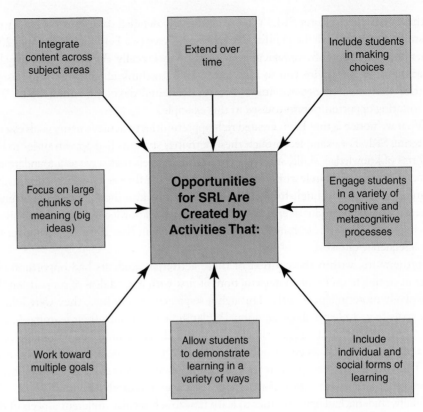

Figure 7-3 Designing Activities That Afford Opportunities for Fostering SRL.

■ *Complex activities add depth by integrating content across subject areas:* In her activities, Lynn integrated goals from across science and English language arts curricula so that students were learning about animals while also developing knowledge and skills in researching, reading, and writing.

■ *Complex activities extend over time:* In Lynn's class, each research project unfolded across an extended period, which required students to plan and sequence their thinking and learning processes.

■ *Complex activities require students to make choices:* Students working in Lynn's classroom needed to make many different kinds of choices while working through research activities (e.g., what topic to take up, who to work with, when to seek help, etc.).

■ *Complex activities engage students in a variety of cognitive and metacognitive processes:* Lynn's young students had opportunities to learn how to engage in metacognitive, self-regulating processes, such as setting goals, planning, monitoring, generating and interpreting feedback, and revising. While researching, reading, and writing, they were also engaged in many kinds of cognitive processes (i.e., thinking and learning).

■ *Complex activities include both individual and social forms of learning:* Lynn's students had opportunities both to work on their own and collaboratively, in different combinations, across the activity sequence. When working with others, students had opportunities to articulate their ideas, think about themselves and others as learners, and learn with and from others.

■ *Complex activities allow students to demonstrate learning in a variety of ways:* Lynn created multiple opportunities for students to share and compare their thinking and learning using different approaches and media (e.g., in writing by hand and on the computer, drawing, diagraming, sharing orally).

How might these qualities of complex activities combine to create opportunities for active learning and the development of SRL? First, when activities work toward multiple goals, focus on large chunks of meaning, and integrate across content areas, students have more opportunities to engage deeply with big ideas from multiple perspectives. They are more likely to develop adaptive expertise or the ability to use knowledge and skills flexibly and adaptively.

Second, to succeed in activities that involve multiple goals, extend over time, include choices, and require multiple processes, students *need* to engage in strategic action cycles. For example, they need to plan, sequence, enact, and refine their use of cognitive and metacognitive strategies (i.e., for planning, monitoring, adjusting their work). They are more likely to experience challenges while learning that demand deliberate self-regulation. When making choices, they need to take control over their learning and performance. In these ways, complex activities provide opportunities for students to learn how to engage strategically in learning. They also create opportunities for students to develop metacognitive knowledge about learning and SRL (e.g., about activities, strategies, and themselves as learners), as well as productive motivational beliefs about themselves as learners (e.g., if I use good strategies, my performance will improve).

Finally, complex activities that focus on multiple goals, offer choices, and require work with peers demand that students self-regulate multiple aspects of their performance. In so doing, these activities offer opportunities for students to develop a range of important knowledge, skills, strategies, values, and beliefs (e.g., about their learning, emotions, motivation, behaviour, or relationships), as well as to refine their approaches to SRL.

How can educators build these qualities of activities into their classrooms? In Starting Small 7-1, Briana Adams, a kindergarten teacher in one of our projects,

>> Starting Small 7-1
Creating Opportunities for SRL in Classrooms by Briana Adams

Opportunities for SRL are created by activities that extend over time, are integrated across subject areas, focus on big ideas, include students in making choices, allow students to demonstrate learning in a variety of ways, and include individual and social forms of learning. It is for those reasons that I chose to try an extended, group-based inquiry activity with my students. For the bear inquiry project, I placed the students in groups of three. I wanted to provide the students with opportunities for autonomy. I also knew that for kindergarten students with limited experience as learners in school and with very limited experiences engaging in inquiry, I would still need to provide a framework and a lot of support in order to make the activity manageable for them. Therefore, I chose four different types of bears and collected appropriate resources (books, pictures, etc.) about each type of bear to have readily available in my classroom. In their groups, the students were then able to select the bear they wished to learn about.

As a class, we then brainstormed the expectations for the project. The students themselves decided that the projects should include a picture of the bear, the name of the bear and at least four facts. Allowing the students to take responsibility for creating the expectations not only helped to make the task clear for them, it also allowed them to be a part of the decision-making and take ownership over the activity. Butler, Schnellert, and Perry (this volume) argue that one way

to bridge from guiding learning to independence is to ask students to make decisions while working through activities. When students are asked to decide, they are more likely to see themselves as responsible for their own learning and this can increase their motivation.

Once the students were clear about the activity expectations, I showed the students the many different choices that were available for them to present their information. For example, when sharing four facts about their bear, they could draw pictures to represent each fact, use invented spelling to write facts, or tell me their facts and I could write them down. Also, in order to create a picture of their bear, I provided the students with a lot of different materials they could use, such as paint, paper, and colouring materials.

Butler, Schnellert, and Perry argue that opportunities for SRL are created in activities that include students in making choices. By allowing the students to choose how they wanted to share their information, they not only had to negotiate choices with their peers, they also had to think about their strengths and weaknesses in relation to the skills required so that they could make choices that best matched their abilities. Again, by creating opportunities for students to make choices in groups, they were encouraged to articulate their thinking and justify their choices, which supports the development of the metacognitive dimension of SRL.

describes how she built from the guidelines described in this book to create SRL–promoting activities for her students.

Designing Activities: Cautions and Considerations

Research has demonstrated that teachers who establish activities that are complex by design create conditions that are supportive of SRL (see Perry, 1998, 2013). These findings are encouraging. It is also encouraging that teachers are building from these ideas to create rich activities in their classroom. For example, Lynn Drummond is a primary teacher who participated in Perry's dissertation research (see Perry & Drummond, 2002). Briana Adams is a kindergarten teacher who built from these ideas to refine her practices in her classroom. Additional examples of other teachers working across grade levels can be found in books by Faye Brownlie, Leyton Schnellert, and their colleagues (see Brownlie & Schnellert, 2009; Brownlie, Fullerton, & Schnellert, 2011; Schnellert et al., 2009; Schnellert, Watson, & Widdess, 2015). Nonetheless, there are important cautions and considerations to keep in mind when designing SRL–promoting activities.

Three Cautions When Designing SRL Promoting Activities   Our first caution is that just "throwing" students into complex activities without preparation or support is not likely to be successful, particularly for learners who are struggling to develop effective forms of SRL. When we described Lynn's research activity above, we explained how she carefully built students' capacities over time before expecting them to take on an animal research project more independently (see Figure 7-2). As Lynn did, it is important to create sequences of activities that build students' capacities to engage in effective forms of SRL over time. If activities do not afford opportunities for students to *learn how to* engage in SRL and to develop the requisite knowledge, skills, values, and beliefs necessary for doing so, then they will not know how to take control over their learning in our classrooms or into the future.

To foster SRL, it is not necessary that all activities be "complex by design". But it is important to ensure students have consistent opportunities to engage in and develop effective forms of SRL across time and activities.

Second, as we have emphasized already, it is not possible to weave every possible SRL–promoting quality or goal into every activity. For example, some activities may focus on very specific goals in just a single content area. To foster SRL, it is not necessary that all activities be "complex by design". But it is important for students to have consistent opportunities to engage in and develop effective forms of SRL across time and activities.

Finally, in this chapter we have described qualities of activities that invite students to engage in and develop effective forms of SRL. We cannot assume, however, that all learners will react to these "inviting" activities in the same way. Some students may be intimidated by complex, multi-step projects, while others may find them stimulating and exciting. Thus, when we design complex activities, we need to be attentive to learners' potential reactions, and anticipate the needs of diverse learners. Fortunately, complex activities can be deliberately designed to offer opportunities for students with a variety of strengths and needs so that they can all participate meaningfully and successfully. For example, when designing complex activities, we can accommodate diverse learning needs in the following ways:

- when students have opportunities to work toward multiple instructional goals, focused on both content and learning processes, it is more likely that all students will find an interest, strength, or preference within them;
- when activities support students to engage in both cognitive and metacognitive processes, then all students can *learn how to learn* through activities;
- when activities include choices (e.g., in how to access information or demonstrate learning), then students have opportunities to control the level of challenge they are experiencing over time, as their knowledge, skills, and strategies are developing; and
- when activities include both individual and social forms of learning, then students can benefit from opportunities to learn with and from one another.

How Do Activities Shape Learning?

How do you think the activities students are assigned in classrooms might impact how they come to think about (1) the nature of learning in different subject areas, (2) what the academic work we give them is all about (e.g., what is expected of a "good" reader), and (3) themselves as learners? Where do these kinds of beliefs *come from*? What do we need to think about when designing activities in order to ensure that the knowledge, skills, strategies, values, and beliefs students construct are supportive of SRL?

An Important Consideration: What Are Students Learning? Students are always constructing knowledge, skills, strategies, values, and beliefs as they participate in activities. Therefore, as educators we need to think carefully about what they may be "learning," for better or for worse, through the activities we assign.

How might activities shape students' construction of knowledge, skills, strategies, values, and beliefs? As one example, imagine an activity that provides opportunities for students to make mistakes and then find ways to correct them, or to experience challenges and then overcome them. What might students learn through these experiences? Given our discussion so far, we suggest that these activities would offer rich opportunities for students to develop their capacities as self-regulating learners. At the same time, they might build an understanding of learning as something that takes time and requires effortful, strategic action. They might also build **growth mindsets**, or a belief that ability can grow through effort and persistence (Dweck, 2006, 2010).

> **Growth mindsets** reflect individuals' beliefs that ability can grow through effort and persistence.

In contrast, imagine an activity designed so that students don't experience mistakes, to ensure that they won't be discouraged. What might students come to think about learning and themselves as learners in this situation? Our worry here is that if their learning is always errorless, then students are not having opportunities to experience challenges or to learn from their mistakes. More than that, they may also come to think of learning as something that should happen relatively quickly, in one try, and without error. They might develop a strong (or even inflated) sense of *self-efficacy*, believing in their capacity to be successful in a given kind of activity. They might also develop **fixed mindsets**, or a belief that ability is stable so there isn't much point in trying hard to improve it (Dweck, 2006, 2010). How would these students later react when facing challenging activities or if they made a mistake? Would they persist through difficulties? Would they be willing to invest time and energy in trying to improve?

> **Fixed mindsets** reflect individuals' beliefs that ability is stable, so there isn't much point in trying hard to improve it.

As a second example, imagine the kinds of metacognitive knowledge students might construct through their experiences with an activity. In her research, Butler (1995, 1998) found that students with learning disabilities who had struggled through school had developed problematic kinds of metacognitive knowledge that was undermining their success. For example, these students tended to think reading was just about decoding words, writing was just about spelling or grammar, and math was just about learning formulas. Where did these conceptions about academic tasks *come from*? In Butler's studies, students seemed to have developed these limited understandings based both on the challenges they were experiencing, which led them to worry most about basic skills in reading, writing, or math, and the activities they were exposed to in school. Those past activities had focused primarily on remediating basic processes at the expense of focusing on big ideas (see also Butler & Schnellert, 2015).

We recognize that it is important to support learners who are struggling to develop basic skills. We also understand why learners would focus most on the skills they find most difficult. But when students are struggling with basic skills, it becomes even more important to make sure they retain a focus on the larger purpose of activities. If the

When students are struggling with basic skills, it is even more important to make sure they retain a focus on the larger purpose of activities.

activities we design for any learner only focus on "mechanics" or just on areas where they are struggling, then they may construct metacognitive knowledge that is too limiting. We may also inadvertently exclude students from opportunities to learn more complex, meaning-based skills and strategies foundational to reading, writing, inquiring, problem-solving, and learning. Finally, if students focus too restrictively on mechanics or basic skills, losing sight of the purpose of activities (e.g., reading to *learn*; working with *big ideas*), then how can they possibly take up their basic skills effectively to achieve those larger purposes? Therefore, as we design and try to differentiate activities to meet the needs of our various learners, we need to ensure that we create opportunities for all of our students to develop rich forms of metacognitive knowledge through their learning experiences.

DESIGNING ACTIVITIES TO FOSTER SRL: PULLING IT ALL TOGETHER

In Chapter 6 we offered four guidelines for designing SRL promoting practices. In this chapter, we built from those guidelines to explain how educators can design activities with promise for fostering SRL. We have emphasized that no single activity can address all the goals we have for learners at one time. We also cannot build all qualities of complex activities into a single lesson. But across activities and over time, educators can do quite a bit to create sequences of activities that foster students' development of effective forms of SRL.

How might you build on the information presented in this chapter to support SRL in your context? In Chapters 4 and 5 we provided two kinds of SRL planning tools you can use to support your efforts to foster SRL. SRL Planning Tool 4-1 is designed to help you *scan for* SRL in action, record your observations, reflect and interpret what you have seen, and consider next steps for your learning or practice (Halbert & Kaser, 2013). Building on information in this chapter, you might want to use that tool to reflect on the kinds of activities you "see" in your context now, how students are responding within those activities, and what more you want to know or learn about SRL–promoting activities.

SRL Planning Tool 5-1 is designed to support your *reflection on action*. You can use SRL Planning Tool 5-1 whenever you try something in practice, to describe your goals, what you tried, what happened, what you learned, and what you might do next. Building on the information in this chapter, you might want to try creating an SRL–promoting activity for use in your classroom. As you take action to support SRL, you can use SRL Planning Tool 5-1 to reflect on what happens when you enact your activity in practice.

In this chapter we introduce one more planning tool you can lean on, this time to design SRL–promoting activities that are complex by design. To that end, SRL Planning Tool 7-1 offers thinking cues that you can refer to when designing an activity or a sequence of activities. The first two rows encourage you to articulate your instructional goals and then to describe your activity in detail. Remaining rows invite you to think through how your activity incorporates some of the features that are characteristic of complex activities as summarized in Figure 7-3.

To give you a sense of how you might use SRL Planning Tool 7-1, in Activity 7-1, we encourage you to apply this tool to think about one or more concrete activities. How do they reflect the qualities of complex activities as we have defined them in this chapter?

We invite you to draw on SRL Planning Tool 7-1 when you are designing or reflecting on activities in your context. Again, as you do so, remember that you cannot take up all of our goals for supporting SRL in a single activity. Similarly, it is not possible to build all of the many kinds of opportunities and supports for SRL into an activity at the same time. But this tool can help you retain a more comprehensive view of the qualities you can aim to

Designing Activities with Promise to Foster SRL

How do activities that are complex by design help in fostering SRL? To help you consolidate your thinking on this topic, in this activity we encourage you to fill out SRL Planning Tool 7-1 with a concrete example in mind.

To begin, imagine a complex activity, from either your experience or building from one of the examples in this book so far (e.g., Lynn Drummond's research project on animals). Start by reflecting on the instructional goals found in that example. Then add a brief description of the activity in the space provided. Next, fill in the remaining rows, describing what you notice about how that activity reflects the qualities of complex activities we described through this chapter (see Figure 7-3). As you go, note how those qualities might work to create opportunities for students' development of effective forms of SRL. Can you also see how those practices might help in achieving one or more of the goals we are working toward when fostering SRL? Can you imagine refinements to the activity that might make it even more effective?

SRL Planning Tool 7-1
Designing SRL-promoting Activities

Your Name	Grade	Subject(s)	Date

Instructional Goals/Objectives:

Activity/Task Description:

How Is Your Activity/Task Creating Opportunities for Active Learning and SRL?

How does your activity/task work toward multiple goals?

How are you focusing on large chunks of meaning (big ideas)?

How are you integrating content across subject areas?

How is learning extended over time?

How are students making choices?

How are students engaging in a variety of processes?

How are students involved in both individual and social forms of learning?

How can students create a variety of products to demonstrate their learning?

incorporate into your activities over time. Furthermore, if you decide to try out this tool, you can bring ideas you generate forward into our next topic. In Chapter 8, we will explain more specifically *how* you can link the *opportunities* for SRL you are creating with *supports* for students so that they become more effective as self-regulating learners.

Recommended Resources

Brownlie, F., Fullerton, C., & Schnellert, L. (2011). *It's all about thinking: Collaborating to support all learners in mathematics and science*. Winnipeg, MN: Portage & Main.

Brownlie, F., & Schnellert, L. (2009). *It's all about thinking: Collaborating to support all learners in social studies, English, and Humanities*. Winnipeg, MN: Portage & Main.

Butler, D. L. (1995). Promoting strategic learning by postsecondary students with learning disabilities. *Journal of Learning Disabilities, 28*, 170–190.

Butler, D. L. (1998). The Strategic Content Learning approach to promoting self-regulated learning: A summary of three studies. *Journal of Educational Psychology, 90*, 682–697.

Butler, D. L., & Schnellert, L. (2015). Success for students with learning disabilities: What does self-regulation have to do with it? In T. Cleary (Ed.), *Self-regulated learning interventions with at-risk youth: Enhancing adaptability, performance, and well-being* (pp. 89–111). Washington DC: APA Press.

Dweck, C. S. (2006). *Mindset: The new psychology of success*. New York: Random House.

Dweck, C. S. (2010). Even geniuses work hard. *Educational Leadership, 68*(1), 16–20.

Halbert, J., & Kaser, L. (2013). *Spirals of inquiry for equity and quality*. British Columbia (BC): BC Principals' and Vice-Principals' Association.

Perry, N. E. (1998). Young children's self-regulated learning and contexts that support it. *Journal of Educational Psychology, 90*, 715–729.

Perry, N. E. (2013). Classroom processes that support self-regulation in young children. *British Journal of Educational Psychology, Monograph Series II: Psychological Aspects of Education—Current Trends, 10*, 45–68.

Perry, N. E., Brenner, C. A., & Fusaro, N. (2015). Closing the gap between theory and practice in self-regulated learning: Teacher learning teams as a framework for enhancing self-regulated teaching and learning. In T. J. Cleary (Ed.) *Self-regulated learning interventions with at risk populations: Academic, mental health, and contextual considerations* (pp. 229–250). Washington, DC: American Psychological Association.

Perry, N. E., & Drummond, L. (2002). Becoming self-regulated readers and writers. *The Reading Teacher, 56*, 298–310.

Perry, N. E., Nordby, C. J., & VandeKamp, K. O. (2003). Promoting self-regulated reading and writing at home and school. *The Elementary School Journal, 103*(4), 317–338.

Schoenfeld, A. M. (2004). Multiple learning communities: Students, teachers, instructional designers, and researchers. *Journal of Curriculum Studies, 36*(2), 237–255.

Schnellert, L., Datoo, M., Ediger, K., & Panas J. (2009). *Pulling together: Integrating planning, assessment and instruction in English language arts*. Markham, ON: Pembroke.

Schnellert, L., Watson, L., & Widdess, N. (2015). *It's all about thinking: Building pathways for all learners in the middle years*. Winnipeg, MN: Portage & Main Press.

Chapter 8
Providing Supports for Self-Regulated Learning

Syda Productions/Fotolia

INTRODUCTION

In Part Two of this book, we are describing how educators can foster the development of self-regulating learners. We started in Chapter 5 by discussing how educators can establish safe and supportive learning environments that create optimal conditions for learners' engagement in active forms of learning and SRL. Then, in Chapter 6, we outlined four key guidelines to keep in mind when designing practices supportive of SRL. In Chapter 7, we explained how educators can build from those guidelines to design SRL–promoting *activities*. In this chapter, we describe more specifically how educators can weave explicit *supports* for learners' development of SRL into environments and activities.

Providing Supports for Active Learning and SRL

What kinds of social influences affect learners' development of SRL in classroom environments? What can we do as teachers to influence the development of effective forms of SRL by students? Can we also recruit peers to support each other's development of SRL? What are you doing already to create supports for SRL in your context? What do you wonder?

Learning Intentions

After reading this chapter, you should be able to do the following:

LI 1 Describe important social influences on the development of SRL.

LI 2 Explain how you can build supports for SRL into day-to-day classroom life.

LI 3 Illustrate ways in which we can recruit peers to support each other's learning.

ANCHORING OUR DISCUSSION

In this chapter we describe how educators can integrate *supports* into activities and environments in order to achieve our goals in fostering SRL. To anchor this discussion, we again need to keep in mind the goals we are seeking to achieve. To review, when setting goals for students, educators need to attend to (1) how students are constructing knowledge, skills, strategies, beliefs, and values that underlie effective forms of SRL; (2) how students' motivation and emotions are supporting or undermining their performance; and (3) whether students are learning how to engage deliberately and reflectively in cycles of strategic action in relation to multiple aspects of performance. Our goals can serve as a guiding light when making choices about practices, trying them out, judging how well we are achieving our aims, and making adjustments accordingly.

In Chapter 6, we introduced four guidelines that you can refer to when designing SRL–promoting practices (see Table 6-1). To review, these four broad guidelines are to develop practices that (1) create opportunities for SRL; (2) foster autonomy; (3) weave supports for SRL into activities; and (4) support students' flexible use of knowledge, skills, strategies, values, and beliefs. Through this chapter, we invite you to consider how you can build from these guidelines to build *supports* for SRL within the context in which you are working.

To structure our discussion, we start by describing the key role of social influences in learners' development of SRL. Next, we describe powerful approaches educators can use to integrate social supports for SRL into their practices. As part of that discussion, we highlight not only what educators can do themselves to foster SRL, but also the benefits of recruiting peers to support each other's learning. We close by suggesting next steps you might take up should you want to try out some of these ideas in your own work with learners.

SOCIAL INFLUENCES ON STUDENTS' DEVELOPMENT OF SRL

In Chapter 1 we emphasized that *self*-regulation is not synonymous with working alone. Indeed, our goals are to empower individuals to learn how to navigate social environments while working alone and *with others*.

Classrooms as Social Spaces

Classrooms are social spaces. Within them SRL is rarely a solo event. As Dumont, Istance, and Benevides (2012) emphasize, learning in classrooms, including the development of knowledge and skills foundational to effective forms of SRL, is "shaped by the context in which it is *situated* and is *actively constructed* through *social negotiation* with others" (emphasis in the original; p. 3).

When educators build supports for SRL into their classrooms, they have a powerful influence on students' development of more active, deliberate, and adaptive forms of learning. Furthermore, when we create *communities of learners* in classrooms (see Chapter 5), teachers and students have opportunities to build knowledge, skills, and strategies together (see Beishuizen, 2009; Paris, Byrnes, & Paris, 2001; Schoenfeld, 2004). In this chapter, we describe how we can build on the social nature of classrooms to integrate supports for SRL from both teachers and peers into environments and activities.

When educators build supports for SRL into classrooms, they have a powerful influence on students' development of more active, deliberate, and adaptive forms of learning.

Social Forms of Regulation

Models of self-regulation describe how supports from both teachers and peers can be created to foster the development of SRL (e.g., see Schunk & Zimmerman, 1994). According to Volet, Vauras, and Salonen (2009), teachers and students engage together in forms of **social regulation**, when "individuals reciprocally regulate each other's cognitive and metacognitive processes and sometimes engage in genuinely shared modes of cognitive and metacognitive regulation" (2009, p. 216).

More recently, researchers have distinguished between three forms of social regulation (see Hadwin, Järvela, & Miller, 2011; Hutchinson, 2013; McCaslin, 2009; Perry, 2013; Volet et al., 2009). As we explained in Chapter 1:

Social forms of regulation occur when individuals' engagement in activities or environments is socially influenced or interactive. They include *co-regulation, socially shared regulation,* and *socially responsible self-regulation.*

> *Co-regulation* occurs when a person receives support to engage in self-regulation effectively. In classrooms, co-regulation can be multi-directional. Adults can co-regulate children's engagement in effective forms of SRL, peers can co-regulate each other's learning, and children can co-regulate adults; for example, by providing information that helps teachers refine their practice to better meet their needs.
>
> *Socially shared regulation* occurs during collaborative activities, when two or more individuals regulate their engagement together through an activity. For example, when engaged in socially shared regulation, individuals typically co-construct understandings about tasks and combine their respective resources to achieve goals.
>
> *Socially responsible self-regulation* occurs when individuals self-regulate their engagement in activities in prosocial and socially competent ways to achieve personal success or foster success in others.

All three types of social regulation are typically present in classrooms simultaneously. Generally speaking, we can embed *supports* into learning environments by nurturing social forms of regulation among teachers and peers.

Teachers' Roles in Social Forms of Regulation   Teachers can play various roles when providing supports for SRL. Teachers can *co-regulate* students' engagement in SRL by taking up instructional, guiding, or mentoring roles. For example, they might teach students about effective learning strategies, and then guide them in using those strategies effectively while engaged in an activity. Educators can also engage with students in *socially shared regulation*. For example, teachers might position themselves as collaborators, working alongside students on problems or projects (e.g., in experiential learning; see Dumont et al., 2012). In these cases, teachers act as facilitators, sharing responsibility for learning with their students. Teachers can also move between scaffolding learning through co-regulation and sharing responsibility for learning, particularly as students build capacities for SRL. By combining these approaches strategically and responsively, educators can help students *learn how to* take responsibility for their learning and performance.

Recruiting Peers to Support Each Other   Educators do not have to take sole responsibility for guiding their students' learning. Another powerful way to foster SRL is to nurture effective forms of peer-to-peer co-learning. For example, teachers might recruit and support a Grade 5 student to mentor a first grader learning to read. By helping an older student learn to *co-regulate* a younger peer's learning, educators can advance both the mentor's and mentee's capacities and skills. Teachers can also create opportunities for *socially shared regulation* among peers. Students can *learn how to learn* together through collaborative or cooperative learning. Educators nurture students' development of *socially responsible self-regulation* when they encourage and enable students to learn about and with one another, and when they help students develop strategies for supporting one another (e.g., offering kind and constructive feedback).

As we move forward in this and coming chapters, we will continually emphasize that a powerful way to build social supports for SRL into classrooms is to create opportunities, and supports, for students *to learn how to learn* with one another. When they do so, educators can amplify opportunities to foster effective forms of SRL in their contexts.

DESIGNING SUPPORTS FOR SRL: KEY IDEAS

In this chapter, we will give many examples of how teachers can weave supports for SRL into activities and environments. To ground those more specific descriptions, we start here with a few key ideas that you can come back to when designing supports for SRL.

First, it is important to keep in mind that the ultimate purpose of the supports we provide is to build students' capacities to take control over their own learning and performance. When creating supports for SRL, it can help to ask yourself, "What can I do to help learners *learn how to* engage in this activity in the future, when I'm not here to guide them?"

Second, it can be helpful to use a scaffolding metaphor to imagine how to support students' development of effective forms of SRL. Following Vygotsky (1978), many educators and researchers think of the development of SRL as a transition from other regulation to "self"-regulation. Educators working from this perspective often start by creating a **scaffold** that cues and guides learners' engagement in effective forms of SRL (e.g., by instructing, modelling, guiding). Then they dismantle the scaffold and gradually release responsibility for learning to students as they become progressively more independent.

Third, even as we build supports for SRL, it's important to remember that we cannot really "regulate" learning *for* students (i.e., "other" regulation in a literal sense). We can inspire and *guide* students' learning. We can build and then fade supports to help them take progressively more responsibility for their own learning. But students have to choose to engage in learning and participate in activities. Ultimately it is they who have to engage in effective learning processes.

Fourth, we would emphasize that for any of our supports to have an effect, *students need to attend to, interpret, and willingly take up ideas and information*. For example, have you ever given detailed instructions to students, orally or in writing, only to find they still do not know what to do? In order for instructions to influence learning, students have to *know how to* attend to and interpret them (see Butler & Cartier, 2004). Similarly, research shows that simply giving students a rubric as an outline of expectations does not necessarily lead to better performance. Rubrics are more beneficial when students actively interpret and refer to them to guide and self-assess their learning. Rubrics have even more impact when students have a hand in co-constructing them (e.g., see Andrade, Du, & Mycek, 2010; Brownlie & Schnellert, 2009). In short, our influence on students depends on what students "hear" and interpret based on what we say and do. It also depends on students' *willingness* to advance their learning alongside us.

Finally, and most critically, our goal in providing social supports for self-regulation is for *students* to learn to be in control of their thinking and action. Teachers can inform, guide, support, and encourage students in ways that make a huge difference in their development of SRL. But the goal is *not* for teachers to take control over student engagement, even if they could actually do so. Instead, our goal is to create conditions that take advantage of social forms of regulation in order to develop students' capacities to take deliberate control over learning.

When creating supports for SRL, it can help to ask yourself, "What can I do to help learners learn how to engage in this activity in the future, when I'm not here to guide them?"

Scaffolds are supports that cue and guide learners' engagement in effective forms of SRL (e.g., by instructing, modelling, or guiding).

IMAGING SUPPORTS FOR SELF-REGULATION

To help you imagine how you can weave social supports for SRL into activities, in SR Vignette 8-1, we describe how one teacher supported her students' development of SRL through an activity sequence in her combined kindergarten/Grade 1 classroom (Perry, VandeKamp, Mercer, & Nordby, 2002).

SR Vignette 8-1
Imagining Supports for Self-Regulated Learning

Pam[1] had the following four goals for students in mind as she constructed her lesson sequence. She wanted them to:

- Construct effective forms of SRL in the context of classroom work.
- Engage with reading and writing as communicative, meaningful activities.
- Develop knowledge and strategies they could draw on when reading and writing.
- Engage in social and moral reasoning.

To achieve these goals, Pam created a series of activities that centered on the story, *The Three Little Pigs*. In a first activity, Pam read the story to students while they followed along with their own copy. During this first reading, Pam and her students engaged in a rich discussion about the story. On the next day, Pam gave her students a choice about how they would re-read the story. The first option was for her to read the story again, with them following along in their books. The second option was for them to do a shared reading, with volunteers taking turns. Students chose to read together on the carpet. On that day, Pam and her students spent a good deal of time talking about the reading process (i.e., strategies they used when they came to a word or part that was difficult for them). Also, on that day, they had a deep discussion about the social and moral dimensions of the story. In another activity, students completed a sequencing task by listing events in the story and "writing" a sentence for each (in words or pictures, based on students' choice). Finally, Pam engaged her students in generating and writing an alternative ending to the story. Below we describe in more detail how Pam built supports into this last activity, which engaged students in (1) re-reading the story, (2) considering the pros and cons of alternative endings, and (3) revising the story to include an alternative ending of their choice.

To begin this last activity, Pam again asked students whether they wanted to re-read the story together or read on their own. The class preferred to re-read together, so they gathered in a circle. During shared reading in Pam's class, student volunteers took turns reading aloud. As they read, their job was to draw on strategies to help them achieve goals. On this day, Pam gave students a choice in whether or not to "track" with their fingers in order to follow along. Then, as they took turns reading, and particularly if students lost their place, she asked students to self-assess whether their choice about whether to use the tracking strategy was working (or not). While reading,

the group also paused as needed to identify, discuss, and try out strategies for solving problems (e.g., to sound out or use context cues to help decode a difficult word) and build meaning (e.g., by making connections or predicting).

Once the students had finished re-reading, Pam engaged them in discussion about possible alternative endings. To get them thinking, she asked them to say what they thought about the current ending of the story in which the pigs' response to the wolf's misbehaviour was to boil him in a pot. She asked, "When someone is mean to us, should we be mean right back?" As students discussed the pigs' actions and possible alternatives, she encouraged them to express and compare their opinions. When they built from each other's ideas, she asked them to think about how they were learning with and from each other, asking questions like, "Is it okay to change your mind because you heard someone else's ideas?"

As the discussion started to wind down and most students seemed to have chosen an alternative ending, Pam encouraged them to move to their desks to draw and write their revision to the story (they could use "kids" writing—invented spellings— or just drawings). But, to make sure they had an idea in hand, each student needed to tell Pam what they had decided on as a new ending before leaving the circle. Two or three students who had not yet decided stayed with Pam for a few minutes to work on their ideas further. This gave Pam an opportunity to work more closely with learners who needed more assistance.

After the activity sequence had unfolded, Pam was pleased by her young students' ability to navigate a challenging text (from Perry et al., 2002, p. 13):

> The book . . . was quite difficult for them to read. . . . We read it together. . . . I read some and they read some. And they handled it, and it was really neat to see them doing that.

She was impressed by how her very young learners engaged in a weighty debate, for *40 minutes*:

> I found that, particularly during the discussion, there wasn't anybody that wasn't engaged, which is not always the case with my group. . . . I looked around and everybody was really into what we were doing.

Finally, she was excited by the richness and depth of discussion as the students discussed alternative endings together:

> I thought, very naturally, a debate came out of it . . . They realized that some questions are really difficult to answer . . . It isn't so black and white. So it was a really excellent discussion.

[1]Pam is a pseudonym, formerly "PM" in Perry, VandeKamp, Mercer, and Nordby (2002).

Imagining Supports for Self-Regulated Learning

How did Pam weave opportunities and *supports* for SRL into the activity sequence described in SR Vignette 8-1?

1. How did Pam create *opportunities* for SRL through her lesson sequence?

2. How did Pam integrate *supports* into those activities that enabled her students to self-regulate, co-regulate, and share regulation while reading, writing, and learning?

Before moving forward, we recommend you complete Activity 8-1. In this, we invite you to look for how Pam built opportunities and supports for SRL into this lesson sequence.

DESIGNING SUPPORTS FOR SELF-REGULATED LEARNING

In the rest of this chapter, we describe approaches educators can use to integrate supports into classroom activities so as to foster the development of self-regulating learners. There are so many options that space limitations prohibit us from describing them all. And, in any case, we strongly encourage you to imagine possibilities based on your own goals in fostering SRL, what you are already doing, and what you are learning about SRL. But to spark your thinking, we also give examples of powerful, research-informed approaches that you can use to design social supports among teachers and peers. To structure our discussion below, we illustrate practices educators can use to do the following:

- incorporate supports for SRL directly within activities;
- support students' engagement in full cycles of strategic action;
- bridge from guiding learning toward nurturing independence;
- support students' thinking and learning processes; and
- nurture learners' construction of knowledge and *adaptive expertise*.

Incorporating Supports for SRL Directly Into Activities

One of the four key guidelines we outlined for fostering SRL in Chapter 6 is to weave supports for SRL into activities. Why is this so important? If they are to take up effective forms of SRL as a way of working, students need to engage in effective SRL processes *in the context of classroom work*. Thus, as you read in upcoming sections about the various kinds of supports for SRL that you might provide, it can help to imagine how you can integrate them into activities, either while planning or "in the moment," to foster SRL.

As a starting point, we invite you to consider how Pam wove supports for SRL into an activity in her classroom (see SR Vignette 8-1). Before reading the rest of this section, you might review your responses to the second question in Activity 8-1. What did you notice?

We observed that Pam was working strategically to achieve key goals in fostering SRL. First, she was supporting her students in constructing SRL–promoting knowledge, skills, strategies, values, and beliefs, and then mobilizing those in the context of actual work. For example, in earlier activities, Pam had worked with students to construct metacognitive knowledge about reading and writing strategies, which were posted around the room. Then, within *The Three Little Pigs* activity sequence, she built in *supports* for students to choose and use strategies they were mastering. For instance, she asked students to judge whether or not they needed to track during shared reading, to follow along. She supported students to choose and use strategies for decoding, when they experienced problems, and comprehension, as they were building meaning. She supported them in monitoring whether or not their strategy choices were working *in real time*, and to make adjustments as needed.

Second, Pam provided supports for *strategic action* through the activity sequence. For example, she supported students in generating ideas and choosing alternative endings as important goal-setting and planning steps prior to writing. Through interactive discussions, she recruited peers to support each other in thinking about reading and writing strategies. Across activities, she helped students choose and use strategies in order to achieve their reading and writing goals, monitor how those were working, and make new choices if needed.

Third, Pam supported multiple aspects of students' learning and performance at the same time. For example, she provided just-in-time support for students' writing processes when she asked them to check in with her to make sure they had an idea in mind before leaving the carpet. As they were engaged in reading and writing, she "scaffolded" their thinking about the moral and ethical dimensions of *The Three Little Pigs* story. As she engaged students in a class debate about endings, she created opportunities for them to learn with and from one another. She simultaneously fostered students' social-emotional learning (e.g., about social-moral dimensions of the story) and self-regulation of *relationships* (e.g., about how to engage in respectful debate about ideas with others).

We also notice that, by empowering students to become more independently self-regulating, Pam was able to use her time more efficiently and effectively to meet the needs of the diverse learners in her classroom. All of her students were supported to engage in rich forms of learning and SRL. Then, within that context, Pam was able to provide more one-on-one, responsive assistance to the few students who needed more help to participate successfully.

Supporting All Steps in Strategic Action

An essential goal in fostering SRL is to ensure that students learn how to engage in full cycles of strategic action, including interpreting tasks, setting personal goals, planning, monitoring, and adjusting, in relation to different aspects of their performance.

Teachers' and Peers' Roles in Fostering Strategic Action   Educators can draw on a range of strategies to support students' development of capacities to work through strategic action cycles (see Brownlie, Fullerton, & Schnellert, 2011; Butler, 2002; Palincsar & Brown, 1984; Perry, Nordby, & VandeKamp, 2003; Pressley et al., 1992). For example, they can help students engage in activities strategically using the following:

Educators can draw on a range of strategies to support students' development of capacities to work through strategic action cycles.

- Direct Explanations; for example, about why they should carefully interpret assignments to guide further action and how to do that.

- Modelling; for example, by demonstrating how to interpret assignments, to figure out what they are asking you to do.

- Guiding; for example, by scaffolding learners' interpretation of an assignment description or by engaging them in guided, and then independent, practice.

- Coaching or Facilitating; for example, by asking "strategic questions" as students are interpreting an assignment.

You can also recruit students to support one another through strategic action cycles. For example, you can ask students to interpret assignment descriptions in pairs, and then share their understandings with the entire class. Often students can explain expectations to each other in "kid friendly" terms. You might also teach students how to give each other feedback as they are working through tasks. Doing so supports them in constructing rich understandings about performance criteria, about what successful performance looks like and how to achieve it, and about how to revise their work to make it better.

As an example, consider how Pam built supports for strategic action from herself and peers into her *The Three Little Pigs* lesson sequence. She did so by consistently focusing students' attention on task demands and goals as the basis for their decision-making (*task interpretation*). Students understood that their goal was to write an alternative ending to *The Three Little Pigs* story as they were debating possibilities and preparing for writing. Pam supported students in *planning* before reading (for how they would re-read) and writing (by choosing an alternative ending before starting). As they worked, Pam supported them to enact tracking, decoding, and comprehension strategies. Finally, Pam explicitly supported the students' engagement in monitoring and adjusting; for example, by asking them to decide whether their choices, such as to finger track or not, were working, and to make adjustments as needed. Notice that throughout this activity, students also saw it as their responsibility to support each other's learning. For example, when student volunteers were reading, class members supported one another to choose and use strategies to overcome challenges.

Supporting Students to Recognize Expectations It is worth highlighting the importance of supporting students' interpretation of expectations as a key step in strategic action. When students learn *how to* identify expectations, they are empowered to take more responsibility for self-regulating all aspects of their performance (see Butler & Cartier, 2004). For example, when students understand performance criteria associated with a writing assignment, research project, art activity, or math homework, they are able to focus their energy more effectively and strategically. When they understand how classrooms "work" (e.g., norms and routines; rights and responsibilities), they are also better able to self-regulate their behaviour accordingly.

In Starting Small 8-1, we give an example of how one secondary-level teacher recognized the importance of task interpretation in her context. Darcy Vogel had been working with her Grade 12 English students on how to revise their work. To help them actively interpret expectations, she put a strategy in place requiring them to interpret provincial exam criteria in their own words.

It is not only students who benefit when learners understand expectations. Educators benefit as well. For example, imagine taking just 10 to 15 minutes at the outset of a major assignment to help students actively interpret and understand any instructions. An educator might do that, for instance, by using a think-pair-share or place mat activity to engage peers in interpreting assignments together, then share ideas as a class (see Bennett & Rolheiser, 2001). This approach creates opportunities for students to support one another in building metacognitive knowledge about the kind of work they have been given (e.g., what learning "looks like" in that activity). Students also learn *how to* interpret

≫ Starting Small 8-1
Supporting Task Interpretation by Darcy Vogel

Only recently through our [program] and related research did I discover that the students who were not revising their work; in fact, they did not know *how* and *what* to revise. During a peer assessment activity requiring students to score exemplar papers using the provincial exam 6-point scale, a student exclaimed, "I don't understand any of it," making me aware of the need to "backwards" scaffold student learning in order to help them improve their writing. Lo and behold, student revision begins with interpreting the task so that students can transition from teacher to self-assessment. This realization

led to my creating a three-column handout that included (1) the scale, (2) my translation, and (3) space for their own wording. My translation is based on my experience as an evaluator. The space for students' own words was for them to record their own interpretation and hopefully stimulate further discussion and clarification of the assessment criteria.

Students needed to understand writing front to back (task interpretation to assessment criteria) and back to front (assessing strong models along with the scale) before they could substantially revise their work.

assignments. Finally, because they clearly understand expectations, the majority of students will be empowered to channel their efforts effectively and to work more independently. As a result, educators also benefit. They can avoid re-explaining an assignment multiple times to many different students. They can focus time more on those few learners who need a bit of extra assistance.

Supporting Students to Self-Assess and Revise Their Work   When fostering effective forms of strategic action, it is also very important to ensure that students learn how to both self-assess *and* revise their work. If students always turn in work without having to judge its quality or refine it, then they do not have an opportunity to engage iteratively in strategic action *cycles*. In many academic tasks (e.g., writing, researching, problem-solving), we can explicitly support learners to self-monitor progress, self-assess performance against criteria, and make a plan for refining their work based on the progress they perceive. As noted above, we can also teach students how to give good feedback to one another. When giving feedback to peers, students co-construct a better understanding of activity demands, what good performance looks like, and strategies for refining their own work. We will come back to this suggestion when we take up a discussion of assessment practices in Chapter 9.

Bridging from Guiding Learning to Fostering Independence

There are, again, many different strategies that educators can use to bridge from guiding learning to fostering independence. In this section, we focus on a few powerful approaches. Some of these can be built into a series of lessons, in a sequence, over time. Others can be used in any activity, short or long, to encourage students to take more ownership over learning.

Building Then Fading Supports across a Lesson Sequence   The first time students face a new kind of activity, they may need considerable guidance to understand expectations and how to achieve them. Yet, ultimately, our goal is still for them to learn how to navigate those activities strategically and independently. How can we get there?

One effective approach is to carefully build and then fade out supports across a series of parallel activities. In early activities we can provide more guidance, as students get used to the activity. But over time, we can gradually release control to students, as they build the capacities necessary to complete aspects of the activity more independently. Why is this approach so powerful? First, students have a chance to engage in the full activity right away, albeit with assistance. As a result, they build frameworks for thinking about activities that they can draw on as they learn to take up those activities more independently. Second, when rich supports for SRL are built into activities, from both teachers and peers, students can move toward independence at their own pace. Educators can simultaneously include all learners in the same sequence of activities and differentiate instruction to match individuals' needs.

Guiding Students' Learning   There are also many strategies educators can use to guide students' effective engagement in SRL as they move to increasing levels of independence. Some teachers find it helpful to offer mini-lessons on concepts, skills, or strategies that students will need when completing an activity. Mini-lessons are particularly helpful when the information presented is immediately relevant to students' work to achieve the requirements of an activity.

Other teachers use *procedural facilitators* to engage students in effective forms of thinking and learning. **Procedural facilitators** are tools (e.g., graphic organizers) that cue particular thinking or learning processes. For example, in Figure 8-1, we present a reading

Procedural facilitators are tools (e.g., graphic organizers) that educators can use to cue particular thinking or learning processes.

Inferences
Showing My Thinking

Stop (significant explanation) phrase, image, action, idea...)	My Interpretation (I think this is important because...) (Maybe.....) (I'm guessing...)	How I figured it out.... (thinking strategy) *Read*
Helena has followed Demetrius and Demetrius had treated Helena very poorly	He's doing this because he is trying to get rid of her. But he can't do this so she keeps loving him	Her attitude, and her lines gave it away. Her character is revealed to be a bit determined and foolish

Main idea/theme so far... (I think it means...)

Helena wants Demetrius. She doesn't want to be rejected
She will do whatever she can to get him

My thinking about the main idea/message/theme is...
(circle one)

It is a good play so far. To me all the characters have something really special/different about them. All the chunks make me think about the different features each person has to offer. (ie) Oberon is very sneaky and keen, Puck is smart, and immature at the same time, and Helena is trying too hard, and is foolish towards her friendship.

What I want you to notice about my thinking...

The author is trying to say that you shouldn't take love for granted when you have it. And don't hurt other people to get it. I think. As the Rolling Stones once said- you can't always get what you want. but sometimes if you try hard, you'll get what you need.

Next time I plan to.... (goal setting)

Find the main idea better.
and infer better

Linda Watson

Figure 8-1 A Reading Log Developed by Linda Watson to Guide Her Students' Learning

log that Linda Watson developed in her Grade 9 English classroom to guide her students' thinking when interacting with a Shakespeare play. Once they had experienced and understood the value of the reading log, Linda asked them what qualities of a reading log where important and effective. Together they brainstormed criteria for an effective log. Students then created their own reading logs to support them in their interactions with texts while preparing for writing. In this way Linda bridged from initially guiding her students' thinking and learning, to the students taking increasing responsibility for self-regulating their own learning. Notice how she also wove in opportunities for students to learn with and from one another.

Gradually Releasing Responsibility to Students   Guiding students to engage in and experience effective forms of reading, writing, and learning processes is incredibly supportive of their development of SRL. Students can and need to build from rich experiences to appreciate the purpose of activities and how to complete them. But, ultimately, self-regulating learners need to learn how to take responsibility for their learning and performance. Earlier we gave an example of how Linda Watson worked to achieve this goal for her students in her Grade 9 English classroom.

Procedural Facilitators

Educators interested in learning more about strategies for guiding students' learning can find a wide array of practical examples in texts co-authored by Faye Brownlie and Leyton Schnellert and their colleagues (see Brownlie, Feniak, & Schnellert, 2006; Brownlie et al., 2011; Brownlie & Schnellert, 2009; Schnellert, Datoo, Ediger, & Panas, 2009; Schnellert, Watson, & Widdess, 2015). Also, useful tools can be found at the following websites: http://www.nea.org/tools/a-story-road-map.html or http://www.nea.org/tools/graphic-orgnizer-for-pre-reading.html.

Another way to gradually release responsibility for learning is to design a sequence of activities that work through the following steps (see Fisher & Frey, 2008):

I do, you watch (maybe help)

We do together

You do, I watch (help as needed)

You do on your own

For example, if we return to the activity sequence Lynn Drummond created for her combined Grade 2/3 class, described in Chapter 7 (Perry & Drummond, 2002), we can see how Lynn gradually released responsibility to learners across three animal research activities. In Figure 8-2, we revisit our summary of Lynn's activity sequence, this time to illustrate how Lynn built from guiding their learning toward their becoming independent researchers.

Supporting Choice-Making   Another way to bridge from guiding learning toward fostering independence is to ask students to make choices while working through activities. When students are asked to choose among options, even during more direct or guided forms of instruction, they are more likely to see themselves as responsible for their own learning (Anderman & Anderman, 2010; Butler, 1995, 1998, 2002; Perry, 2013).

For example, Pam prepared students for independence by building choices into activities. In previous lessons, Pam had worked with students to identify and use reading and writing strategies (listed on posters on the wall). Then, in *The Three Little Pigs* activity sequence, she encouraged students to make decisions about how to apply the knowledge and skills they had learned (e.g., in whether or not to track; what reading and writing strategies to use; what to write as an alternative ending). Similarly, when students lost

Sept–Oct	Nov–Dec	Jan–Mar	May–Jun
Creating a community of learners.	Research Project 1	Research Project 2	Research Project 3
	Topic: Chipmunks	Topic: Penguins	Topic: Students' choice
Developing frameworks for researching and writing about animals.	All activities are carried out as a class and guided by Lynn.	Lynn guides activities but encourages students to do more fact-finding, organizing, and writing on their own.	Students work independently on all aspects of their research and writing.
			They report back to Lynn and the group, who supply support when/where needed.

Figure 8-2 Building toward Independence.

Source: Adapted with permission from Perry and Drummond (2002).

their place during shared reading, Pam did not jump in to tell them to track. Instead, she asked students to self-assess the success of their choice (i.e., not to track) and then, on that basis, *to decide* if they should do anything differently. By continually giving choices and requiring decision-making, Pam was fostering SRL by consistently positioning students as "owners" of their learning.

Supporting Thinking and Learning Processes

It is very important to consistently infuse talk about thinking and learning processes into classroom discourse and activities.

Educators can also draw on many different kinds of practices to support students' development of thinking and learning processes. As described earlier, they can use direct instruction, modelling, guiding, and coaching approaches. They can also use *procedural facilitators* to guide students' learning and draw their attention to how they are learning in that context. Whatever the approach, it is most important to consistently infuse talk about thinking and learning processes into classroom discourse and activities.

For example, in SR Vignette 8-1, Pam consistently drew students' attention to the processes underlying their engagement in reading and writing. Before shared reading, the class discussed and decided how they wanted to read (alone or together). While reading, students discussed and decided among strategies to use for tracking, decoding, and comprehension. To prepare for writing, students considered together what would constitute a good alternative ending. The result was that students were continually participating in rich discussions about reading and writing processes, their purpose, and when and how to use them.

Strategic Questioning   One very powerful approach to fostering SRL is to ask students **strategic questions** that direct their attention to thinking and learning processes while they are engaged in activities (see Figure 8-3). *Strategic questions* compel students to think about how they are learning and why. Strategic questioning is an effective strategy because it not only makes learning processes visible, but it can also be used as a support to achieve many goals. You can use strategic questions to support any step in strategic action, facilitate decision-making, assist students in making good choices, or focus students' attention on their growth and progress.

Strategic questions direct learners' attention to thinking and learning processes while they are engaged in activities. They compel students to think about how they are learning and why.

For example, imagine how a teacher might use strategic questioning to support students' ability to work through full cycles of SRL. When students are facing a new activity or task, teachers can cue and support their task interpretation by asking questions, such as: *What is your job?*, *What is this assignment asking you to do?*, or *How will you know if you've done a good job?* Educators can cue and support goal-setting and planning by asking questions such as: *How will you approach this task?* To help students mobilize what they had

Interpreting Activities and Tasks	Choosing and Using Strategies	Monitoring and Adjusting
• What is your job? • What is this assignment asking you to do? • How will you know if you've done a good job?	• How will you approach this task (given your goals)? • What strategies have worked for you before? • What don't you show me what you can try? • I noticed you did this. Is that a strategy you are using? • What are you doing here that you can do again and again?	• How are you doing? How do you know? • What criteria are you using here to judge your work? • What can you do differently to solve that problem?

Figure 8-3 Strategic Questioning

Using Strategic Questioning by Amy Semple

It is recess time. The children are asked to put their coats on and line up. This routine has been the same since September. Every single day, Alex (pseudonym) does not do this. He wanders around the classroom and rarely even has his coat in his hands.

In the past, I would always ask him to put his coat on. Since all I have learned, I decided to change my language; I now ask him what his job is. He always knows the correct answer. For this example, his answer would be, "I should put on my coat and line up." Once he offers that information, he will go, get his coat, and ask for help to put it on.

I have found that this slight change in my language has created a powerful shift! The children (including Alex) are starting to take ownership over what they are supposed to be doing (rather than relying on having the information repeated over and over again). Alex is very capable of following the directions but constantly relies on adults to help him.

learned previously for use in a new situation, educators might ask, *What strategies have worked before for you in a similar situation?* Educators can use strategic questions to get students thinking about how strategies they are using might be helpful in the future (e.g., *What are you doing here that you can do again and again?*), or to cue and support monitoring and adjusting (e.g., *How are you doing? How do you know? Given how things are going, what could you do differently?*).

Note that more open-ended strategic questions invite exploration (e.g., *How can we think about this problem differently? What might be ways in which we can approach this problem?*). But strategic questions can also be quite pointed, directing students' attention very specifically to a way of thinking or possible courses of action (e.g., *I noticed that you weren't following along while reading. Do you think using a tracking strategy might help you in this instance?*). Thus, strategic questioning can be used both to guide learning and to bridge toward independence. Either way, the beauty of strategic questions is that they not only direct students' attention to learning processes, but they also position students as decision-makers. Even when teachers guide learning using pointed questions, students *perceive* that they are making choices about their thinking and learning (Brownlie et al., 2011; Brownlie & Schnellert, 2009; Butler, 1995, 1998).

In Starting Small 8-2, we provide an example of how one teacher, Amy Semple, used strategic questioning in her combined kindergarten/Grade 1 classroom, in this case to provide more personalized supports to a student who was experiencing behavioural challenges. As you read this example, notice how her approach was working to support *self*-regulation by her student.

Nurturing Students' Construction of Knowledge and Adaptive Expertise

Again, there are many strategies that educators can use to support learners' construction and flexible use of knowledge, skills, strategies, values, and beliefs. We highlight just a few particularly useful approaches here.

Engage Students in Talking about Learning We know that students construct new content knowledge more actively when they try to teach something to others or summarize ideas in their own words. The same insight holds true when students are building capacity for SRL. If students are asked to articulate what they are doing and why, they construct and refine understandings about tasks, strategies, and themselves as learners (e.g., see Butler, 2002; Cleary & Zimmerman, 2004; Harris & Pressley, 1991; Paris et al., 2001). Educators support students' active construction of knowledge and beliefs whenever they engage them in conversation about learning processes or require them to articulate emerging understandings based on their new experiences.

For example, in Chapter 6 we described how Sheri Gurney, a Grade 7 teacher, wove support for SRL into her curriculum to enhance her students' problem-solving in math. Sheri supported students in learning *how to* interpret math problems by getting them to *ask themselves* strategic questions (e.g., What do I know for sure? What's happening in this problem?). She also created supports for peers to learn about problem-solving with one another. Within numeracy circles, Sheri asked students to share their proofs, compare approaches, reflect together on what was and wasn't working, and decide what actions to take next. Using these strategies, Sheri required students to explicitly articulate their thinking about math problems and math problem-solving while engaging with her and their peers. The result was that her students were building rich forms of metacognitive knowledge about problem-solving in math and themselves as learners (for more information about Sheri's use of numeracy circles, see Schnellert et al., 2015).

Nurturing Adaptive Expertise   In Chapter 4 we described one of our broad goals in supporting SRL as fostering students' development of *adaptive expertise*. For students to develop into flexible, adaptive 21st-century learners, it is not sufficient for them to just acquire knowledge and skills. They must also develop the capacity to draw on their knowledge and skills to think deeply and richly with big ideas (Dumont et al., 2012; Hargreaves, 2003; Schoenfeld, 2004).

How can educators provide supports that foster adaptive expertise? Educators set the stage for that when they create opportunities for rich forms of thinking and learning; for example, by creating activities that are complex by design or offer *experiential* forms of learning. In those contexts, teachers can draw on many of the approaches we have described in this chapter to support students' flexible and adaptive use of their knowledge and skills. Many of these approaches create opportunities for students to take up the knowledge and skills they are developing flexibly and adaptively in the context of authentic activities. For example, when they employ powerful strategies like *strategic questioning,* educators can nurture learners' creativity and problem-solving in context (e.g., What can you imagine? What do you already know that can help you in interpreting that problem?).

For instance, in Sheri Gurney's Grade 7 math classroom, her students were asking themselves strategic questions to navigate problem-solving tasks (e.g., What's happening in this problem?). As students negotiated problem-solving tasks, they discussed, adapted, applied, and refined their knowledge and skills together while working through problems. In this way, Sheri created opportunities and supports for students to both (1) apply knowledge and skills adaptively and flexibly, and (2) learn how to take control over strategic action. To foster the development of adaptive expertise, educators need to provide *supports* for students to learn how to seek, apply, adapt and/or generate knowledge flexibly and strategically.

BUILDING SUPPORTS FOR SRL INTO ACTIVITIES: NEXT STEPS

How might you design *supports* for SRL in your context? In this chapter, we offer one more tool that you might find useful, this time in planning ahead for how you might provide SRL–promoting supports in your context (see SRL Planning Tool 8-1). You can use this tool to imagine in advance how you might weave supports for SRL into activities you are designing. You can also refer to this tool as you are constructing supports day-to-day with individuals or groups of students. Alternatively, you can just refer to this tool as you move forward in reading this book, to help you retain a big-picture view of effective approaches to weaving supports for SRL into activities and environments.

SRL Planning Tool 8-1
Weaving Supports for SRL into Activities and Environments

Your Name	Grade	Subject(s)	Date

Instructional Goals/Objectives:

Activity/Task Description:

How will you weave supports for active learning and SRL into activities? Consider, in each area, how you might also recruit students to support each other's learning.

How will you integrate support for SRL into activities?

How will you support students to engage in full cycles of strategic action (interpreting tasks, setting goals, planning, enacting strategies, monitoring, revising)?

How will you bridge from providing guidance to fostering independence?

How will you support students' thinking and learning processes?

How will you nurture learners' construction of knowledge and adaptive expertise?

Recommended Resources

Anderman, E. M., & Anderman, L. H. (2010). Motivational classrooms for all learners. In *Classroom motivation* (pp. 186–205). Upper Saddle River, NJ: Pearson.

Andrade, H. L., Du, Y., & Mycek, K. (2010). Rubric-referenced self-assessment and middle school students' writing. *Assessment in Education: Principles, Policy, & Practice, 17(2)*, 199–214.

Beishuizen, J. (2009). Does a community of learners foster self-regulated learning? *Technology, Pedagogy, and Education, 17(3)*, 183–193. DOI: 10.1080/14759390802383769

Bennett, B., & Rolheiser, C. (2001). *Beyond Monet: The artful science of instructional integration.* Toronto ON: Bookation.

Brownlie, F., Fullerton, C., & Schnellert, L. (2011). *It's all about thinking: Collaborating to support all learners in mathematics and science.* Winnipeg, MN: Portage & Main Press.

Brownlie, F., & Schnellert, L. (2009). *It's all about thinking: Collaborating to support all learners in English, social studies and humanities.* Winnipeg, MN: Portage & Main Press.

Brownlie, F., Feniak, C., & Schnellert, L. (2006). *Student diversity* (2nd ed.). Markham, ON: Pembroke Publishers.

Butler, D. L. (1995). Promoting strategic learning by postsecondary students with learning disabilities. *Journal of Learning Disabilities, 28*, 170–190.

Butler, D. L. (1998). The Strategic Content Learning approach to promoting self-regulated learning: A summary of three studies. *Journal of Educational Psychology, 90*, 682–697.

Butler, D. L. (2002). Individualizing instruction in self-regulated learning. *Theory into Practice*, *41*(2), 81–92.

Butler, D. L., & Cartier, S. (2004). Promoting students' active and productive interpretation of academic work: A key to successful teaching and learning. *Teachers College Record*, 106, 1729–1758.

Cleary, T. J., & Zimmerman, B. J. (2004). Self-regulation empowerment program: A school-based program to enhance self-regulated and self-motivated cycles of student learning. *Psychology in the* Schools, *41*(5), 537–550.

Dumont, H., Istance, D., & Benavides, F. (Eds.) (2012). The nature of learning: Using research to inspire practice. Practitioner Guide from the Innovative Learning Environments Project. OECD: Centre for Educational Research and Innovation.

Fisher, D., & Frey, N. (2008). *Better learning through structured teaching: A framework for the gradual release of responsibility*. Association for Supervision and Curriculum Development, Alexandria, VA.

Hadwin, A. F., Jarvela, S., & Miller, M. (2011). Self-regulated, co-regulated, and socially shared regulation of learning. In B. J. Zimmerman & D. H. Schunk (Eds.), *Handbook of self-regulation of learning and performance* (pp. 65–84). New York: Routledge.

Hargreaves, A. (2003). *Teaching in the knowledge society*. New York: Teachers College Press.

Harris, K. R., & Pressley, M. (1991). The nature of cognitive strategy instruction: Interactive strategy construction. *Exceptional Children, 57*, 392–404.

Hutchinson, L. R. (2013). Young children's engagement in self-regulation at school. (Unpublished doctoral dissertation). University of British Columbia, Vancouver. Available at https://circle.ubc.ca/handle/2429/44401.

McCaslin, M. (2009). Co-regulation of student motivation and emergent identity. *Educational Psychologist, 44*, 137–146.

Palincsar, A. S., & Brown, A. L. (1984). Reciprocal teaching of comprehension-fostering and comprehension-monitoring activities. *Cognition and Instruction*, *1*, 117–175.

Paris, S., Byrnes J., & Paris, A. (2001). Constructing theories, identities and actions of self-regulated learners. In Zimmerman, B., & Schunk, D. (Eds.), *Self-regulated learning and academic achievement: Theoretical perspectives* (pp. 253–288). Mahwah, NJ: Erlbaum.

Perry, N. E. (2013). Classroom processes that support self-regulation in young children [Monograph]. *British Journal of Educational Psychology, Monograph Series II: Psychological Aspects of Education—Current Trends, 10*, 45–68.

Perry, N. E., & Drummond, L. (2002) Becoming self-regulated readers and writers. *The Reading Teacher, 56*, 298–310.

Perry, N. E., Nordby, C. J., & VandeKamp, K. O. (2003). Promoting self-regulated reading and writing at home and school. *The Elementary School Journal*, *103(4)*, 317–338.

Perry, N. E., VandeKamp, K. O., Mercer, L. K., & Nordby, C. J. (2002). Investigating teacher-student interactions that foster self-regulated learning. *Educational Psychologist*, *37*, 5–15.

Pressley, M., El-Dinary, P. B., Gaskins, I. W., Schuder, T., Bergman, J. L., Almasi, J., et al. (1992). Beyond direct explanation: Transactional instruction of reading comprehension strategies. *The Elementary School Journal*, *92*, 513–555.

Schnellert, L., Datoo, M., Ediger, K., & Panas, J. (2009). *Pulling together: Integrating assessment, planning and instruction in English language arts*. Markham, ON: Pembroke Publishers.

Schnellert, L., Watson, L., & Widdess, N. (2015). *It's all about thinking: Building pathways for all learners in the middle years*. Winnipeg, MN: Portage & Main Press.

Schoenfeld, A. H. (2004). Multiple learning communities: Students, teachers, instructional designers, and researchers. *Journal of Curriculum Studies*, *36*(2), 237–255.

Schunk, D. H., & Zimmerman, B. J. (Eds.) (1994). *Self-regulation of learning and performance: Issues and educational applications*. Hillsdale, NJ: Erlbaum.

Volet, S., Vauras, M., & Salonen, P. (2009). Self- and social regulation in learning contexts: An integrative perspective. *Educational Psychologist*, *44*(4), 215–22.

Vygotsky, L. S. (1978). *Mind in society*. Cambridge, MA: Harvard University Press.

Chapter 9

Designing Assessment and Feedback to Nurture Self-Regulated Learning

flairimages/Fotolia

INTRODUCTION

In Part Two of this book, we have been describing how educators can support the development of self-regulating learners. In Chapter 5 we outlined how educators can establish safe and supportive environments to create a foundation for active learning and self-regulated learning (SRL). In Chapter 6 we identified four key guidelines for shaping SRL–promoting practices. Across Chapters 7 and 8, we explained how educators can design *activities* that create rich opportunities for SRL and then integrate *supports* for SRL into activities and environments. To conclude Part Two of this book, in this chapter we describe how educators can construct *assessments and feedback* to nurture active learning and SRL.

Assessments and Feedback That Foster Active Learning and SRL

Why and how are assessments and feedback so important in fostering the development of self-regulating learners? How can educators design assessments and feedback to foster active learning and SRL? What might *less* supportive forms of assessments or feedback look like? Why might they be less supportive? What else do you wonder?

Learning Intentions

After reading this chapter, you should be able to do the following:

LI 1   Explain how educators can design and use assessments to foster SRL.

LI 2   Describe qualities of feedback that encourage active learning and SRL.

LI 3   Define why and how assessments and feedback play such pivotal roles in the development of self-regulating learners.

ANCHORING OUR DISCUSSION

As we have done throughout Part Two, we anchor our discussion by considering our goals in fostering SRL. Doing so is particularly important in this chapter, because assessments and feedback have a profound impact on students' engagement in learning environments, and, correspondingly, their opportunities to develop as self-regulating learners. To review, when setting goals for students, educators need to attend to (1) how students are constructing knowledge, skills, strategies, beliefs, and values that underlie effective forms of SRL; (2) how students' motivation and emotions are supporting or undermining their performance; and (3) whether students are learning how to engage deliberately and reflectively in cycles of strategic action in relation to multiple aspects of performance. Assessments and feedback can have a powerful influence on students' development of capacities in each of these areas.

As we imagine how to design assessment and feedback practices, it will also help to refer back to the four key guidelines we outlined in Chapter 6 that combine so powerfully to support SRL (see Table 6-1). To review, these four broad guidelines are to (1) create opportunities for SRL; (2) foster autonomy; (3) weave supports for SRL into activities; and (4) support students' flexible use of knowledge, skills, strategies, values, and beliefs.

Finally, to anchor our discussion, it is also important to reconnect with ideas presented in Chapters 7 and 8 (see SRL Planning Tools 7-1 and 8-1). To create SRL–promoting environments, it is important to coordinate all of our classroom practices in coherent ways. For example, to foster effective forms of SRL, *assessments* and *feedback* need to integrate well with the *activities* we develop (Chapter 7). We need to connect the dots between the content and process goals we establish for students in activities and the criteria we use to judge progress through assessment. Furthermore, assessments should enable educators to provide *supports* for students' development of SRL (Chapter 8). Indeed, feedback is a powerful form of *support* with particular potential to foster or undermine students' development of SRL.

> To create SRL–promoting learning environments, it is important to coordinate activities, supports for SRL, and assessments and feedback in coherent ways.

ASSESSMENT FOR SRL

Kohn (2012) suggests that assessments be designed to generate and share information. But *what information* do we want and need to generate if we are to foster SRL? Given those purposes, *how* can we conduct SRL–promoting assessments? And, ultimately, *who* is it that needs to generate and use information? How we answer these questions when designing assessments can have an enormous impact on students' motivation, learning, and achievement (see Hargreaves, 2005; Kohn, 2012; Wiliam, 2011). Thus, in this chapter, we need to uncover *why*, *how*, and *for whom* information needs to be generated by assessments if they are to support the development of self-regulating learners.

In this chapter, we uncover why, how, and for whom information needs to be generated by assessments if they are to support the development of self-regulating learners.

Purposes for Assessment

In today's schools, a key purpose for assessment is to generate and share information about students' progress. Teachers need to keep multiple audiences in mind when designing classroom assessment practices. For example, parents, administrators, policy-makers, and the students themselves all have a vested interest in how students are achieving.

At the same time, assessment should inform teaching, learning, and decision-making by focusing on what we value in terms of *learning* (Heritage, 2007; Landrigan & Mulligan, 2013; Shepard, 2000). Indeed, the primary purpose of assessment is to improve teaching and learning, not to grade or rank-order students (Black, Harrison, Lee, Marshall, & Wiliam, 2003, 2004; Brownlie & Schnellert, 2009; Davies, 2011). When deciding how to use assessments to foster SRL, educators need to generate and share information in ways that inform *teachers* in shaping their practices, and *students*, so they themselves can take control over their learning.

When using assessments to foster SRL, educators need to generate and share information to inform *teachers* in shaping their practices, and *students*, so they themselves can take control over their learning.

Unfortunately, in some jurisdictions teachers may feel so much pressure to account for learning outcomes that they take up assessment practices with little potential to foster SRL. For example, Davis and Neitzel (2011) conducted an observational study of teachers in the southeastern United States to investigate whether the classroom assessment practices they were using were optimal for supporting SRL. What they found was that teachers' assessments were limited, not by a lack of knowledge about assessment, but by pressures they were feeling to report on outcomes. As a result, rather than using assessments to empower students as owners of their learning, teachers were focusing narrowly on measuring attainment of content, and prioritizing formalized assessments that did not give them information that they could use to inform their teaching (see also Hargreaves, 2005).

What about Grades?

Using "grades" or "marks" is a common strategy for communicating about students' learning with all sorts of audiences, including students. Unfortunately, another obstacle to enacting SRL–promoting assessment practices can be an over-emphasis on grades. There is a good deal of evidence suggesting that grading practices can have a detrimental effect on motivation and learning (e.g., see Butler, 1987, 1988; Kohn, 2012; Wiliam, 2011). For example, Ruth Butler (1988) compared the effects of three types of grading practices on 6th-grade students' engagement in a divergent thinking task. After engaging in the task a first time, students were provided with (1) just constructive comments, (2) just grades, or (3) both grades and comments. What she found was that the learning of students given just grades did not improve between the first and a second task, while the performance of students who received just constructive comments improved by 30 percent. Students given just constructive comments were interested in doing the task again, as were students who had received high scores in the "just grades" condition. But low-scoring students in the just-grades condition were less interested in doing the same task again. Notably, students in the third condition, who received *both* grades and comments, responded like students who received only grades. In other words, the constructive effect of comments was eliminated when scores were also provided.

Balancing Assessments for Reporting and Learning   What can educators do to balance requirements for reporting to other stakeholders with their use of assessments to support active learning and SRL? Wiliam (2011) concludes that, while it may be difficult to

escape grading requirements, it is nonetheless possible to build assessments to foster growth and learning. For example, one way to achieve this is to trace growth over time and to hold back scores (i.e., grades or marks) until an extended learning episode is completed (Wiliam, 2011). Another approach is to assess, not just for attainment of concepts, but also for *how* students are engaging in learning and/or making progress over time (Schnellert, Datoo, Ediger, & Panas, 2009).

One example comes from Jacqueline Clymer and Dylan Wiliam (2006/2007; see also Wiliam, 2011). In this example, one teacher created an assessment framework to both generate grades and foster SRL in a Grade 8 physical science classroom. In the school where this classroom was located, the academic year was broken into seven-week marking periods. During each period, teachers worked toward 10 content standards linked to state requirements. These standards included both content (e.g., learning about density) and process (e.g., to build inquiry skills) goals. To assess for growth as activities unfolded, this teacher identified indicators (i.e., evidence) of students' learning related to each standard. Then, throughout the marking period, the teacher created an accumulating record of each student's mastery in each content area. Students were also encouraged to provide evidence of learning in each area. To track students' progress, the teacher created a visual map, using colours (red, yellow, or green) to represent students' achievements in each area (i.e., *beginning*, *developing*, or *consistently meeting and often exceeding* the content standard). The teacher shared this record with each student and gave feedback each week to support further learning. At the end of the marking period, grades were based on records of students' mastery across standards, a cumulative test designed to provide converging evidence for the growth record, and follow-up interviews, if needed, during which students could further demonstrate learning.

Clymer and Wiliam's assessment framework made criteria for grading transparent, tracked growth over time, assessed for content and process, included both teachers *and students* in generating and sharing evidence of learning, and reserved assigning formal grades until the end of a marking period. Notable, too, was that the evidence generated was related to learning standards and could be replaced with new evidence as understanding and skills improved. The effect was that students viewed their teacher more as a coach than a judge, were more relaxed, focused more on learning than performing, and engaged more in self-monitoring. Wiliam (2011) concluded that "perhaps the most profound impact of such a grading system is that it pushes both teacher and students into thinking about longer-term learning" (p. 125).

The Great Grade Debate   What do you think about grades and their place in education? In Activity 9-1, we invite you to consider how you might design assessments that are useful for informing teaching and learning and also communicate in important ways with other stakeholders in education.

Assessments for Learning

So, how can we construct assessments if our goal is to foster active learning and SRL? A powerful approach to fostering SRL is to build *assessments for learning* into classroom practice. In their influential work, Black and Wiliam (1998) defined **assessment for learning** as follows:

> All those activities undertaken by teachers, *and by their students in assessing themselves*, which provide information to be used as feedback to modify the teaching and learning activities in which they are engaged. (p. 2, emphasis in original)

Ideally, *assessments for learning* both (1) inform teachers' efforts, by extending their understanding about students' strengths and needs and providing guidance on how to most effectively direct their practice; and (2) inform *learners' efforts*, so they can more effectively self-regulate their learning.

Assessment for learning includes practices that teachers and their students can use to generate information important to guiding both *educators*, in their teaching, and *students*, in their learning.

The Great Grade Debate

Above, we suggested that in today's schools a key purpose of assessment is to generate and share information about students' progress with multiple stakeholders. How can we achieve that goal while still fostering effective forms of SRL? To consider that question, we invite you to engage in a debate (with yourself, with others) about grades. One way or another, try to take up both sides of the argument presented in the Table 9-1 as strongly as you can. Then consider what you conclude about the role of grades as a part of assessment practices in your context.

Table 9-1 The Great Grade Debate

Grades Are Inevitable and Can Be Useful	We Have to Get Rid of Grades
While it may be difficult to escape grading requirements, it is nonetheless possible to build assessments to foster growth and learning (Wiliam, 2011)	*Over-emphasizing grades can be an obstacle to enacting SRL–promoting practices. There is a good deal of evidence suggesting that grading practices can have a detrimental effect on motivation and learning.*
Your argument: We can keep grades, but need to refine how we create assessments to foster student learning and nurture motivation. Explain *how* you would do that.	**Your argument:** We need to get rid of grades to foster student learning and motivation. We need to meet our responsibility to report marks to others in a different way. Explain *how* you would do that.

Source: Republished with permission of John Wiley & Sons, Inc, from "Becoming self-regulated readers and writers", *The Reading Teacher*, 56 no.3 permission conveyed through Copyright Clearance Center, Inc

Assessments *of* and *for* learning are both important in education today. Thus, the trick is to create a balance between them. In terms of fostering SRL, assessments *for* learning are essential. Thus, in this chapter we highlight how using assessments *for* learning can both inform teachers in constructing their practice and empower learners to understand, take control over, and improve their learning.

How Can Teachers Build from Assessments for Learning to Inform Their Practice?

As emphasized above, assessments need to provide high-quality information for both teachers (to shape teaching) *and* students (to shape learning). To help in imagining how teachers can build from assessments for learning to inform their practice, in SR Vignette 9-1 we revisit an example we introduced in Chapter 4. In that chapter, we described how teachers in one school district were using two complementary assessment tools to "scan" for SRL in their contexts. In this chapter, we describe more specifically how those teachers were building from those assessments to develop practices with promise to foster their students' development of self-regulated *learning through reading* (LTR) in subject-area classrooms (see Butler & Schnellert, 2012; Schnellert, Butler, & Higginson, 2008).

> SR Vignette 9-1

Building from Assessments to Inform Practice

As we described in Chapter 4, as part of a district-level initiative, teams of teachers from four secondary schools were working to advance students' capacities to grapple with informational text in subject-area classrooms (e.g., textbooks in science, original source documents in social studies). The teachers started by designing assessments that would help them learn more about how their students were engaging in these kinds of learning through reading (LTR) activities.

The teachers used two paired assessments to inform their teaching: the *Learning through Reading Questionnaire* (LTRQ) and a *Performance-Based Assessment* (PBA). The LTRQ is a self-report tool that assesses how students think and feel about their engagement in LTR activities (see Butler & Cartier, 2004a; Cartier & Butler, 2004). Questions on the LTRQ tap into all aspects of students' self-regulated engagement in LTR (i.e., motivation, emotions, cognition, and strategic action). The companion PBA is a curriculum-based measure of LTR performance (see Brownlie, Feniak & Schnellert, 2006). The PBA in this project assessed competencies reflective of provincial performance standards for reading informational text.

While the LTRQ was already tailored to secondary-level activities, the teachers needed to work together to personalize PBA assessments for their classrooms. To that end, teachers started by selecting curriculum-based topics and texts meaningful for a given subject area and grade level. Then, school-based teams built from sample open-ended question stems (see Brownlie et al., 2006) to create prompts that would uncover the quality of students' comprehension and learning. When completing the PBA, students read one or more texts in order to learn about a topic. They answered some questions independently. Teachers also circulated to observe students at work and ask other questions orally. Teachers used a common template to record observations and students' responses, focusing both on how students were building meaning and their learning processes. Teachers met with their school-level teams to co-score evidence gathered through the PBA, assigning scores on each dimension as well as creating an overall "snapshot" score.

Teachers at each school reviewed class-, grade-, and school-level patterns they observed across the LTRQ and PBA assessments. Based on what they observed, they set some common goals for students at a particular grade level (e.g., to work on inferring for all Grade 8 students in social studies). Teachers also set unique goals for the learners in their classrooms. Examples of classroom-level goals teachers set based on the assessment data were to:

■ Instruct students on *how* cognitive strategies are applied, especially "invisible" ones like self-questioning, linking background knowledge, or applying new knowledge;

■ Develop a common language around literacy strategies and concepts;

■ Share with students that cognitive strategies are learnable— you're not just born as a good reader, you develop into one. Also, share that improving as a reader is a life-long task;

■ Share that understanding and learning are different from memorizing;

■ Help students develop strategies to manage stress and emotions;

■ Give students encouragement to help them feel optimistic when approaching literacy tasks. Make sure they understand how their work will be assessed—what is important;

■ Work on how "the scene is set" with students to create interest, establish purpose, and help them plan and connect with previous knowledge;

■ Help students work on identifying main ideas and supporting details and note-making.

To achieve their goals, teachers developed and refined practices based on assessment information and how their students were learning. For example, in Figure 9-1 we reproduce a framework for Grade 9 Social Studies lessons that was created collaboratively by a classroom teacher and a learning resource teacher based on assessment data.

Throughout the year, teachers also used classroom-based assessments to monitor how students were progressing. At the end of the year, teachers again used the LTRQ and PBA to monitor their success in achieving learning goals for students. They also drew on the end of the year PBA assessment when summarizing students' learning attainments on report cards. School-based administrators and literacy leaders also built from the assessments as part of their report to the school district on how they were advancing adolescent literacy goals in their schools.

Social Studies Grade 9 Lesson Framework
Get students ready for new material by: • activating prior knowledge   • surveying the text   • setting a purpose for reading/learning   • setting reading goals
Help students monitor their reading by: • identifying important ideas   • comparing new knowledge to prior knowledge   • asking questions   • summarizing and paraphrasing
Help students use and integrate information by: • demonstrating understanding in a variety of ways   • organizing information to remember it   • identifying what they still need to learn   • putting ideas into their own words

Figure 9-1 Building from Assessments: A Framework for Grade 9 Social Studies Lessons

Building from Assessments to Inform Practice

What did you notice in SR Vignette 9-1 about how teams of teachers in the LTR project were using assessments formatively to better understand and advance students' learning? How were they creating assessments that could support them both in guiding and reporting on learning? Can you imagine how teachers could have included students in self-assessing and taking ownership of their learning?

How Can Teachers Design Assessments for Learning to Inform Practice?

Assessments for learning are best designed by considering the purpose they are enlisted to serve. Many different practices can serve the essential function of "providing information to be used as feedback to modify teaching and learning activities" (Black & Wiliam, 1998, p. 2). Assessments for learning can be relatively structured and formalized, as was the case in the LTR project described above. But assessments for learning can also be conducted daily and dynamically to inform teaching and learning.

> Assessments for learning can be relatively structured and formalized. But they can also be conducted daily and dynamically to inform teaching and learning.

A Variety of Approaches   There are many strategies available to educators interested in creating assessments with promise to foster students' development of SRL (Zimmerman, 2008). For example, teachers can learn from informal conversations, more formalized interviews, questionnaires, observations, classroom-based assessments, and records of students' learning generated in work samples (e.g., in notes, diagrams, or drawings created when planning or enacting work). In the LTR project, you might notice how the teachers combined several of these approaches to provide a fuller picture of their students' approaches to SRL (see SR Vignette 9-1). In this section, we describe some approaches that educators have found useful when assessing for learning in their contexts.

Strategic Questioning as an Assessment for Learning   One way educators can assess students' knowledge and learning processes is by asking strategic questions. *Strategic questions* direct students' attention to thinking and learning processes while they are engaged in activities. As described in Chapter 8, they can be used to provide *supports* for students' development of SRL (e.g., by guiding strategic action, fostering better decision-making, or drawing students' attention to growth and progress). But they also are useful as a dynamic, contextualized tool for assessment. Through questioning, teachers can reveal how students are thinking about activities, learning, and themselves as learners (e.g., *what is your job in this activity? what are you trying to do here?*). Strategic questions can provide important feedback to teachers about how classroom practices are working (e.g., *what do you understand about…?*). They can identify important information that students need to guide their learning (e.g., *what do you need to do next here, to overcome that challenge?*).

Talking with Students about Learning   Whenever students talk with teachers or peers about their learning or learning process, the resulting dialogue can serve as an *assessment for learning*. For example, Hargreaves (2005) describes how one teacher, Remy, engaged her primary students in talking about learning environments. Remy asked her students to draw pictures of locations where they felt most comfortable learning, then to explain to their peers what it was about that location that helped them learn. While certainly not a "formalized" assessment, notice the multiple benefits created by this one activity. It created an opportunity for Remy to hear what students were thinking about environments in relation to learning. As a teacher, Remy could build on that information. At the same time, Remy created an important opportunity for *students* to co-construct metacognitive knowledge and build capacities to self-regulate environments in the service of learning (i.e., talking together about, reflecting on, and choosing good places for learning).

Activities That Create a Window into Students' Thinking and Learning

Trauth-Nare and Buck (2001) describe a range of strategies that can be utilized to create *assessments for learning* within problem- and project-based activities. These include engaging students in "KWL" (What do you *know*? What do you *wonder*? What have you *learned*?) or "think-pair-share" activities as well as facilitated, whole-class discussions (see http://www.nea.org/tools/k-w-l-know-want-to-know-learned.html; http://www.nea.org/tools/tips/Think-Pair-Share.html). Trauth-Nare and Buck highlight how, by engaging students in these kinds of activities, educators generate information for both themselves and students. Teachers can build from what students are saying to refine their instruction. Students are supported to reflect on what they are learning, keep key goals in mind, self-assess progress, and decide on next steps for learning.

Observations

David Whitebread and his colleagues (see Whitebread et al., 2009) have created an observational protocol that is helpful for "seeing" metacognition and SRL in the actions of young children. Building on his work, we suggest that an observational approach can be particularly useful when assessing learning processes in individuals who have difficulty, due to age or other reasons, in articulating their approaches to learning. You can learn a great deal by watching for different dimensions of SRL as your students engage in activities.

More Formalized SRL Assessments for Individual Learners

For educators who might want to create a more detailed assessment of an individual's approaches to SRL, Timothy Cleary, Barry Zimmerman, and their colleagues have developed an approach to assessing SRL called *Self-Regulated Learning Microanalysis* (e.g., see Cleary, Callan, & Zimmerman, 2012; Cleary & Zimmerman, 2001, 2004). This approach uses a semi-structured interview to assess how students are working through five key self-regulation sub-processes *as they work through* activities: goal-setting, strategic planning, monitoring, self-evaluation, and attributions (see Cleary et al., 2012). This approach might be particularly helpful when designing more intensive supports for SRL for students who are struggling.

Designing Assessments for Learning: Closing Reflections

Any of the approaches we have introduced in this section can be woven into classroom practice to assess learning processes, growth, and outcomes. When deciding among the many approaches you might use to *assess for learning*, you can ask yourself, "What strategy can I use to generate information that is important, relevant, and valuable in this context, to help me in refining my practices, and to help students learn how to self-regulate their learning?"

Empowering Students through Assessment

To foster SRL, assessments need to empower students to understand and take control over their learning.

Assessments for learning provide information to teachers to inform their instruction. As such, they help teachers in developing and refining practices over time. But, to foster SRL, assessments also need to *empower students* to understand and take control over their learning. Assessments need to generate information that *students* can use as feedback to help them in developing and refining their own approaches to learning (Brownlie & Schnellert, 2009; Davies & Herbst, 2013; Davis & Neitzel, 2011; Earl, 2003, 2013; Halbert & Kaser, 2013; Hattie & Timperley, 2007; Wiliam, 2011).

Wiliam (2011) offers a compelling example of how a small change to a common classroom practice can bridge from "just grading" to empowering learning. Imagine a math classroom in which students have completed a set of 20 problems. A typical grading scenario might include the teacher assessing the accuracy of students' responses and then feeding that information back to students. For example, a student who gets five questions wrong might get his or her paper back with check marks by 15 questions and five red "X's" by problems with incorrect answers. How could students make use of that information to improve their approaches to learning in mathematics? Students might advance their learning based on the information provided, for example, if they took the time to redo questions with incorrect answers. But it's not clear how this approach would empower students to self-regulate learning more effectively.

In contrast, Wiliam's alternative is to identify the number of correct and incorrect answers in students' work. Then, rather than telling students which answers are right or wrong, he suggests tasking *them* with finding the incorrect answers (e.g., "You got 15 out of 20 of the questions right. That's a great start! Can you find the other five and correct them?"). How might this alternative foster SRL? In this scenario, students are positioned as owners of their learning (i.e., as responsible for checking their work). They are engaged in strategic action (i.e., self-assessing and refining their solutions accordingly). They are more likely to construct perceptions of control over learning (e.g., if they link newly corrected answers to strategies for finding and fixing them). Imagine the added benefit if students were also provided with *supports* to learn *how to* check their answers or debug their problem-solving strategies.

How Can Teachers Include Students in Assessment Processes?

There are many strategies that educators can use to involve students in assessment practices. Building on Davies and Herbst's (2013) recommendations, in this section we highlight three powerful and complementary approaches: (1) engaging students in talking about, interpreting, and co-constructing learning goals; (2) involving students in self-assessment; and (3) ensuring students have opportunities to build from assessments to refine their learning.

Engaging Students in Talking about, Interpreting, or Co-Constructing Learning Goals
Students need to have a clear sense of purpose if they are to engage in effective forms of SRL. As Butler (1998, 2002) emphasizes, how can students possibly self-direct learning if they are not clear on what they are trying to do? How can they choose and enact strategies well-matched to their goals? And how can they judge progress or refine efforts so as to achieve goals more effectively? In short, to self-regulate learning effectively, students need to learn how to:

- identify, interpret, or construct learning goals;
- self-direct action with those goals in mind;
- self-monitor and self-assess progress toward goals; and
- refine goals and actions based on progress perceived.

Students need to have a clear sense of purpose if they are to engage in effective forms of SRL.

Assessment frameworks foster SRL when they engage students in full and iterative cycles of strategic action (e.g., see Davies & Herbst, 2013). In so doing, they create opportunities *for students* to engage in assessments for learning (e.g., Earl, 2003).

Interpreting Criteria and Rubrics.   How can educators engage students in identifying, interpreting, or constructing learning goals? One strategy that is increasingly popular is to provide students with rubrics or explicit descriptions of criteria necessary for effective performance. Rubrics typically cross-reference a list of performance criteria (e.g., to set and maintain a clear purpose in an essay) with descriptions of what performance would look like at different levels (e.g., approaching expectations, meeting expectations, fully meeting expectations, exceeding expectations). Criteria lists and rubrics can be very helpful because they make the qualities of "good" performance transparent to learners.

However, research shows that just outlining expectations for students is insufficient (e.g., see Andrade, Du, & Mycek, 2010). Instead, for rubrics or criteria lists to be useful, students have to learn how to actively interpret and build from that information to guide their performance effectively. Why is this so necessary? One problem is that students often fail to attend to rubrics or criteria, or use them to guide their performance (Butler & Cartier, 2004b). Students need support to take up "interpreting expectations" as an important first step in learning. Another challenge is that interpreting activity demands is very complex. To interpret requirements successfully, students need to attend to many different kinds of clues, not just those that are articulated explicitly in criteria lists or instructions. On top of those, they need to recognize more implicit and contextual clues within a particular subject area, classroom, and activity (Hadwin & Winne, 2012; Perry, 2013).

Yet another challenge is that it is very hard to describe rich forms of learning in words (Nicol & Macfarlane-Dick, 2006). Correspondingly, it can be very hard for students to imagine what good performance "looks like" based just on written descriptions. For example, what really makes a poem "powerful"? Can we communicate that easily in a list of criteria? Finally, even when students understand criteria deeply, achieving them in practice can be quite difficult (Andrade et al., 2010). For example, we may be able to recognize a particularly powerful poem when we see one, but applying "criteria" to create one can be challenging.

Thus, for criteria lists and rubrics to be useful, students need to work with them somehow to develop a deeper understanding about the qualities of expected work. They need opportunities to talk about criteria with their teacher and peers. They need support to "see" criteria in concrete examples and in their own and others' work. Furthermore, if we are to foster SRL, learners need support, not only to understand criteria, but also to *mobilize* them as they are working to set goals, choose strategies, monitor their progress, and improve their work.

Co-Constructing Criteria.   An excellent way to empower learning is to engage students in co-constructing criteria. When students are involved in generating criteria with teachers, they have opportunities to actively construct a deep understanding of what they mean. Furthermore, if learners are given some choice in defining their own learning intentions, they can develop important capacities needed by 21st-century learners, such as learning how to find and define problems, not just solve them (see Chapter 4).

How can educators engage students in co-constructing criteria? To begin, it definitely helps for students to have opportunities to work from examples (e.g., of poems) and experiences (e.g., of trying to write poems) to anchor their thinking about what good performance looks like. If students have opportunities to view exemplars that differ in how well

> For rubrics or criteria lists to be useful, students have to learn how to actively interpret and build from that information to guide their performance effectively.

they achieve criteria, they can better "see" and describe important differences in the quality of performance. Then, based on their growing understandings, educators can engage students in talking about and defining criteria together.

For example, in her combined Grade 5/6 classroom, Nicole Widdess supported her students to co-construct criteria for writing free verse poetry. Students read and wrote several poems across a series of lessons. Then they participated in a "placemat" activity in groups of four (see Bennett & Rolheiser, 2001). Students started by recording their own ideas about the qualities of evocative poems in the quadrant closest to them. Then, they worked together as a group to list criteria they agreed on in the "centre" of the placemat (see Figure 9-2). Finally, Nicole worked with the entire class to generate a list of criteria at the front of the room, linking each to rich examples from actual poems (for more information, see Chapter 10; Schnellert, Watson & Widdess, 2015).

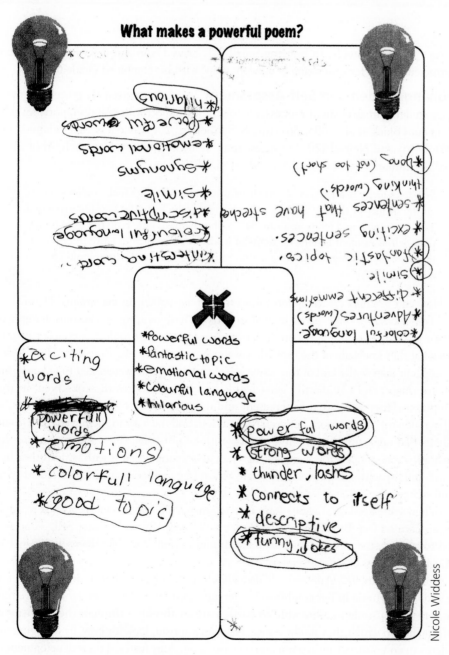

Figure 9-2 Co-Constructing Criteria.

Building Criteria with Children in Four Steps by Dave Dunnigan

Steps	Activity	Example: Concept Maps
One	Brainstorm	What would make a powerful/ excellent concept map?
Two	Sort ideas into categories or groups	Key concepts, connections, illustrations, etc.
Three	Create and post a T-Chart with categories on one side, details on the other	Illustrations—colourful, relevant, support concept
Four	Add, revise, refine (teacher input here if students missed something)	

As a second example, in Starting Small 9-1, Dave Dunnigan describes how he co-constructed criteria for generating a "concept map" with his combined Grade 6/7 class.

Involving Students in Self-Assessment   Another extremely powerful way to engage students in assessment processes is to provide opportunities and supports for self-assessment (Black et al., 2003; Brownlie & Schnellert, 2009; Nicol & Macfarlane-Dick, 2006). Davis and Neitzel (2011) suggest that "self-assessment is the linchpin of SRL" (p. 202). Similarly, according to Andrade et al. (2010),

> Self-assessment is a process of formative assessment during which students reflect on the quality of their work, judge the degree to which it reflects explicitly stated goals or criteria, and revise accordingly. … The emphasis here is on the word formative. Self-assessment is done on drafts of works in progress in order to inform revision and improvement: it is not a matter of having students determining their own grades. (p. 199)

How can teachers create opportunities for self-assessment in classrooms? Hargreaves (2005) describes how one teacher invited students to both monitor and account for growth in their learning over time. In Ben's class, students were asked to draw a concept map to show what they knew about the topic they were about to study (the Romans). They drew a new concept map at the end of the activity. Next, the students were asked to (1) compare their two maps, and (2) identify what had led to the differences they observed. In this example, students were asked to represent and reflect on their own learning progress, as well as to identify connections between their actions and the learning achieved. As a result, students had opportunities to build metacognitive knowledge (e.g., about strategies for learning), a sense of control over learning (e.g., associating progress with actions they had taken), and capacities to engage in strategic action (e.g., self-assessing progress, identifying useful strategies).

When self-assessing, students learn how to generate information for themselves to guide further learning.

When self-assessing, students *learn how to generate information for themselves* to guide further learning (see Brookhart, 2008; Butler & Winne, 1995). To foster SRL, educators need to support students *to learn how to* build from information they themselves generate through the process of self-assessment.

In SR Vignette 9-2, Amy Semple describes how she engaged her students in generating and using criteria in her combined kindergarten/Grade 1 classroom. Notice here how her very young students were able to participate in thinking through the qualities of performance to which they might aspire. Also, as you read, look for how, by engaging her students in co-constructing criteria and self-assessing, Amy fostered their development as self-regulating learners.

From Co-Constructing Criteria to Self-Assessment by Amy Semple

The next strategy I put in place was one that I adapted from [a program] that I attended. Within that workshop, there was a discussion about sharing the criteria with the students. There, was a picture shared showing an example of a partially drawn flower (which represented work that was "approaching expectations"), a picture that had some detail but was complete (which represented work that was "meeting expectations") and a picture of a flower that had great detail and even included some landscape behind it (which represented "exceeding expectations").

I loved the idea of this but I needed to adapt it a bit to meet the needs of my students (and lend itself more easily to my work). I introduced the idea of 3-Star Printing, 3-Star Drawing, and 3-Star Colouring. I started showing three different examples of my own printing on the board. The children then looked at the three examples and talked with a friend about what they saw. (I told them that one was a 1-Star printing example, another was a 2-Star printing example, and the third was a 3-Star example.)

The children were then asked to show me a number (one to three) representing which number each example received. (I tried to make this process more authentic by asking the children to put their fingers up to represent a number, but in front of their bodies so that no one but me could see it). They were almost completely unanimous in what they indicated. It was very clear that they understood the examples. We then made a list of all the things we needed to remember when we were printing. The list was quite long but it was amazing to see how engaged they were. We talked about capital letters, printing on the line, finger spaces, correctly sized letters, correctly placed letters, and punctuation. They loved looking at my examples. It made them giggle to see that sometimes I make mistakes (which I started to do more often) and they began to talk about how to redo my printing.

I am finding that this has really started to make an impact on the printing that I am seeing. All of my students (including those in kindergarten) are now printing on the line. Each child (with the exception of one) consistently writes his or her name with a capital and all the rest lowercase. This is huge growth! I always ask the child to check his or her work to ensure that it is 3-Star Printing. Of course we are still working on this but I have seen definite improvements in their work. (I should mention that we did the same type of activity with 3-Star Drawing and 3-Star Colouring. Within 3-Star Drawing, we talked about having a picture fit the size of the space we have—not too big or small—adding detail, labelling the picture, and making sure our drawing matches the words.)

There are many times that children, independently, will do this activity over and over again at centre time. One child will write a sentence over and over again, each sentence reflecting a 1-star, 2-star, or 3-star sentence. They love this. It all promotes lots of discussion and reflection among the children. I have never been made aware of an example in which two children disagreed with the marking, or rating, of the sentence. They also are starting to show interest in "fixing" the problem.

Ensuring Students Have Opportunities to Build from Assessments to Refine Their Learning   Finally, to foster SRL, students also need opportunities to build from information generated through assessment (by teachers, peers, or themselves) to *refine* their learning approaches (e.g., Davies & Herbst, 2013; Trauth-Nare & Buck, 2001). In other words, they need opportunities to refine action based on a thoughtful analysis of gaps between current and desired performance and why those might be occurring (Butler, 2002; Butler & Winne, 1995). Linking back to our goals for 21st-century learners, the development of *adaptive expertise* hinges on students' ability to flexibly and adaptively set and refine goals and strategies in the face of new problems or challenges. This requires that they can accurately and honestly match their progress with their goals to identify what, if any, adjustments should be made.

Assessments for SRL

Based on what you have read so far, how do you think you could design assessments in your context to foster students' development as self-regulating learners? How might you use assessments to inform your development of SRL–promoting practices? How could you design assessment practices to empower *learners*?

FEEDBACK FOR SRL

> The purpose of feedback is to increase the extent to which learners are the owners of their own learning.
>
> —(Halbert & Kaser, 2013, p. 21)

Feedback is information about performance generated by teachers, peers, or students themselves that is fed back to learners to give them a sense of progress and inform further action and learning.

What is **feedback**? Ideally, educators design assessments in ways that allow for the generation of information (by teachers and by students) that is fed back to learners to give them a sense of progress and inform further action and learning. According to Brookhart (2008), feedback from a student's perspective should be, "just-in-time, just-for-me information delivered when and where it can do the most good" (p. 1).

Brookhart also emphasizes that the purpose of feedback is not for teachers to "regulate" students' actions. Instead, the potential of feedback, as part of a formative assessment process, is to build in social forms of support, from teachers and peers, that *foster students' ability to feel and be in control of their learning* (see Chapter 8). Consistent with Brookhart's description, Nicol and Macfarlane-Dick (2006) argue that high-quality feedback enables *students* to troubleshoot their own performance and close the gap between intentions and outcomes.

What Is Powerful Feedback?

Based on their review of research on feedback, Hattie and Timperley (2007) concluded that effective feedback helps students answer three questions necessary in detecting and reducing discrepancies between progress and goals:

- Where am I going (goals)?
- How am I doing (progess)? and
- Where to next (what can I do to improve)?

Consistent with this conclusion, Wiliam (2011) emphasizes that it's not enough for feedback to reveal gaps in performance (i.e., discrepancies between goals and outcomes). To be effective, feedback also needs to help learners imagine future action. Brownlie and Schnellert (2009) agree, suggesting that feedback needs to be descriptive in answering three questions for the learner: (1) what's working? (2) what's not working? and (3) what's next?

How Can Educators Provide Powerful Feedback?

What makes powerful feedback? In some respects, the answer depends on the situation (Brookhart, 2008). For example, in some cases giving feedback immediately may be essential. This might be the case if students have wrong information they are working from to solve a bigger problem. In other cases, it may be more productive to encourage students to think something through. Students can sometimes solve their own problems, particularly if you nudge them in the right direction. For example, instead of weighing in, you could suggest, "Why don't you start by summarizing what this problem is asking for, then I'll come back to help you in a minute?" (Wiliam, 2011). When choosing how to provide feedback, it can help to ask yourself, "What will advance students' ownership over their learning in this situation?"

When choosing how to provide feedback, it can help to ask yourself, "What will advance students' ownership over their learning in this situation?"

That said, there are definitely important principles to consider when deciding how to provide feedback in any given instance. For example, Wiliam (2011) cautions that too much feedback at once can overwhelm learners. Better is focused, targeted feedback offered over time to support learning. Based on an extensive review of the feedback literature, Hattie and Timperley (2007) found that some forms of feedback can have damaging effects on both motivation and learning. Destructive forms of feedback include grades with no comments (e.g., see also Butler, 1987, 1988), feedback associated with external rewards, and feedback that focuses on the qualities of a person rather than on the task at hand (e.g., praise for being "good" at something; see Dweck, 2006).

In contrast, effective feedback "causes thinking" (Wiliam, 2011). Feedback has little effect if students do not interpret, make sense of, or take up the information so as to advance their learning (see also Butler & Winne, 1995). As Wiliam argues, "Feedback functions formatively *only if the information fed back to the learner is used by the learner in improving performance*" (p. 120, emphasis in the original). Nicol and Macfarlane-Dick (2006) add that effective feedback creates a "dialogue" among teachers and learners. This contrasts with a view of feedback as something that is transmitted from teachers to students. When educators use feedback to initiate or sustain a "dialogue" about learning and learning processes, students have time to work with and make meaning of information provided.

> When educators use feedback to initiate or sustain a dialogue about learning and learning processes, students have time to work with and make meaning of information provided.

Supporting Peers to Give High-Quality Feedback to One Another

In Chapter 8 we emphasized the value of recruiting peers to support one another's learning. Along those same lines, we recommend engaging peers in giving feedback to each other. Why can this be helpful? According to Nicol and Macfarlane-Dick (2006),

- peers can often offer feedback using language that other students can better understand;

- when discussing their work with peers, students have opportunities to access and compare multiple perspectives;

- engaging in a constructive dialogue about learning with peers can "depersonalize" feedback, making it easier to detect, accept, and interpret critiques.

We would add that when students generate and share feedback with peers, they co-construct important kinds of metacognitive knowledge (e.g., about criteria; about strategies). They also learn *how to* engage in strategic action together (e.g., as they look for specific kinds of discrepancies between progress and learning goals).

In Chapter 8 we also noted that educators benefit when they recruit peers to support each other's learning. When they do, they are not solely responsible for guiding or scaffolding their students' active learning and development of SRL. Educators don't always have the time or opportunity to give personalized, powerful feedback to every student in the midst of activities. But, when peers are empowered to give feedback to one another, educators can ensure students are still getting timely feedback to help them in improving their performance.

That said, it is often necessary to support peers to know how to give high-quality feedback to one another. For example, in Chapter 7 we described how Lynn Drummond supported her Grade 2/3 students' development of SRL across a year through a sequence of research on animals activities. As part of the mid-year research activity (the "penguin" project), Lynn explicitly supported her students *to learn how to* engage positively and constructively in peer editing. To that end, she asked permission to use one student's writing as an example. She modelled for students how she might provide constructive criticism to the author, emphasizing the importance of acknowledging what is good ("because if you've worked hard on something, it's important to hear ..."). She suggested that authors should hold the pen when receiving feedback, since it was their job to decide what changes to make in their writing. Ultimately, she built "peer editing" as a participation structure that students could take up whenever they had opportunities to provide and receive feedback from one another (see Perry & Drummond, 2002).

As one other example, in SR Vignette 9-3, we describe how April Chan supported her Grade 1 students to give each other constructive feedback. To that end, she showed a helpful video to her students, *The Story of Austin's Butterfly* (Berger, 2012; see https://www.youtube.com/watch?v=hqh1MRWZjms). As you read, you might notice that April used SRL Planning Tool 5-1 to structure her reflection (see Chapter 5).

⟫ SR Vignette 9-3
Supporting Peers to Give Each Other Feedback by April Chan

Context: What was your goal? What did you try?

Goal: To use peer feedback as a way to promote and support self-regulated learning.

Quick Scan:

■ The video, "Austin's Butterfly," demonstrates effective peer modelling in a way that is accessible for students of all ages. By helping students provide specific and criteria-based feedback, Berger (2012) fosters a growth mindset in the peer models as well as the student receiving the feedback.

■ I was curious to know how peer modelling may affect my students' learning, and how I can empower them to take ownership of their learning through peer feedback.

The Activity:

■ Before showing my class the video, I informed them that they, along with the children in the video, would help Austin draw his best scientific drawing of a butterfly.

■ Although we had practised "observing and drawing like a scientist" in a few of our previous class inquiries, we reviewed the difference between scientific drawing and imaginative drawing.

■ It was important for students to recognize and to create the criteria of a scientific drawing before beginning the task:

Division 11's 3-Star Scientific Drawing

1. Draw what you see only
2. Look closely and draw the details
3. Add labels

■ As we watched the video, I stopped at certain points to allow my students to provide suggestions for how Austin could improve his drawing.

■ After the video, we went on a nature walk to a nearby pond to look for "signs of spring," brainstorming different signs along the way (see Figure 9-3).

■ The students' task was to create a scientific drawing of something they saw that was a sign of spring.

■ Students worked with partners (chosen by them) to provide feedback for each other as they drew.

■ Before they showed me their final drawing, students had to consult with their peer at least three times and revise their drawings as needed.

Figure 9-3 Drawing like a Scientist

■ We also had a whole-class discussion and reflection time when we returned to our classroom.

Observation: What happened?

What did you notice about the students' reaction and learning

Watching the Video:

■ Their reactions to Austin's first drawing of a butterfly were very interesting. While some students noted that it was not close to what the actual image looks like, other students thought that it really did look like a butterfly. *How might their interpretation of a picture affect the feedback they provide? How can I help them in understanding the task and the criteria?* At this point, we revisited our 3-Star Scientific Drawing, and I reminded them about the criteria they had set.

■ As we paused at certain parts of the video, most students were able to provide specific feedback. However, I found it somewhat challenging for students who are English language learners (ELLs) to simply describe what needed to be revised, so those students were able to come to the front to point out what Austin could change.

> *"He needs to make the wings pointy."*
>
> *"He needs to make the bottom go down."*
>
> *"He did make the top straight."*

■ An ELL level one student said, *"This long and this short"* as he pointed to the bottom part of the butterfly's wings.

■ It's interesting to note that while students provided feedback for Austin, one student commented, "Make sure you only use green-light words so you don't hurt his feelings."

■ Even though we had not yet discussed ways to provide feedback for their peers, I was impressed that students were able to recognize the importance of criteria-based feedback. They were excited to practise using "sparkle statements" and "helpful words" before doing their activity.

■ Working with partners allowed all students to be able to interpret and understand their task before beginning. As we walked toward a nearby pond, students helped each other remember what their job was for the day.

■ Although I did not realize at the time, I now recognize that strategic action was beginning to take place in an authentic way. Students helped each other in interpreting the task, planning what signs of spring they would look for, planning how they would draw like a scientist, and how they would know if they had done a 3-Star Drawing.

■ As I walked around, I noticed that students were pointing out specific details of plants for their peers. *"Look closely at this little leaf. You forgot to draw it."*

■ One group was particularly interested in the yellow daffodils. While one partner wanted to draw the whole garden, the other partner wanted to zoom in on the details. I was surprised to learn that they had navigated through their differences in their chosen task, and one student even asked his partner for advice on drawing a specific leaf!

Feedback for SRL: Summary of Key Qualities

What are the key qualities of powerful feedback? Just like SRL–promoting assessments, effective feedback positions students as owners of their learning, supports their engagement in cycles of strategic action, and fosters within students a sense of control over learning. In addition, effective feedback:

■ "causes thinking" (Wiliam, 2011);

■ surfaces learning goals (i.e., "where am I going?") (Hattie & Timperley, 2007);

■ highlights "what's next?" (Hattie & Timperley, 2007; Wiliam, 2011);

■ engages students and peers in dialogue about learning processes (Nicol & Macfarlane-Dick, 2006);

■ is targeted and focused (Wiliam, 2011); and

■ is offered "just in time," as needed, in the context of activities (Brookhart, 2008).

DESIGNING ASSESSMENT AND FEEDBACK: NEXT STEPS

At the outset of this chapter, we suggested that assessments and feedback are particularly influential in establishing SRL–promoting learning environments. Unfortunately, assessment practices can quickly lead students to perceive environments as "threatening," particularly if they cue students to prioritize performance and compare themselves to others. As Wiliam (2011) describes, when students receive marks, the first thing they look at is the mark they are given. The next thing they look at are the marks received by the others around them. As Butler's (1987, 1988) studies document, grading practices can quickly undercut the potential benefits of constructive comments.

In contrast, assessment *for* learning can play a powerful role in creating SRL–promoting learning environments, as can effective forms of feedback. As we close Part Two of this book, we invite you to imagine how you might design assessments and feedback in your context to foster the development of self-regulating learners. To help you in that, we offer one last tool that you might find useful. SRL Planning Tool 9-1 can help you plan for an

SRL PLANNING TOOL 9-1
Assessments and Feedback for SRL

Your Name	Grade	Subject(s)	Date

Instructional Goals/Objectives:

Activity/Task Description:

How Will You Create Assessments and Feedback Supportive of Active Learning and SRL?
How will you use assessment to generate information for both yourself *and students*?
How will you distribute assessments and feedback through activities?
How will you engage students in recognizing, interpreting, and/or co-constructing learning goals?
How will you assess for both content and process goals?
How will you grade for growth and progress?
How will you use assessment and feedback to empower students (e.g., through self-assessment? by engaging them in full cycles of strategic action)?
How will you use assessment and feedback to create a "dialogue" with students?
How will you ensure feedback is powerful (e.g., helps learners understand learning intentions, progress, and what to do next)?

activity or activity sequence in a class. You can also refer to the tool through day-to-day practice as you are interacting with learners, watching for SRL, and thinking about how to provide feedback to advance their thinking or learning. Finally, you can rely on this tool for a helpful overview of the qualities of SRL–promoting forms of assessment and feedback. We will refer back to this, and the other planning tools we have introduced through this second part of the book, as we pull all these ideas together in upcoming chapters.

Recommended Resources

Andrade, H. L., Du, Y., & Mycek, K. (2010). Rubric-referenced self-assessment and middle school students' writing. *Assessment in Education: Principles, Policy, & Practice, 17*(2), 199–214.

Bennett, B., & Rolheiser, C. (2001). *Beyond Monet: The artful science of instructional integration.* Toronto ON: Bookation.

Berger, R. (2012, Dec 8). Critique and descriptive feedback: The story of Austin's butterfly. Core Practices in Action. Expeditionary Learning. Retrieved from: https://www.youtube.com/watch?v=hqh1MRWZjms

Black, P., & Wiliam, D. (1998). *Inside the black box*. London: King's College.

Black. P., Harrison, C., Lee, C., Marshall, B., & Wiliam, D. (2003) *Assessment for learning–putting it into practice.* Buckingham: Open University Press.

Black, P., Harrison, C., Lee, C., Marshall, B., & Wiliam, D. (2004). Working inside the black box: Assessment for learning in the classroom. *Phi Delta Kappan, 86*, 9–21.

Brookhart, S. M. (2008). *How to give effective feedback to your students*. Alexandria, VA: ASCD.

Brownlie, F., Feniak, C., & Schnellert, L. (2006). *Student diversity* (2nd ed.). Markham, ON: Pembroke Publishers.

Brownlie, F., & Schnellert, L. (2009). *It's all about thinking: Collaborating to support all learners in Enlgish, Social Studies and Humanities*. Winnipeg, MB: Portage & Main Press.

Butler, D. L. (1998). The Strategic Content Learning approach to promoting self-regulated learning: A summary of three studies. *Journal of Educational Psychology, 90*, 682–697.

Butler, D. L. (2002). Individualizing instruction in self-regulated learning. *Theory Into Practice, 41*(2), 81–92.

Butler, D. L., & Cartier, S. C. (2004a, May). Learning in varying activities: An explanatory framework and a new evaluation tool founded on a model of self-regulated learning. Paper presented at the annual meetings of the Canadian Society for Studies in Education. Winnipeg, MB.

Butler, D. L., & Cartier, S. (2004b). Promoting students' active and productive interpretation of academic work: A key to successful teaching and learning. *Teachers College Record, 106,* 1729–1758.

Butler, D. L., & Schnellert, L. (2012). Collaborative inquiry in teacher professional development. *Teaching and Teacher Education, 28*, 1206–1220.

Butler, D., & Winne, P. (1995). Feedback and self-regulated learning: A theoretical synthesis. *Review of Educational Research, 65*(3), 245–281.

Butler, R. (1987). Task-involving and ego-involving properties of evaluation: Effects of different feedback conditions on motivational perceptions, interest and performance. *Journal of Educational Psychology, 79*(4), 474–482.

Butler, R. (1988). Enhancing and undermining intrinsic motivation; The effects of task-involving and ego-involving evaluation on interest and performance. *British Journal of Educational Psychology, 58*, 1–14.

Cartier, S. C., & Butler, D. L. (2004, May). Elaboration and validation of the questionnaires and plan for analysis. Paper presented at the annual meetings of the Canadian Society for Studies in Education. Winnipeg, MB.

Cleary, T. J., Callan, G. L., & Zimmerman, B. J. (2012). Assessment self-regulation as a cyclical, context-specific phenomenon: Overview and analysis of SRL microanalytic protocols. *Education Research International*, Article ID 428639. doi: 10.1155/2012/428639.

Cleary, T. J., & Zimmerman, B. J. (2001). Self-regulation differences during athletic practice by experts, non-experts, and novices. *Journal of Applied Sport Psychology, 13*, 61–82.

Cleary, T. J., & Zimmerman, B. J. (2004). Self-regulation empowerment program: A school-based program to enhance self-regulated and self-motivated cycles of student learning. *Psychology in the* Schools, *41*(5), 537–550.

Clymer, J. B., & Wiliam, D. (2006/2007). Improving the way we grade science. *Educational Leadership, 12*. 36–42.

Davies, A. (2011). *Making classroom assessment work*. Merville, BC: Connections Publishing.

Davies, A., & Herbst, S. (2013). Co-constructing success criteria. Education Canada, 53 (5). Available at http://www.cea-ace.ca/education-canada/article/co-constructing-successcriteria.

Davis, D. S., & Neitzel, C. (2011). A self-regulated learning perspective on middle grades classroom assessment. *The Journal of Educational Research, 104*, 202–215.

Dweck, C. (2006). *Mindset: The new psychology of success*. New York: Random House.

Earl, L. (2003). *Assessment as learning: Using classroom assessment to maximize student learning*. Thousand Oaks, CA: Corwin-Sage.

Earl, L. (2013). *Assessment as learning: Using classroom assessment to maximize student learning* (2nd ed.). Thousand Oaks, CA: Corwin-Sage.

Hadwin, A. F., & Winne, P. H. (2012). Promoting learning skills in undergraduate students. In M. J. Lawson & J. R. Kirby (Eds.), *The quality of learning: Dispositions, instruction, and mental structures.* New York: Cambridge University Press.

Halbert, J., & Kaser, L. (2013). *Spirals of inquiry for equity and quality*. BC Principals and Vice-Principals Association.

Hattie, J., & Timperley, H. (2007). The power of feedback. *Review of Educational Research, 77*(1), 81–112.

Hargreaves, E. (2005). Assessment for learning? Thinking outside the (black) box. *Cambridge Journal of Education, 35*(2), 213–224.

Heritage, M. (2007). Formative assessment: What do teachers need to know and do? *Phi Delta Kappan, 89*(2), 140–145.

Kohn, A. (2012). The case against grades. *Educational Leadership, 69*(3), 28–33.

Landrigan, C., & Mulligan, T. (2013). *Assessment in perspective: Focusing on the readers behind the numbers*. Portland, ME: Stenhouse.

Nicol, D. J., & Macfarlane-Dick, D. (2006). Formative assessment and self-regulated learning: A model and seven principles of good feedback practice. *Studies in Higher Education, 31*(2), 199–218.

Trauth-Nare, A., & Buck, G. (2001). Assessment "for" learning: Using formative assessment in problem- and project-based learning. *Science Teacher, 78*(1), 34–39.

Perry, N. E. (2013). Classroom processes that support self-regulation in young children [Monograph]. *British Journal of Educational Psychology, Monograph Series II: Psychological Aspects of Education—Current Trends, 10,* 45–68.

Perry, N. E., & Drummond, L. (2002). Becoming self-regulated readers and writers. *The Reading Teacher, 56*, 298–310.

Schnellert, L., Butler, D. L., & Higginson, S. (2008). Co-constructors of data, co-constructors of meaning: Teacher professional development in an age of accountability. *Teaching and Teacher Education, 24*(3), 725–750.

Schnellert, L., Datoo, M., Ediger, K., & Panas, J. (2009). *Pulling together: Integrating assessment, planning and instruction in English language arts*. Markham, ON: Pembroke Publishers.

Schnellert, L., Watson, L., & Widdess, N. (2015). *It's all about thinking: Building pathways for all learners in the middle years*. Winnipeg, MN: Portage & Main Press.

Shepard, L. A. (2000). The role of assessment in a learning culture. *Educational Researcher 29*(7), 4–14.

Whitebread, D., Coltman, P., Pasternak, D. P., Sangster, C., Grau, V., Bingham, S., Almeqdad, Q. & Demetriou, D. (2009). The development of two observational tools for assessing metacognition and self-regulated learning in young children. *Metacognition Learning, 4*, 63–85.

Wiliam, D. (2011). Providing feedback that moves learning forward. In D. Wiliam (Ed.), *Embedded formative assessment* (pp. 107–132). Bloomington, IN: Solution Tree Press.

Zimmerman, B. J. (2008). Investigating self-regulation and motivation: Historical background, methodological developments and future prospects. *American Educational Research Journal, 45*(1), 166–183.

Chapter 10
Meeting the Needs of Diverse Learners

E.D. Torial/Alamy

INTRODUCTION

In Part One of this book, we identified essential goals in developing self-regulating learners. In Part Two, we offered detailed descriptions of how educators can establish learning environments and classroom practices supportive of learners' development of effective forms of SRL. Starting here, in Part Three, we pull all of these ideas together to show how developing self-regulating learners can help in tackling three important challenges facing educators today: *motivating* and *engaging learners* (Chapter 11), *empowering 21st-century learning* (Chapter 12), and, the subject of this chapter, *meeting the needs of diverse learners* in today's schools.

How do you think supports for SRL can assist educators in orchestrating rich forms of learning in classrooms that include learners with diverse experiences, challenges, strengths, knowledge, skills, values, and beliefs? What are you already doing to recognize and accommodate diverse learners in your context? What do you wonder?

Imagine how fluidly a classroom would function if all of the learners within it understood what they were being asked to do, recognized their own strengths and challenges, and were able to deliberately and adaptively mobilize their knowledge and skills to engage effectively in activities.

Educators sometimes ask us how they can possibly foster effective forms of self-regulated learning if they have to take into account all of the differences learners bring to classrooms. Our response is that supporting SRL *enables* us to navigate that diversity. Imagine how fluidly a classroom would function if all of the learners within it understood what they were being asked to do, recognized their own strengths and challenges, and were able to deliberately and adaptively mobilize their knowledge and skills to engage effectively in activities. By fostering SRL, we recruit students to help us in advancing their learning. By fostering SRL, we empower all learners to successfully navigate activities and environments to their full potential.

Learning Intentions

In this chapter, we consider how fostering SRL can help educators in meeting the needs of diverse learners in today's schools. After reading this chapter, you should be able to do the following:

LI 1 Describe how, by adopting SRL–promoting practices, educators can help learners with diverse needs participate successfully in learning activities and achieve their full potential.

LI 2 Imagine how you can use SRL–promoting practices to celebrate and build from the diversity that students are bringing to your learning community.

ANCHORING OUR DISCUSSION

In this book, we have consistently emphasized the power of SRL–promoting practices to assist *all* students in reaching their full potential as self-determining, 21st-century learners. We have explained how teachers can build from scanning for SRL in their contexts, more or less formally, to set goals and design SRL–promoting practices. We have described the qualities of SRL–promoting activities, supports, and assessments.

In this chapter, we describe more fully how educators can pull together SRL–promoting practices to build inclusive learning communities and empower all learners to succeed to their full potential. To begin, we suggest strategies for creating rich, *inclusive* learning communities. Then we provide three extended examples. These describe how teachers can use SRL–promoting practices to (1) support an individual learner struggling to succeed in academic activities, (2) weave supports for SRL into support settings, and (3) accommodate very diverse learning needs in inclusive classrooms.

Before getting going, it will help to remind yourself of the essential goals we have in fostering SRL, as described in Chapter 4 (see Figure 4-2). We also encourage you to review the SRL–promoting practices we described through Part Two of this book (e.g., see Table 6-1 and SRL Planning Tools 7-1, 8-1, and 9-1). Doing so will help you recognize how educators were taking up these kinds of practices in our extended examples.

THE PROMISE OF SRL: BUILDING INCLUSIVE LEARNING COMMUNITIES

When we create safe and supportive classrooms (see Chapter 5), we have the potential to build learning communities in which all members are, and feel, included and valued. We can realize that potential by (1) celebrating the differences learners bring to classrooms,

(2) supporting all learners to grow and learn to their full potential, and (3) assisting all learners to develop personalized strategies based on their unique talents, interests, and needs.

Celebrating the Differences Learners Bring to Classrooms

If we are to create inclusive classrooms that foster SRL, it is important *not* to think about diversity as a problem to be solved or avoided. Instead, imagine how diversity enriches the life of a classroom community. On one level, diversity provides students with opportunities to learn about each other's experiences and develop empathy and understanding. All students can develop perspective-taking and deeper learning through encounters with diverse peers. On another level, the most desired 21st-century skills—critical and creative thinking, collaboration, and social responsibility—are best nurtured in a diverse classroom community. When students encounter diverse ways of thinking, are required to seek out and consider multiple perspectives, and are encouraged and supported to approach tasks and represent ideas in different ways, they grow their capacity to think critically and creatively (Lundy, 2009; Moje et al., 2004; National Middle School Association, 2010; Schnellert, Datoo, Ediger, & Panas, 2009).

At the heart of inclusive pedagogy is a recognition that students come with diverse funds of knowledge and experience. Approaches such as culturally responsive teaching (Gay, 2010), universal design for learning (Rose & Meyer, 2002), and differentiated instruction (Tomlinson, 1999, 2014) support teachers to value and design learning opportunities that build from learners' unique contributions. When educators employ inclusive pedagogies, such as open-ended teaching, writing workshop, information circles, project-based learning, and cooperative learning, they create opportunities for students to find unique learning pathways within them (Brownlie & Schnellert, 2009). At the same time, these open-ended pedagogical practices, akin to the "complex by design" activities described in Chapter 7, afford opportunities for students to engage in rich forms of learning and SRL (Perry, 1998, 2013). By nurturing the development of self-regulating learners within more open-ended activities, educators enable all students to participate and thrive in inclusive learning communities.

Our goals in fostering SRL are consistent with efforts to build classroom learning communities that value, draw on, and nurture difference. In this chapter, we illustrate how educators can seize the opportunity to advance active learning and SRL as diverse students are learning together across difference within inclusive classrooms (Perry, 2004).

Supporting All Learners to Grow and Learn to Their Full Potential

When educators foster SRL, they help *all* learners participate and learn within classroom-based activities to the best of their abilities. For example, consider how Mehjabeen Datoo enables successful participation by the diverse learners in her secondary humanities classroom. At the start of each year, Mehjabeen invites all of her students to identify their strengths and interests and set goals for learning. She also co-constructs expectations and participation structures with students whenever they engage in new kinds of activities (e.g., when learning cooperatively, in literature circles; see Chapter 5). As the year progresses, she works with her students to co-construct criteria for judging success in activities and build strategies for achieving them. Students also regularly self-assess progress and set refined goals for themselves in relation to those criteria (Chapter 9).

Using these and other strategies, Mehjabeen ensures students with diverse backgrounds and skills know how to focus their efforts and learn actively in her classroom. Her SRL–promoting practices encourage students to take responsibility for their own learning. They help all learners, including students with diverse cultural backgrounds, English

The Promise of SRL: Including All Learners

What enables *you* to successfully navigate different kinds of activities (e.g., plan a big event with friends, build furniture, read poetry, write an essay)? Can you describe your strengths and challenges in these or other activities? Have you noticed any differences between how you learn best and how others do (e.g., other family members, peers, or colleagues)? Have you developed any personalized strategies that help *you* to be more successful?

language learners, and students identified as having disabilities, recognize expectations, participate productively in activities, and achieve personalized forms of academic success (Schnellert et al., 2009).

Assisting All Learners to Develop Personalized Strategies

Fostering SRL is particularly advantageous for students experiencing learning challenges, whether or not they have been designated as having a particular kind of disability. When we nurture SRL, we shift away from a focus on deficits or trying to "fix" students toward helping them learn how to build on their unique strengths and skills to achieve goals. When students understand their own strengths and needs and know how to set goals, make plans, enact strategies, self-assess, and adjust approaches accordingly, they can participate in building unique pathways for their own learning and development. Students who are struggling benefit enormously when they are provided with *opportunities* and *supports* to learn how to make decisions about their learning, to control challenge, and to evaluate their own work (Perry, 2004).

But, again, it is not just students with designated disabilities who need to know how to build from their unique strengths and challenges to engage in activities successfully. All students benefit when they learn how to identify and develop capacities in areas of challenge (e.g., in attention control, reading social cues, or problem solving), take control over performance, and develop personalized strategies for navigating activities. For example, in Food for Thought 10-2 we ask you to consider what enables you to navigate different kinds of activities. What kinds of personalized strategies have you developed to be successful? By fostering SRL, educators help all students understand and adjust for their own strengths and weaknesses so that they can take control over their success in academic settings.

All students benefit when they learn how to identify and develop capacities in areas of challenge, take control over performance, and develop personalized strategies for navigating activities.

FOSTERING SRL FOR STUDENTS WITH LEARNING CHALLENGES

As noted earlier, educators have often asked us whether the ideas we have been presenting about SRL apply to students with significant learning needs, such as developmental disabilities, learning disabilities, autism, or attention deficit disorder. Our response is YES. In fact, it is often students with special education needs who need support for SRL. For example, students struggling with self-regulation of emotions, behaviour, or learning need to develop metacognitive knowledge about these aspects of performance if they are to navigate life and learning successfully. They need to construct motivational beliefs, like *growth mindsets*, that energize their persistence through difficulties. They need to develop personalized strategies that enable them to participate successfully (see Butler, 1998b, 2002; Butler & Schnellert, 2015; Graham & Harris, 1989; Montague, 2008; Reid, Harris, Graham & Rock, 2012).

Research has consistently documented how support for SRL can help learners with a variety of special learning needs to learn how to manage multiple aspects of their engagement (i.e., environments, behaviour, emotions, motivation, strategic action, cognition/thinking, and relationships) (Graham, Harris & Troia, 1998; Perry, 2004). For example, students who need support with *executive functions* (e.g., in resisting distractions, focusing behaviour, planning, or organizing thinking) achieve substantial gains when they learn how to self-regulate more effectively (see Reid et al., 2012). Similarly, when provided with supports for SRL, students with learning disabilities achieve gains in metacognition, motivation, strategic action, and achievement (e.g., see Butler, 1995, 1998a; Butler, Novak Lauscher, & Beckingham, 2005; Harris & Graham, 1996; MacArthur, Philippakos, Graham, & Harris, 2012; Montague, 2008; Wong, 1991). With appropriate supports, students with cognitive disabilities can participate meaningfully in interpreting expectations, defining goals for learning and behaviour, and developing personalized strategies to achieve them; students with autism can learn to self-regulate emotions and behaviour within SRL–promoting classroom environments (Copeland & Hughes, 2002; Wehmeyer, 2007; Wehmeyer, Yeager, Bolding, Agran, & Hughes, 2003).

An Extended Case Example

In SR Vignette 10-1, we provide an extended example of how educators supported Joshua, a Grade 2 student with significant challenges, to focus his attention more successfully. As you read, notice how Joshua was supported to take more deliberate control over his thoughts and actions during classroom-based learning activities. Also, notice how Joshua's classroom teacher asked for help from a member of her district's inclusion support team to help her in designing strategies to help him. When general and special educators work together to design supports for SRL, they can combine their respective areas of expertise in powerful ways.

SR Vignette 10-1
Building Supports for Joshua into an Inclusive Classroom

Reena's classroom was a vibrant learning community that encouraged active learning, both physically and intellectually. She included many opportunities for students to move about during the day. She created opportunities for active learning and SRL using inclusive pedagogies like writing workshop; literacy centres; cooperative learning; and multi-modal, constructivist-based math learning. Through all of these activities, Reena supported all of her students to identify learning objectives, make plans, and advocate for their learning needs.

Reena noticed that Joshua benefited from all of these strategies, and others. But he still struggled to engage productively in learning during independent work. An educational assistant (EA) was assigned to the classroom; she watched over Joshua and redirected him to his work whenever he lost focus. Still, Joshua was not sustaining his attention to classroom work without on-going support from the EA. So, Reena called on Shelley Moore, a member of her school district's inclusion support team, to help her in creating a support plan for Joshua.

To help Reena design more personalized support for Joshua, Shelley joined the class during a variety of activities over the course of four days. What she noticed was that during group work Joshua successfully interacted with peers to engage in collaborative learning. When he could ask questions and paraphrase tasks to his peers, he participated more productively. But when Joshua was asked to move from mini-lessons on the carpet to independent work at his desk, he had trouble getting started and maintaining attention on his work. He refocused if the EA prompted him to do so, but only for short periods.

During her first visits, Shelley asked Joshua what he liked to do in school and at home. Joshua replied that he liked to play outside, use *Lego*, play with cars, read, and work and play with friends. It seemed that Joshua had a good sense of his strengths and interests. When Shelley and his teacher met after the first observation, Reena described Joshua as highly visual and particularly strong with expressive language and socializing.

To further her assessment, Shelley joined Joshua when he was assigned a math task. Her goals were to identify barriers to his learning and explore strategies that might work for Joshua. She noticed that Joshua was able to complete the task with prompting, which suggested that the task was not too difficult for him. She concluded that there must be another barrier preventing him from completing the task independently. The next time he was stuck, rather than prompting, Shelley asked

Joshua what he was thinking about. He replied, "I am thinking about all of my toys at home and my favourite TV show that I get to watch after school." Shelley asked him if he thought about those things a lot and he replied, "Yes." Shelley asked, "What do you want to be thinking about?" Joshua replied, "I should be thinking about math."

On her next visit, Shelley came to Reena's classroom when Joshua was working on math independently. After carpet time Joshua went to his desk, but instead of working on the math task he gazed off into the distance. When Shelley came to sit beside Joshua, he looked at her and then guiltily at his math task.

To explore what might help Joshua, Shelley asked him, "Should we try some things to see what works so that you can think about math? I have an idea. Let's try something." Shelley had prepared some materials ahead of time based on Joshua's description of his interests, her discussion with Reena, and her observations. Shelley showed Joshua a box. Inside were objects related to his favourite activities (e.g., a *Thomas the Train* DVD case, a *Mr. Potato Head* doll, a *Cars* DVD, pictures of his favourite cartoon characters, pieces of *Lego*). They pulled everything out of the box. Joshua was very excited to see his favourite things. Shelley asked Joshua to tell her about them.

To help him to find a strategy for refocusing, Shelley said, "Right now we are having a great time thinking and talking about your favourite things." Joshua enthusiastically agreed. Shelley asked, "What is everyone else doing right now?" Joshua looked around and saw his classmates working on math. Shelley suggested, "Maybe we should focus on doing

math too." Joshua nodded. He was invested in being part of the class, but frustrated with how distracted he became when working by himself.

"What can we do?" asked Shelley. Joshua shrugged. Shelley thought out loud, "When I get distracted by my phone, texting and Facebook, I turn off my phone and put it in my bag. I really want to use it, but it helps me to put it away." Joshua nodded and put all of the toys back in the box. "What are you doing?" asked Shelley. Joshua replied, "I'm putting my thoughts away in the box. It's math time." Shelley took her phone, turned it off, and put it in her bag. "Good idea," she said to Joshua. They gave each other a high five.

The next day when Shelley visited, she asked Joshua to help her build a book (i.e., a social story) about the strategy they had discovered. She pulled out her camera and they undertook a photo shoot to reenact the event. Shelley and Joshua went through each step and acted it out, so Shelley could take pictures. Shelley asked Joshua what "focused" looked like. Joshua showed what it looked like to be distracted and what it looked like for him to put his thoughts away. Shelley asked what his teachers and peers felt like when Joshua has finished his work, and took more photos of that. Once the photo shoot was complete, they integrated the pictures into PowerPoint slides and together came up with wording to describe thinking steps for Joshua.

Finally, each PowerPoint slide became a page in a book. The text on each page, which Shelley and Joshua wrote collaboratively, was accompanied with vibrant pictures (see Figure 10-1 for an example). The book concluded with a visual checklist of

I need to put my thoughts on stop so I can do my work.

Shelley Moore

Figure 10-1 A Page from Joshua's Book

Here are my thinking steps:

1. I am not focused ☐

2. I tell my thoughts to STOP ☐

3. I put my thoughts in a box ☐

4. I finish my work ☐

5. I take my thoughts out of the box ☐

Figure 10-2 Joshua's Thinking Steps: A Visual Checklist

the thinking steps they co-constructed (see Figure 10-2). Here is a list of the text that appeared on each page:

Title Page: Me and My Head!!!!

Page 2: Hi! I'm Joshua. And this is my head!

Page 3: My head is FILLED with lots of cool stuff.

Page 4: My head helps me tell stories, and play games. I am never bored!

Page 5: BUT sometimes I need to do work.

Page 6: It is hard for me to focus on my work because of all the thoughts in my head.

Page 7: I need to put my thoughts on stop so I can do my work.

Page 8: I can think about them again later, when all my work is done.

Page 9: I know one thing that helps me!!

Page 10: My head has a special box for me to put my thoughts in when I need to work.

Page 11: Then, when my work is done, my thoughts can come back out of the box.

Page 12: This helps me focus on my work by putting my thoughts on stop.

Page 13: It makes my friends and my teachers very happy!

Page 14: It makes me happy too because then I don't miss out on any fun.

Page 15: Thank you so much! Thank you head.

Page 16: [A visual checklist of Joshua's thinking steps (see Figure 10-2).]

Shelley created two copies of the book—one for Joshua to keep in his desk and a backup copy for his teacher. This was a book he could refer to independently. To support Joshua to learn how to use his book, he and Shelley read through the book together. While reading, Shelley asked Joshua about each of the pages and what he would do and why. She reinforced his strategy by saying, "Every time you catch yourself thinking about activities other than math, stop and put them in the box." Joshua was very proud of his strategy and the book he wrote with Shelley.

Finally, to build Joshua's strategy into the life of his classroom, Shelley modelled for the EA how to shift from prompting Joshua to do his work or redirecting his attention toward instead asking *strategic questions* (see Chapter 8), such as these: What's the task? What strategies could you use right now? What's your next step? These questions were designed to encourage Joshua to recognize when and where he might apply the strategy he had developed with Shelley. The goal was for Joshua, not the EA, to self-regulate his thinking and action.

Building Support for Joshua into an Inclusive Classroom

As you read SR Vignette 10-1, what did you notice about how Shelley supported Joshua to better understand and take control over his thoughts and behaviour? What was going wrong when the EA tried to support him? What did Shelley do that was different? How does this example reflect the principles and practices for supporting SRL that we identified through Part Two of this book?

Structuring Supports for Individuals within Inclusive Classrooms

What can Joshua's case example tell us about the ways in which educators can structure supports for students with significant learning challenges en route to their developing more effective forms of self-regulation? We highlight a few notable observations here.

First, Reena used strategies in her classroom to foster the development of SRL for all students. For most students, those supports were enough for them to understand and participate successfully in active, strategic forms of learning. But sometimes learners with significant challenges need more intensive supports to learn how to self-regulate learning effectively. In Joshua's case, just a bit of added assistance from Shelley, a district-level consultant, enabled Joshua to take more deliberate control over his thinking and behaviour. Reena and the EA assigned to her classroom could then build from Joshua's individualized support plan to include him meaningfully in regular classroom activities. Educators can use a similar approach to support students who struggle to self-regulate different aspects of their participation (e.g., emotions, motivation, strategic action), building from their unique strengths and challenges.

Second, when educators involve students in co-creating strategies, then students are more likely to take ownership over them (see Butler, 1995, 1998b). Joshua was proud of his book and used his strategy enthusiastically to help him learn successfully. Joshua's case also illustrates how even a Grade 2 student with significant challenges was able to participate in problem solving and developing a strategy. Young children can and need to learn about their thinking and how to control it (Perry, 1998, 2013). Learning to self-regulate is a developmental process.

Third, notice how continued redirecting from an EA did not help Joshua become an independent, self-regulating learner. In fact, having an EA continually watch over him seemed to have the opposite effect, because Joshua came to rely on the EA to notice when his attention had wandered and redirect him accordingly. In contrast, when Shelley brought Joshua into the problem-solving process, Joshua learned to monitor and redirect his own attention.

Furthermore, Shelley built on her work with Joshua to help the educational assistant learn how to support Joshua more effectively. In this way, she helped in reframing the supports Joshua received in the future to better foster his independence. For example, rather than monitoring Joshua's attention for him and then reminding him to focus, Joshua's EA shifted to nurturing his capacity to self-regulate his own learning and behaviour (e.g., by using strategic questioning; see Chapter 8). The result was that Joshua learned how to monitor his attention and keep focused, as needed, while working through activities.

Finally, students who are experiencing significant learning challenges can become very demoralized over time and are at risk for giving up on themselves and school. It is very empowering for these learners to experience and celebrate progress and growth. Joshua was so proud when he successfully put his thoughts in a box so that he could focus on his math. Can you imagine the effect on Joshua's motivation and sense of control over outcomes, particularly when he realized that he was being more successful because of what *he* was doing? Can you imagine how these successful experiences might fuel his persistence through difficulties and positive investment in learning?

It is important to recognize that, although students with significant challenges benefit from supports to self-regulation, the approaches educators use to foster SRL will need to vary depending on individuals' particular strengths and needs. Furthermore, growth for different students will likely progress in different ways and at different rates. For example, Joshua will likely need continued support to use his strategy, not only in math, but in other activities. But, if his teacher and EA continue to build on Joshua's strengths to support his development of SRL, Joshua can progress toward controlling his performance and increase his capacity to focus across activities. Furthermore, because Shelley supported Joshua to better understand himself in relation to expectations and start learning how to trouble shoot solutions in the face of challenges, he will be better able to develop and use strategies for other challenges he experiences in other settings (see Butler, 1995, 1998b, 2002; Butler & Schnellert, 2015).

Social Stories

The work Shelley did with Joshua was informed by research on *social stories* (Gray, 2000; Sansosti, Powell-Smith, & Kincaid, 2004). Although now used to support learners with a wide variety of needs, Carol Gray originally developed *social stories* to help students with autism learn how to navigate expectations more successfully. **Social stories** do this by describing "a situation, skill, or concept in terms of relevant social cues, perspectives, and common responses in a specifically defined style and format" (see http://www.thegraycenter.org/social-stories/what-are-social-stories). They are easily interpretable by students and so help them in understanding expectations and how to act in particular situations. They are typically told from the learner's perspective. Because they often include visual representations, they can be used with learners who have more limited communication capacities (e.g., for reading or writing).

> **Social stories** help students learn how to navigate expectations, environments, and activities more successfully. They do this by providing a written or visual guide that helps students interpret important social cues, recognize their own reactions and others' perspectives, engage in action appropriate to a particular situation, and link action to hoped-for-outcomes.

Social stories can be used to achieve essential goals in fostering SRL, particularly when educators construct them with students. They invite learners to reflect on their needs and then consider and select a plan of action. As a result, they foster learners' development of metacognitive knowledge. They also provide a concrete plan learners can refer to when choosing and self-assessing their thoughts and actions. In this respect, they provide cues that help learners develop effective forms of strategic action. In this example, Shelley used social stories as a tool to help Joshua problem solve and develop a personalized strategy (i.e., his thinking steps) for controlling his attention. Joshua's strategy both addressed his particular needs and built on his interests (e.g., in certain movies and toys). Because it was built for him and he had a hand in creating it, Joshua felt great ownership over this strategy and used it enthusiastically.

Fostering SRL for Students with Learning Challenges: Closing Reflections

We can and need to include students with significant challenges in developing effective forms of SRL. When we do, we can support their development of growth mindsets, coupled with the self-belief that they are capable of engaging in effective forms of thinking and learning. Students who are struggling, not only in the early grades but also as they progress through school, are in particular need of support to *be*, and *feel*, in control over learning.

> Students who are struggling, not only in the early grades but also as they progress through school, are in particular need of support to be, and feel, in control over learning.

FOSTERING SRL IN A SUPPORT SETTING

When supports for SRL are integrated into classrooms, all students have opportunities to learn how to participate in rich forms of learning. Still, there are also times when educators work with groups of students in support settings, such as resource rooms or learning assistance rooms. How can educators take advantage of those opportunities to build learners' capacity for SRL and success in academic work? In SR Vignette 10-2, we provide an example of how Denise Briard reconstructed her practices in a learning assistance setting in order to help struggling learners better succeed in their regular classroom work. As you read this example, try to identify how Denise integrated SRL–promoting practices into her setting.

Fostering SRL in a Support Setting

Denise was a very experienced learning resource teacher who was responsible for teaching several "learning strategies" blocks in a secondary school. These blocks were 75-minute classes that students attended in addition to their subject-area classes in order to help them learn how to learn more effectively. Denise's classes typically included 10 to 15 students from across grade levels (8–11), each of whom brought in work from their different subject-area classrooms (e.g., math, English, science, social studies). Many of her students had been designated as having learning disabilities following district and provincial criteria. All were significantly behind in their academic work.

Denise's goal was to help her students take control over their learning so that they could be more successful in their regular classes. To that end, she asked students to bring their classroom work with them. She provided individualized support, as best she could in the time she had, as students were trying to tackle those authentic classroom tasks. She also engaged them in mini-lessons about strategies they could use to learn more effectively.

But Denise wasn't satisfied with how her students were taking responsibility for their learning. First, when her students came into the class, they sat down at their desks and immediately raised their hands, waiting for her to help before taking any action. Similarly, whenever her students encountered a problem, they relied on her to tell them what to do to solve it. Second, her students had no interest in learning strategies. Instead, they usually wanted quick, direct help with what they perceived to be urgent (e.g., preparing for a test in the next block). Whenever Denise tried to engage them in mini-lessons about strategies, they complained bitterly. They failed to see the connection between the strategies Denise was describing to them and the work they wanted to get done.

Denise was also very unhappy with her relationships with students, which she described as confrontational. Denise felt pressured to run from student to student since they were all waiting until she could get to them. But as she dashed from one to the other, she only had time to glance down at their work, guess at the root problem, and offer direction. Students' responses were typically to dismiss her or push back. Denise believed strongly in empowering students, but felt trapped in what she knew wasn't working. When the opportunity arose for her to participate in a district-level project on SRL, Denise jumped on board.

What did Denise ultimately do to better foster SRL in her context? One thing she did was to replace mini-lessons with support for SRL in the context of classroom work. Students still brought their general education classroom work with them to her classroom. They still came to the room, sat down, and started working. Denise still circulated around the room to help students as needed. But, instead of offering quick solutions or teaching the same strategies to everyone, Denise supported her students to approach activities strategically. She re-positioned herself from someone who gave explanations and solutions to someone who facilitated students' learning how to learn through the activities they cared about most.

For example, whenever students pulled out a classroom activity, Denise used strategic questioning, asking, "What are you supposed to be doing here?" If students weren't sure, she worked through "clues" (e.g., instructions) with students to identify expectations, criteria, and goals. Then, once students were clear on expectations, instead of telling them what strategies to use, Denise helped them develop personalized strategies with task goals in mind. To that end, she watched them engage in the activity, asking them to think out loud so that both she and they could see the learning processes they were using. She worked with students to identify what was working, as well as important gaps and needs. To address gaps, Denise supported students to make informed decisions about other strategies they might try. She asked students to think of options; as needed, she made suggestions of things they might do. In this way, Denise engaged students in monitoring their own progress, diagnosing gaps, and troubleshooting alternatives.

Denise still wanted students to build better strategies for learning. So, whenever students had an "a ha" moment, when they recognized an action they were taking was leading to learning or progress, she asked students to pause. She encouraged them to recognize and celebrate their progress. She also asked them to describe, *in their own words*, what they were doing to achieve that success so that they could do it again, next time, if they were taking up a similar kind of activity. Students recorded "advice" to themselves on personal "strategy sheets" that they kept with them in their binders. Sometimes, the students wrote down their strategies themselves. Other times the students dictated their ideas to Denise, who wrote them down just as the students described them. Denise noticed that her students found it very empowering when she was sitting with her pen raised, listening to them, waiting to write down *their* words. In Figure 10-3, we provide an example of strategies for writing English paragraphs that one student developed in Denise's classroom over a series of classes.

At the end of the year, Denise reflected on her experiences in the SRL project. She explained that she had originally joined the project because she liked how it positioned students as problem solvers, rather than as "empty vessels." She had also liked the focus on empowering learners as "capable strategists." By the end of the year, Denise was delighted with the changes she observed in her students and her classroom. For example, Denise described how her switch from "telling students what to do" to facilitating their problem solving had "taken the struggle out of dealing with students." She perceived her classroom environment as "more studious and business-like." Instead of raising their hands and passively waiting for Denise to help them, her students were now coming into the classroom, pulling out their assignments and strategy sheets, and getting down to work. Students only asked for help when they couldn't solve a problem themselves. The result was that Denise found she could spend more time providing high-quality, individualized assistance.

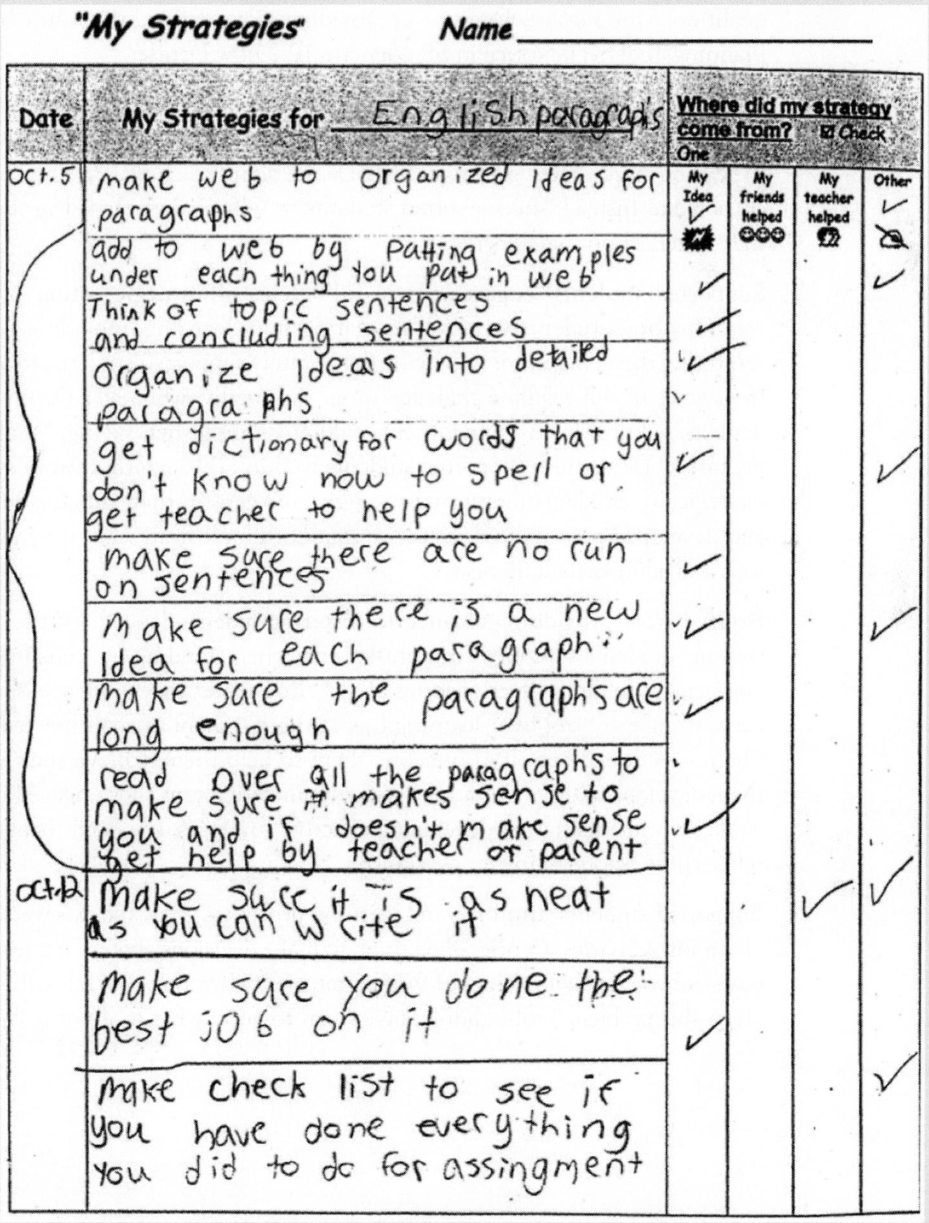

"My Strategies" **Name** ____________________

Date	My Strategies for English paragraph's	Where did my strategy come from? ☑ Check One — My Idea	My friends helped	My teacher helped	Other
oct.5	make web to organized Ideas for paragraphs	✓			✓
	add to web by Patting examples under each thing you put in web	✓			✓
	Think of topic sentences and concluding sentences	✓			
	Organize Ideas into detailed paragraphs	✓			
	get dictionary for words that you don't know how to spell or get teacher to help you	✓			✓
	make sure there are no run on sentences	✓			
	make sure there is a new Idea for each paragraph	✓			✓
	make sure the paragraph's are long enough	✓			
	read over all the paragraphs to make sure it makes sense to you and if doesn't make sense get help by teacher or parent	✓			
oct.12	Make sure it is as neat as you can write it			✓	✓
	make sure you done the best job on it	✓			
	make check list to see if you have done everything you did to do for assingment				✓

Deborah Butler

Figure 10-3 One Student's Strategies for Writing English Paragraphs

Fostering SRL in a Support Setting

As you read SR Vignette 10-2, what did you notice about how Denise changed her approach to fostering SRL? What was going wrong in Denise's earlier attempts to support students' strategy development (e.g., in mini-lessons, when offering one-on-one support)? What did Denise change that made a difference? How does this example reflect the SRL–promoting practices that we identified through Part Two of this book?

How Denise Wove Supports for SRL into Her Classroom

How was Denise building supports for SRL into her classroom? Below, we summarize key qualities of the *supports* Denise was providing as we defined them in Chapter 8 (see SRL Planning Tool 8-1). Notice in SR Vignette 10-2 how Denise:

Integrated support for SRL into activities   Students brought work they cared about to her learning strategies block. It was within the context of that work that Denise guided students to develop more effective forms of SRL. Denise didn't teach SRL as something outside of the curriculum. Instead, she supported students to self-regulate their learning effectively and then to reflect on that experience.

Supported students' engagement in full cycles of strategic action   Denise started by watching how students were self-regulating their learning, including how they were interpreting the demands of tasks. She deliberately supported students to identify and build from goals to self-regulate their learning. Eventually, whenever Denise approached students to see how it was going, they would poke fun at her, saying, "Yeah, I know; what's my task?!" Denise also supported students to think through their work systematically and strategically. Students monitored strengths and gaps in their progress in relation to goals and developed personalized strategies that both built from what they were already doing well and addressed challenges.

Bridged from providing guidance to fostering independence   Denise transitioned from "telling" students solutions (in mini-lessons, when standing by students) to guiding their engagement in more effective forms of SRL. To support independence, she encouraged students to take control over learning by positioning them as goal-directed problem solvers. She re-positioned herself as someone there to help them achieve their goals. She helped them develop, apply, and refine strategies cumulatively, as they engaged in their classroom work. As students started developing effective strategies, she cued them to refer to and/or refine those before asking for assistance.

Supported students' thinking and learning processes   As students were working through classroom activities, Denise asked them to make decisions about their learning (e.g., What goals are you trying to achieve? What strategies will you use? What will you do differently given this problem?). She didn't leave them to guess what to do or make up strategies for themselves. Instead, she engaged in a dialogue with students, using strategic questioning to guide their thinking. Students articulated what they were doing in their own words, particularly when they discovered something that was working. They were positioned as owners of their learning and strategies.

Nurtured learners' construction of knowledge and adaptive expertise   Denise grounded her support in what students were already doing that was working for them. In that way, she helped students recognize and build on the knowledge, skills, and strategies they were bringing to their work. Denise also asked students to describe strategies they were using whenever they observed that they achieved success through something *they chose to do*. Through these experiences, students constructed important kinds of metacognitive knowledge (about activities, strategies, and themselves as learners). Furthermore, because her students could see the connection between their actions and positive outcomes, they built more positive self-perceptions of competence and control over learning. Finally, as Denise engaged her students in more strategic approaches to learning, she supported them to identify and flexibly apply their growing knowledge and capacities flexibly and adaptively.

Fostering SRL in a Support Setting: Closing Reflections

One of the most powerful qualities of Denise's reframed instruction was that she consistently engaged students in talking about and making sense of their thinking and learning. She asked them to explain activities, what they were trying to do, *and how they knew* that (e.g., what cues they were using to interpret the activity demands). She asked them to tell, or show her, strategies they were using (e.g., for solving a problem in math). She asked them to judge how strategies were working and *to tell her how they knew* (e.g., how they knew that an answer to a math problem was correct or not). Ultimately, students articulated strategies they were using, grounded in their experiences, in their own words. What mattered to Denise was not so much whether students' strategies were eloquently described or accurate in her terms, but whether the language students were using made sense *to them*, mapped onto strategies that were useful and meaningful for accomplishing their work successfully, and resulted in high-quality learning and performance.

ACCOMMODATING DIVERSITY IN AN INCLUSIVE CLASSROOM

In our final example, we describe how Nicole Widdess was able to nurture active learning and SRL for a very diverse group of learners within an inclusive classroom environment (see SR Vignette 10-3). Notice here how, like Pam and Lynn (from Chapters 7 and 8), Nicole built supports for SRL across a sequence of activities. Notice too how, to help her in building her practice, Nicole took advantage of opportunities to collaborate with other educators.

Accommodating Diversity in an Inclusive Classroom

Nicole, a second-year teacher, was concerned about how she could support the culturally and cognitively diverse learners in her combined Grade 5/6 classroom. To help her develop her practices, she reached out to a district-level instructional coach (Leyton Schnellert), who came on board to co-teach with Nicole through a series of lessons.

Nicole's very diverse class included Marshall, a boy diagnosed with autism, 5 other students on individualized education programs, 1 First Nations[2] boy (Jerry) with very significant social-emotional challenges, 2 students identified as gifted, and 22 English language learners (most classified at level 1, 2, or 3 in British Columbia's system). Nicole and Leyton were particularly concerned about Jerry, who they feared was at risk for dropping out of school. Jerry had lost touch with his mother and worried about her safety. This was Jerry's third school in as many years, and there were no other First Nations students in the class. While he participated in art activities, Jerry would not engage in other subjects, write anything (particularly "paragraphs" or essays), or engage with his peers.

Planning the Lesson Sequence to Accommodate Diversity When they first met to plan, Nicole described how she worried that she too often did the thinking *for* students. Nicole also said that her students knew they were *supposed* to be metacognitive while learning, but didn't know how to do that. She wanted to shift her instruction so that her students could and would take more ownership over their learning. As part of their work together, Nicole and Leyton set a goal to infuse support for students' development of more effective forms of self-regulated reading, writing, and learning into their lesson planning.

Nicole and Leyton decided to co-plan and co-teach a new unit and lesson sequence that could integrate across social studies, language arts, art, and dance curricula. They initially thought of focusing on the Japanese interment in North America during WWII. But, because they wanted to reach out to Jerry without singling him out, they decided instead to focus on First Nations students' experiences in Canada's residential school system. Ultimately, Nicole and Leyton's goals were to support all students' construction of knowledge about Canada's Indigenous peoples, empathy toward and understanding about Indigenous students' experiences in residential schools, and capacities to communicate emotions and understandings through free verse poetry as a writing genre.

As they planned, Nicole and Leyton recognized that, by integrating across art, dance, and language arts curricula, they could create rich opportunities for Jerry, Marshall, and their peers, including students just learning English, to express their understandings in different ways. Poetry as a writing genre also seemed like a good fit to their goals of generating empathy and understanding (while reading and writing). They hoped Jerry might be more willing to write poems than paragraphs. They also thought that they could use poetry to foster language and literacy development for English language learners.

Thus, through the lesson sequence students had opportunities to express their thinking and feelings using different media, including art and dance. Over time, they were also asked to write a series of free verse poems *to*, *as*, or *about* individuals who had experienced life in residential schools. Note here that the main academic adaptation for Marshall had to do with volume. While most students started by drafting six poems, Marshall was only asked to draft two. This allowed him to keep working with a single poem over two weeks, receiving more extended support through conferencing with peers and teachers.

Creating Inclusive Participation Structures Because they had selected a First Nations theme, Nicole and Leyton reached out to Lynn Wainwright, their district's teacher consultant for Indigenous Education. Nicole, Leyton, and Lynn decided to launch the lesson sequence with the students seated in a circle. They hoped the circle participation structure would be welcoming and inclusive for all members of the classroom community, as well as for Jerry, who was likely to be comfortable and familiar with this approach to sharing ideas and learning. Within the circle, Lynn started by telling stories orally, honouring an Indigenous storytelling tradition.

To be successful in self-regulating his learning, Marshall had learned to use strategies for self-regulating his emotions and behaviour. For example, if he felt that he was getting frustrated or angry—if he was heading toward a "bad path"—he used a "break card" to move to the back of the room with a visual schedule, consequence map, and *social stories* in hand. During the poetry lesson sequence, Marshall used his break strategy during the oral story-telling, because he had a particularly difficult time sitting and attending during that activity. Otherwise, he was able to participate positively in other lesson activities.

On the third day of story-telling, Lynn shared a story about residential schools. In subsequent classes, Nicole, Leyton, and the class read related picture books

---

[2]First Nations refer to the Indigenous (Aboriginal) peoples of Canada, who are the descendants of the original inhabitants of North America (from the website of the Department of Aboriginal Affairs and Northern Development, Government of Canada).

(e.g., *Mush-Hole* by Harper [1993]). By hearing and reading these stories, all learners developed background knowledge and language they could draw on as they moved into further reading and writing activities. Students found the picture books to be intriguing, inspiring, visually powerful, and evocative. Most importantly, the images and ideas were accessible to all students.

Weaving in Explicit Supports for SRL   To foster students' development as self-regulating readers, writers, and learners, Nicole and Leyton decided to engage students explicitly, throughout the lesson sequence, in interpreting tasks, establishing criteria, setting goals, making plans related to their goals, trying out their plans, reflecting on actions, and adjusting their performance. To set the stage for students' engagement in these cycles of strategic action, they co-taught an anchor lesson. Every reading and writing activity that followed was connected back to that anchor lesson.

During the anchor lesson, Nicole and Leyton engaged students in co-constructing criteria that they could lean on when composing and self-assessing their own work. To begin, Nicole and Leyton asked students to look at poems together and then, in small groups, decide—What makes these poems powerful? For each idea they generated, students were asked to provide an example (e.g., a quote from one of the poems). Within their groups, students had opportunities to think alone and then come to agreement about their different ideas (using a placemat activity; see Chapter 8). Then, groups shared their ideas, which were recorded on an overhead projector for the whole class to see (see Figure 10-4). After considering the relative merits and drawbacks of the criteria they had come up with, the students collectively settled on four central attributes they thought were most important in creating powerful, free verse poetry. Not accidently, given that Nicole and Leyton asked questions to inspire and guide students' thinking, the attributes students identified were well aligned with those identified in provincial curricula.

Next, Nicole and Leyton supported students *to learn how to* use the criteria they had generated while reading and writing poems. Students were asked to refer back to their criteria to focus their reading; plan for writing; and engage in peer-, self-, and teacher-assessment. For example, Nicole and Leyton asked students to find examples of attributes of powerful poems while they were reading. As a procedural facilitator (see Chapter 8), they constructed a graphic organizer that listed students' criteria in four quadrants, along with mnemonic icons. During one lesson, they worked with students to generate examples of how those attributes were reflected in the poems and picture books

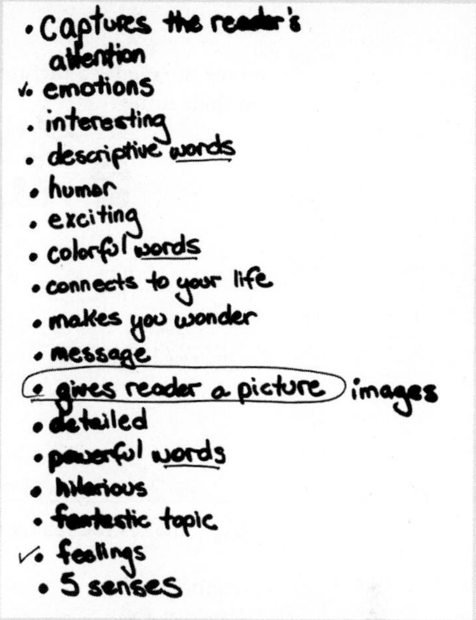

Figure 10-4 Criteria for Free Verse Poems Generated with Students in Nicole's Classroom

they were reading to fuel their writing (see Figure 10-5). Linking back to their co-constructed criteria, they said to the students, "You told us that *images*, *feelings*, the *five senses*, and *powerful words* are important aspects of poetry. So we are using this strategy to help us find and collect them."

Nicole and Leyton also supported students to link back to criteria while they were writing. For example, as students were refining their writing about midway through the lesson, they asked students to list the criteria they were working toward. As students generated ideas, Nicole transcribed them onto the blackboard (so that all students could see them). For each idea, they asked students to generate an example, which Nicole also wrote down on the board. The students' ideas included the four criteria that they had previously generated, agreed upon, and been working on as a class (that emphasized meaning and style, but also aspects of form). Their goals in starting the lesson this way were to (1) reinforce the importance of working to achieve particular goals, (2) honour and bring forward criteria students were co-constructing, and (3) make sure that all learners could see criteria and examples to help them with their writing.

Next, they asked students to choose the strongest of the poems they had begun over the last three weeks and to continue to refine that poem. To that end, Nicole and Leyton reminded them to be mindful of how they were

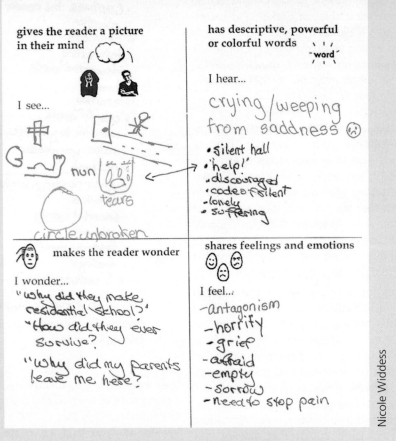

Nicole Widdess

Figure 10-5 Building from Co-Constructed Criteria to Generate Content

incorporating each of the criteria as goals into their writing. As students were writing, they circulated and conferenced with students on their works-in-progress. While circulating, they asked students which criteria they were working on. If they noticed a problem in students' writing, they asked learners to think about how they were doing in relation to particular criteria.

At the end of the lesson, Nicole and Leyton asked students to write down advice for themselves and others about how to write a free verse poem (see Figure 10-6). Each student recorded different kinds of ideas in their advice. Rather than being comprehensive (i.e., covering every step needed to write a poem), students' strategies tended to include advice based on points they wanted to remember or approaches they had used to overcome a challenge. The next day, students were asked to take out and share their advice with one another before choosing the same or another one of their poems to refine.

Building in Supports from Both Teachers and Peers Leyton and Nicole engaged students in working with them and each other throughout the lesson sequence (e.g., when co-constructing criteria). Furthermore, across the unit, all students signed up for a weekly conference with either Nicole or Leyton. During those conferences, students shared their poetry drafts, explained what they thought was effective or not, and set goals for the next iteration. In this context, Nicole and Leyton supported students primarily by asking them questions designed to help them think through and develop their self-regulated approaches to writing. After each conference, students were also asked to return to their "how to" advice and refine it as a means to support them as authors.

By the end of the unit, students knew they would have opportunities to publish what they considered to be the best two poems they had written over time. To help them in preparing their submissions, they were required to conference

How to write a free verse poem:

1. _____
   _____
2. _____
   _____
3. _____
   _____
4. _____
   _____
5. _____
   _____
6. _____
   _____
7. _____
   _____
8. _____
   _____
9. _____
   _____

Figure 10-6 How Nicole and Leyton Supported Students to Build Personalized Strategies

with two other students and one of the teachers and then rework their poems based on that feedback. But, as authors, they could make decisions about how to use feedback so as to improve their writing.

Reflections on Students' Engagement Through these activities, students built understandings of Indigenous ways of knowing and learning, appreciation for the experience of First Nations peoples in residential schools, and their own capacities as readers and writers. Nicole and Leyton were pleased that they had been able to build on students' knowledge and interests in ways that let students' thinking drive the unit. They were impressed by students' ability to find and focus on the strengths of others' poems. They were delighted by the level of ownership students felt over the co-constructed criteria. Nicole and Leyton observed that, as students became progressively more proficient at working toward criteria, they began to write more powerful pieces. Students also began adapting the task to suit their personal interests and ideas as authors. For example, instead of writing to, as, or about students who had experienced life in residential schools, some students wanted to write as the land or the residential school and/or connect their personal experiences to those of others (Schnellert, Watson & Widdess, 2015; Schnellert & Widdess, 2005).

How Did Nicole and Leyton Weave Supports for SRL into an Inclusive Classroom?

In this chapter, we have been describing how educators have used SRL–promoting practices to inspire and support the diverse learning needs we find in today's classroom. In Activity 10-1, we invite you to identify the qualities of SRL–promoting practices built by Nicole and Leyton into their poetry lesson sequence. Can you see qualities of SRL–promoting practices in this example, as we identified them across Part Two of this book?

You'll notice that in Activity 10-1 we ask you to consider a very long list of SRL–promoting features you might be able to discern in Nicole and Leyton's practice. At first glance, this list will likely feel a bit daunting. But, as you really think through this example, can you identify how some of the practices they used served multiple purposes all at once? For example, just by asking students to articulate advice about how to write poems, based on their goals and co-constructed criteria, they were all at once:

- supporting students in making choices;
- integrating support for SRL into activities;
- supporting students to engage in full cycles of strategic action;
- bridging from guiding to fostering independence;
- supporting students' thinking and learning processes;
- involving students in the assessment process (e.g., self-assessing);
- creating a dialogue with students about learning; and
- asking students to draw flexibly on knowledge and beliefs.

We stress here that SRL–promoting practices can be enormously effective because simple approaches serve multiple purposes and, correspondingly, can achieve multiple benefits.

> SRL–promoting practices can be enormously effective because simple approaches serve multiple purposes and, correspondingly, can achieve multiple benefits.

Accommodating Diversity in an Inclusive Classroom

As you read SR Vignette 10-3, what did you notice about how Nicole and Leyton supported students to engage in effective forms of SRL while engaged in this lesson sequence? Using Table 10-1, see if you can link back to the SRL–promoting practices we identified in Chapter 7 (activities), Chapter 8 (supports), and Chapter 9 (assessments and feedback). Overall, how did the practices they used enable them to reach out to and include such a diverse range of learners?

Table 10-1 SRL–Promoting Practices in Nicole's Classroom	
How did Nicole and Leyton. . .	**Examples?**
Design *activities* that. . . • worked toward multiple goals? • focused on large chunks of meaning? • integrated across content areas? • extended over time? • engaged students in making choices? • engaged students in a variety of processes? • involved individual and social forms of learning? • allowed students to create a variety of products to demonstrate learning?	
Provide *supports* that. . . • integrated support for SRL in activities? • supported students to engage in full cycles of strategic action? • bridged from guiding learning to fostering independence? • supported students' thinking and learning processes? • nurtured learners' construction of knowledge and adaptive expertise? • recruited peers to support one another?	
Structure assessment and feedback to. . . • generate information for both themselves and students? • distribute assessment and feedback through activities? • engage students in recognizing, interpreting, and/or co-constructing learning goals? • assess for both content and process goals? • grade for growth and progress? • empower students (e.g., using self-assessment)? • create a "dialogue" with students? • provide powerful feedback?	

Accommodating Diverse Learners in an Inclusive Classroom: Closing Reflections

Nicole and Leyton realized that, if they had not used these kinds of inclusive pedagogical strategies, up to 50 percent of their learners (particularly English language learners and students with disabilities) might not have achieved curricular objectives. Instead, by creating flexibility in how learners could work through and engage with activities, they were able to scaffold support for multiple learners simultaneously. For example, although perhaps for different reasons, many students benefited from the class's collaborative construction of criteria and corresponding clarity in expectations, having access to language they could borrow to express their ideas, and multiple opportunities to progressively build and refine their writing and learning.

The result was that learners with very different needs were supported to thrive simultaneously. For example, Jerry, the First Nations boy at risk for dropping out of school, was drawn into the community of learners through inclusive participation structures (e.g., oral story-telling; sharing circles; small group interactions; large group, supported dialogues). Although he was the only First Nations learner in the classroom, he felt less isolated when the lesson sequence brought stories of Indigenous peoples into the learning community. Jerry could relate to these stories and link them in powerful ways to his life. Jerry also had opportunities to express his voice through art and poetry. Ultimately, this initially disenfranchised learner "published" an extremely powerful poem through which he connected his own life experiences and challenges to the stories of students in residential schools.

At the same time, Marshall (a boy with autism) was able to achieve curricular goals. Like Joshua, earlier in this chapter, Marshall used emotion and behaviour control strategies in ways that enabled him to participate in active forms of *learning*. In this lesson sequence, Marshall successfully wrote a free verse poem, like the other students, using the same content as his peers. He shared and received feedback like all other students. Most importantly, he learned about and understood the experiences of Indigenous students in residential schools.

Many of the practices built into the lesson structure enabled success for Jerry, Marshall, *and their peers* (e.g., having access to visuals, being able to express ideas in different ways, having opportunities to collect and use language from picture books, recursive explorations of the theme and poetry). For example, students new to English were also able to use or build from criteria that the class had generated together. Because they had permission to borrow or extend from concrete examples that the class had examined and generated, these learners were better able to generate ideas for their own writing or find English words for expressing their ideas. Ultimately, although all students were working toward common criteria, they had opportunities throughout the lesson sequence to achieve them at their own pace and in their own ways.

MEETING THE NEEDS OF DIVERSE LEARNERS: NEXT STEPS

In this chapter, we have illustrated how, by nurturing SRL, educators can better capitalize on the rich opportunities created when learners with different experiences, backgrounds, strengths, and interests have opportunities to learn together. In SRL–promoting classrooms, all learners are empowered to build their capacities within an inclusive learning community.

At the start of this chapter we asked you how you thought supports for SRL could assist educators in orchestrating rich forms of learning in classrooms that include learners with diverse experiences, challenges, strengths, knowledge, skills, values, and beliefs. What do you think now? As we close this chapter, we invite you to consider implications for you in your context. Could you see your own practices reflected in our examples? Have you taken away any new ideas on which you could build to design or refine your approaches to meeting diverse learning needs in your context? What more do you want to know? What could you do to advance your learning further?

Recommended Resources

Brownlie, F., & Schnellert, L. (2009). *It's all about thinking: Collaborating to support all learners in English, Social Studies and Humanities*. Winnipeg, MB: Portage & Main Press.

Butler, D. L. (1995). Promoting strategic learning by postsecondary students with learning disabilities. *Journal of Learning Disabilities, 28*, 170–190.

Butler, D. L. (1998a). Metacognition and learning disabilities. In B. Y. L. Wong (ed.), *Learning about learning disabilities* (2nd ed.) (pp. 277–307). Toronto: Academic Press.

Butler, D. L. (1998b). The Strategic Content Learning approach to promoting self-regulated learning: A summary of three studies. *Journal of Educational Psychology, 90*, 682–697.

Butler, D. L. (2002). Individualizing instruction in self-regulated learning. *Theory into Practice, 41*(2), 81–92.

Butler, D. L., Novak Lauscher, H. J., & Beckingham, B. (2005). Promoting strategic learning by eight-grade students struggling in mathematics: A report of three case studies. *Learning Disabilities Research and Practice, 20*, 156–174.

Butler, D. L., & Schnellert, L. (2015). Success for students with learning disabilities: What does self-regulation have to do with it ? In T. Cleary (Ed.), *Self-regulated learning interventions with at-risk youth: Enhancing adaptability, performance, and well-being* (pp. 89–111). Washington DC: APA Press.

Copeland, S. R., & Hughes, C. (2002). Effects of goal setting on task performance of persons with mental retardation. *Education and Training in Mental Retardation and Developmental Disabilities, 37*, 40–54.

Gay, G. (2010). *Culturally responsive teaching: Theory, research, and practice* (2nd ed.). New York: Teachers College Press.

Gray, C. (2000). *The new social story book*. Arlington: Future Horizons Inc.

Graham, S., & Harris, K. R. (1989). Components analysis of cognitive strategy instruction: Effects on learning disabled students' compositions and self-efficacy. *Journal of Educational Psychology, 81*, 353–361.

Graham, S., Harris, K. R., & Troia, G. A. (1998). Writing and self-regulation: Cases from the self-regulated strategy development model. In D. H. Schunk & B. J. Zimmerman (eds.), *Self-regulated learning: From teaching to self-reflective practice* (pp. 20–41). New York: Guilford Press.

Harper, M. (1993). Mush-hole: Memories of a residential school. Toronto, ON: Sister Vision Press.

Harris, K. R., & Graham, S. (1996). *Making the writing process work: Strategies for composition and self-regulation*. Cambridge, MA: Brookline.

Lundy, K. G. (2009). *Teaching fairly in an unfair world*. Markham, ON: Pembroke.

MacArthur, C. A., Philippakos, Z., Graham, S., & Harris, K. R. (2012). Writing instruction. In B. Y. L. Wong & D. L. Butler, *Learning about learning disabilities*, 4th ed. (pp. 243–270) Elsevier Academic Press.

Moje, E. B., McIntosh Ciechanowski, K., Kramer, K., Ellis, L., Carrillo, R., & Collazo, T. (2004). Working toward third space in content area literacy: An examination of everyday funds of knowledge and discourse. *Reading Research Quarterly, 39*(1), 38–71.

Montague, M. (2008). Self-regulation strategies to improve mathematical problem-solving for students with learning disabilities. *Learning Disability Quarterly, 31*, 37–44.

National Middle School Association. (2010). *This we believe: Keys to educating young adolescents*. Westerville, Ohio: Association for Middle Level Education.

Perry, N. E. (1998). Young children's self-regulated learning and contexts that support it. *Journal of Educational Psychology, 90*, 715–729.

Perry, N. E. (2004). Fostering self-regulated learning in exceptional students in general education classrooms. *Exceptionality Education Canada, 14*, 65–87.

Perry, N. E. (2013). Classroom processes that support self-regulation in young children [Monograph]. *British Journal of Educational Psychology, Monograph Series II: Psychological Aspects of Education—Current Trends, 10*, 45–68.

Reid, R. R., Harris, K. R., Graham, S., & Rock, M. (2012). Self-regulation among students with LD and ADHD. In B. Y. L. Wong & D. L. Butler, *Learning about learning disabilities*, 4th ed. (pp. 141–173) Elsevier Academic Press. San Diego, CA.

Rose, D. H., & Meyer, A. (2002). *Teaching every student in the Digital Age: Universal design for learning*. Alexandria, VA: Association for Supervision and Curriculum Development.

Sansosti, F., Powell-Smith, K. A., & Kincaid, D. (2004). A research synthesis of social story interventions for children with autism spectrum disorders. *Focus on Autism and Other Developmental Disabilities, 19*(4), 194–204.

Schnellert, L., Datoo, M., Ediger, K., & Panas, J. (2009). *Pulling together: Integrating assessment, planning and instruction in English language arts.* Markham, ON: Pembroke Publishers.

Schnellert, L., Watson, L., & Widdess, N. (2015). *It's all about thinking: Building pathways for all learners in the middle years*. Winnipeg, MN: Portage & Main Press.

Schnellert, L., & Widdess, N. (2005). Student-generated criteria, free verse poetry, and residential schools. *English Practice, 47*(2), 19–28.

Tomlinson, C. (1999). The differentiated classroom: Responding to the needs of all learners. Alexandria, VA: ASCD.

Tomlinson, C. (2014). The differentiated classroom: Responding to the needs of all learners (2nd ed.). Alexandria, VA: ASCD.

Wehmeyer, M. L. (2007). *Promoting self-determination in students with developmental disabilities*. New York: The Guilford Press.

Wehmeyer, M. L., Yeager, D., Bolding, N., Agran, M., & Hughes, C. (2003). The effects of self-regulation strategies on goal attainment for students with developmental disabilities in regular education classroom. *Journal of Developmental and Physical Disabilities, 15*(1), 79–91.

Wong, B. Y. L. (1991). The relevance of metacognition to learning disabilities. In B. Y. L. Wong (Ed.), *Learning about learning disabilities* (pp. 231–256). New York: Academic Press.

Chapter 11
Motivating and Engaging Learners

Steve Debenport/E+/
Getty Images

INTRODUCTION

In Part Three of this book, we are explaining how fostering the development of self-regulating learners can help educators in addressing three important challenges they face today. We started in Chapter 10 by describing how nurturing SRL enables teachers to *meet the diverse needs of learners*. In Chapter 12, we will discuss the promise of SRL–promoting practices in *empowering 21st-century learning*. In this chapter, we consider why fostering SRL is so intimately connected with *motivating and engaging learners*.

Research has shown that motivation is central in effective forms of self-regulation and learning (e.g., see Linnenbrink & Pintrich, 2003; Perry & Winne, 2004; Zimmerman, 2011). Learners won't engage in self-regulation, or active learning of any sort, if they aren't

The Promise of SRL in Motivating and Engaging Learners

What kinds of beliefs, values, or expectations do individuals bring to contexts that might influence their willingness to try hard, invest in learning, or persist through challenges? Where do these come from? How can SRL–promoting practices motivate and engage learners? What kinds of practices might inadvertently undermine motivation for learning? When you think about learners' motivation and engagement in your context, what do you wonder?

motivated to do so. In contrast, self-regulating learners initiate and engage actively in rich kinds of learning processes, treat errors as opportunities to learn, and persist through challenges. It follows that, to foster SRL, we need to pay attention to nurturing motivation. As Zimmerman (2011) observed, based on his literature review:

> Interventions that relied only on cognitive strategies produced small effects, but interventions that emphasized motivational strategies or a combination of metacognitive and motivational strategies exerted large effects on students' overall academic attainments (p. 59).

Fortunately, there is much we can do as educators to inspire students' motivation and engagement in rich forms of learning and SRL.

In order to foster SRL, we need to pay attention to nurturing motivation and engagement.

Learning Intentions

After reading this chapter, you should be able to do the following:

LI 1 Describe different kinds of beliefs, values, and expectations that influence the quality of learners' motivation and engagement;

LI 2 Imagine how, by engaging in SRL–promoting practices, educators can inspire and sustain students' engagement in active learning and SRL.

ANCHORING OUR DISCUSSION

Throughout this book we have identified *motivation* as central to effective forms of SRL. For example, in Chapter 1 we defined *motivation* as a "broad term used to describe what drives individuals' willingness to invest and engage in activities." We also identified motivation as among the key dimensions of self-regulation (i.e., cognition and metacognition, emotion and *motivation*, and strategic action). In Chapter 2, we described how students need to self-regulate multiple aspects of their performance, including their *motivation*, if they are to engage effectively in SRL (e.g., if they are to sustain their engagement in learning through obstacles or boredom). Correspondingly, in Chapter 4, we emphasized the importance of students learning *how to* self-regulate their motivation as an essential goal in fostering SRL.

Across chapters, we have also introduced different kinds motivational beliefs, such as growth mindsets and self-efficacy perceptions, which influence the ways in which students engage in learning. In this chapter, we build from those previous discussions by considering a wider range of beliefs, values, and expectations that influence how learners take up activities. We also describe why SRL–promoting practices have such great potential to cultivate motivation.

WHAT IS MOTIVATION?

Students are always motivated. But the key question is, "What are they are motivated to do?" To consider that question, it might help to take a step back to think about the nature of and influences on motivation. What is motivation? What does motivation look like? What personal and environmental factors influence individuals' motivation to engage in different activities?

Students are always motivated. But the key question is, "What are they are motivated to do?"

Courtesy of Harv Craven

Figure 11-1 Imagining Lucy's Motivation

To help in addressing these questions, Figure 11-1 presents a picture of Lucy taken when she was visiting a popular tourist attraction with her family. Her father has just given her a map of the park, hoping to create a rich educational experience for his daughter. What does Lucy's motivation look like in this context? Does Lucy look excited about or interested in learning from her experiences at the park? Is she ready to throw herself enthusiastically into learning activities? Might she prefer to just run through the park without thinking too hard about it? Even if she's not all that interested, do you think she might go along with her father's wishes anyway (e.g., to make him happy)? If Lucy gives a couple of activities a try and ends up enjoying them, do you think she might develop interest in others? How do you think her motivation might be affected if she were to receive a colourful stamp (e.g., in a little booklet or passport) for completing each activity?

Or, for another perspective, Activity 11-1 invites you to identify situations and circumstances in which *you* feel motivated. What factors are associated with your "willingness to invest and engage in activities"?

> Activity 11-1
> # What Does Motivation Mean to You?

What does motivation mean to you? When and why do you feel motivated to engage in some kind of task or activity? Is it always necessary for you to be interested in an activity for you to make a significant effort? For what other reasons might you still do your best and engage willingly in an activity?

Given your responses to Activity 11-1, what did you notice about your own motivation? Did you identify times when you throw yourself into activities because you are *intrinsically* motivated to do so (e.g., for interest or enjoyment)? Are there occasions when you willingly engage in less-than-preferred activities because you think you *should* (e.g., your job requires it, it is good for your health, unwanted consequences may occur if you don't)? Did you identify times when you might want to take up an activity but don't, because you think it might be too difficult or you are afraid of looking foolish? Do you sometimes engage begrudgingly in an activity at first, only to develop genuine fondness for it over time?

When thinking about concrete examples, it doesn't take long to realize that motivation is complex. People take up actions for many different reasons (e.g., see Ryan & Deci, 2000). For example, based on just a single snapshot, such as Figure 11-1, it's not hard to imagine how Lucy's motivation might evolve through her time at the park, based on a combination of personal (e.g., interest) and environmental (e.g., her father's persuasion) factors. Similarly, if you reflect on your own experience, you can likely identify personal (e.g., interest, confidence, values) and environmental factors (e.g., who else is there, others' expectations on you, supports for you to be successful) that combine to influence your motivation.

MOTIVATION IN CONTEXT

How can educators nurture motivation and engagement? Students' motivation and engagement is partly a function of beliefs, values, and expectations they bring to activities. But classroom environments also play an important role in shaping learners' motivation. Indeed, in our integrative model of SRL (see Figure 1-2), we described how students' motivation and SRL depend on complex interactions between their experiences, strengths and challenges, knowledge, beliefs, and values and the many features of classrooms in which they are working. Thus, to consider how to inspire motivation, we need to think about how "what individuals bring to learning" interacts with the environments we create. Note here that motivation is not static; it ebbs and flows through activities. We also need to remember that not all learners experience and engage with activities in just the same way (Perry & Winne, 2004; Turner & Patrick, 2008).

> To consider how to inspire motivation, we need to think about how "what individuals bring to learning" interacts with the environments we create.

In this context, a pivotal question is: Where do motivationally charged beliefs, values, and expectations *come from*? The perspectives that children bring to classrooms are not just given to them at birth. Instead, they are shaped over time through their experiences in different environments and activities. Consciously or less consciously, students continuously construct and refine beliefs, values, and expectations related to learning and themselves as learners both within and outside of schools (Paris, Byrnes, & Paris, 2001). Fortunately, this means that educators can play an important role in helping students develop productive forms of beliefs, values, and expectations that influence their motivation.

BELIEFS, VALUES, AND EXPECTATIONS THAT INFLUENCE MOTIVATION

In previous chapters, we have mentioned some of the kinds of beliefs that learners bring to activities that influence their motivation and engagement, including *growth mindsets* and *self-efficacy*. But growth mindsets and self-efficacy are not the only kinds of beliefs, values, and expectations that can be linked to "self-regulated learners' display of personal initiative, perseverance and adaptive skill" (Zimmerman, 2011, p. 49). Indeed, researchers have identified all sorts of beliefs, values, and expectations that influence motivation (see Linnenbrink & Pintrich, 2003; Perry & Winne, 2004; Schommer, 1990; Zimmerman, 2011).

In Table 11-1 we list the most heavily researched of these, grouped roughly by common underlying themes. These include *epistemological beliefs*; *goal orientations and mindsets*; *interest*; *intrinsic/extrinsic motivation and task value*; and *outcome expectations, self-efficacy and causal attributions*. Our goal in this chapter is not to thoroughly review all of these ideas,

Table 11-1   Motivationally Charged Beliefs, Values, and Expectations

Beliefs, Values, and Expectations	Description in Relation to Motivation and SRL
Epistemological beliefs	**Epistemological beliefs** reflect individuals' assumptions about the nature of knowledge and how it is developed or learned (e.g., learning is "easy" or "hard"; knowledge is given or constructed) (Schommer, 1990).
Goal orientations	**Goal orientations** reflect the purposes students implicitly pursue in activities. **Learning (or mastery) goals** focus on advancing one's development and learning. They focus on personal progress and are associated with an *incremental* view of ability (i.e., as changeable). **Performance goals** focus on either gaining positive, or avoiding negative, judgments of one's competence by others. They are associated with *entity views* of ability (i.e., as fixed) (Dweck & Leggett, 1988; Pintrich, 1999; Zimmerman, 2011).
Mindsets	Like goal orientation, *mindsets* are linked to individuals' beliefs about ability and other personal qualities. **Growth mindsets** reflect beliefs that ability or personality can be cultivated and developed through effort. **Fixed mindsets** reflect beliefs that ability or aspects of personality are innate and unchangeable (Dweck, 2006, 2010).
Interest	**Interest** is "a psychological predisposition to re-engage with particular classes of objects, activities, and ideas" (Zimmerman, 2011, p. 51). It can be situational (i.e., emergent, based on qualities of a particular activity) or more enduring (i.e., reflected in choices and engagement over time) (Renninger & Hidi, 2002; Zimmerman, 2011).
Intrinsic and extrinsic motivation	**Intrinsic motivation** is self-determined, fully endorsed by the self, and grounded in one's interests in and enjoyment of an activity for its own sake. **Extrinsic motivation** is taken up when actions are instrumental to achieving goals. Extrinsic motivations can vary in locus of control (e.g., from compliance with external demands to taking up goals and actions aligned with one's sense of self) (Deci, Vallerand, Pelletier, & Ryan, 1991; Ryan & Deci, 2000; Zimmerman, 2011).
Task value	Expectancy-value theories link motivation to the value individuals associate with a given task. **Task value** refers to an individual's perceptions of the worth of a task given its intrinsic/personal value, importance, usefulness, and relative cost (Eccles, 2009; Wigfield & Eccles, 2000).
Outcome Expectations	Expectancy-value theories of motivation suggest perceptions of task value interact with *outcome expectations* to influence motivation. **Outcome expectations** reflect individuals' perceptions of what are likely outcomes, given their skills, characteristics, and competencies. Individuals' outcome expectations influence their actions (Eccles, 2009).
Self-efficacy	**Self-efficacy** beliefs reflect "personal judgments of one's capabilities to organize and execute courses of action to attain desired goals" (Zimmerman, 2000, p. 86). In contrast to outcome expectations, which reflect generalized expectations, self-efficacy perceptions reflect individuals' beliefs in their capacity to marshal resources to achieve desired outcomes in particular situations (Zimmerman, 2011).
Causal attributions	**Causal attributions** reflect the explanations one gives for outcomes (e.g., success or failure). They can vary in terms of the locus of origin (e.g., internal or external), stability (e.g., changeable or enduring), and control (e.g., within one's control or not) (Borkowski, 1992; Zimmerman, 2011).

Beliefs, Values, and Expectations That Influence Motivation

As you can see in Table 11-1, researchers have taken up many different lenses to view motivation. Even so, across all this complexity, can you discern any common themes or big picture ideas? If so, what do you notice?

which you may have encountered before. For more detail, interested readers will find useful references in Table 11-1. Instead, as we move through this chapter, we consider why and how these kinds of beliefs, values, and expectations play such an important role in learners' motivation and approaches to SRL.

Reading the literature on motivation can be daunting, particularly given the wide variety of beliefs, values, and expectations that have been identified as important. But, across all that complexity, we can pull away five important goals for educators interested in nurturing motivation. Motivation and engagement can be enhanced if we support learners to:

1. *understand learning and how it works for them and others;*
2. *develop growth mindsets;*
3. *find or develop their interests in activities;*
4. *take up autonomous forms of motivation;*
5. *build a sense of competence, confidence, and control over learning.*

In this section, we illustrate how SRL–promoting environments and practices can help in achieving these goals for learners.

Understanding Learning and How It Works for Themselves and Others

> *Learning this material takes me so much time! Everyone else can just read a chapter and remember everything! Why is this so hard for me?*

In her early research, Deb Butler conducted over 100 case studies of students who had not been successful through their school years but were trying again in post-secondary settings (see Butler, 1995, 1998). What struck her was how many of them were bringing unproductive beliefs about learning to activities when setting goals or judging their progress. For example, when she heard the quote above, Deb realized that this student held an underlying belief that was undermining her confidence and motivation, namely that everyone else learns quickly without much effort. This student didn't seem to recognize that learning takes time and is hard for everyone.

Deb was observing students' problematic *epistemological beliefs*, which reflected their understandings about the nature of knowledge and how it is developed or learned. For example, in Table 11-2 we list four kinds of epistemological beliefs that can influence students' approaches to learning (e.g., see Duell & Schommer-Aikins, 2001; Schommer, 1990, 1993; Schommer, Crouse, & Rhodes, 1992).

Table 11-2 Four Kinds of Epistemological Beliefs	
Beliefs about . . .	**Examples**
The degree to which effort is necessary to learn	Learning is easy; Learning is hard
How quickly knowledge is acquired	Learning takes time; Learning happens quickly
The certainty of knowledge that is learned	Knowledge is given; Knowledge is provisional, socially constructed, and developing
The complexity of knowledge	Topics are complex; There is one right answer

Understanding How Learning Works

Greg was a kindergarten student in Ms. Madelay's classroom. He found writing to be difficult, explaining that "most of my [writing is] bad." But he worked hard to improve his writing. He recognized that writing is hard for most people ("no one could do writing perfect"). In spite of his difficulties, he was willing to take on moderately challenging tasks. He valued feedback he received from his teacher and peers because it helped him improve. He expected that his writing would and could get better over time (from Perry & Winne, 2004).

Why do these kinds of beliefs matter? In SR Vignette 11-1 we describe Greg, a kindergarten student in Ms. Madelay's classroom. What kinds of beliefs about learning do you see in this example? How are they influencing Greg's engagement in learning?

Research has shown that productive *epistemological beliefs* are associated with greater motivation and SRL. For example, in SR Vignette 11-1, Greg was struggling with writing. But he believed that writing is hard for most people and takes time to learn. The result was that he was willing to invest time and effort in improving his skills. In contrast, Schommer and her colleagues found that students who believed that learning should progress quickly tended to use more-superficial strategies for studying. Students who believed learning should be simple, with one right answer, tended to be overconfident and have lower achievement.

What Educators Can Do: Nurturing Metacognition and Epistemological

Beliefs   Students' epistemological beliefs are linked to the *metacognitive knowledge* they construct over time about themselves, tasks, and learning processes. In earlier chapters, we explained how SRL–promoting practices foster students' development of metacognitive knowledge. Educators can use the very same practices to nurture students' construction of more-productive epistemological beliefs. The trick in this case is for educators to recognize the kinds of epistemological beliefs students bring to learning and to target them directly.

Taken together, students' metacognitive knowledge and epistemological beliefs reflect their understandings about learning and how it works for themselves and others.

How can educators nurture students' development of epistemological beliefs? First, educators can engage students in working with knowledge as something that is provisional, socially constructed, and developing rather than certain, fixed, or given. For example, in Chapter 5, we explained how SRL–supportive environments create *communities of learning* in which students are grappling together with the big ideas, often through collaborative, inquiry-based learning. In that environment, students have opportunities to experience how knowledge and learning are constructed through their efforts, over time. They can see where knowledge comes from (e.g., research, inquiry, reflection), and that it is something that is complex and evolving.

Similarly, in Chapter 7 we described how educators create opportunities for SRL when they engage students in activities that are "complex by design" (Perry, 2004, 2013). Complex activities work toward multiple goals, focus on large chunks of meaning, integrate across content areas, and extend over time. Within activities that incorporate these qualities, students are also more likely to experience knowledge and learning as challenging, complex, socially constructed, and developing.

Second, educators can design *supports* as well as *assessments* and *feedback* to stimulate students' active construction of metacognitive knowledge and epistemological beliefs. As we described in previous chapters, learners develop awareness of and knowledge about learning processes when educators:

- focus explicit attention on students' thinking and learning processes;

- engage students in dialogue about knowledge and learning;

- guide students' thinking in new or different ways; and

- support students to consolidate emerging knowledge and beliefs (i.e., by requiring them to articulate developing ideas).

Educators can create opportunities to uncover, discuss, challenge, and nurture students' development of metacognition and epistemological beliefs using these approaches.

Developing Growth Mindsets

In her hugely influential book, *Mindset: The New Psychology of Success*, Carol Dweck (2006) describes what led her to focus on *mindsets*. Early in her career, she observed students as they were grappling with a series of progressively more difficult puzzles. She noticed something unexpected, at least given her own past experience. She explains:

> Confronted with the hard puzzles, one ten-year-old boy pulled up his chair, rubbed his hands together, smacked his lips, and cried out, "I love a challenge!" Another, sweating away on these puzzles, looked up with a pleased expression and said with authority, "You know, I *was* hoping this would be informative!" *What's wrong with them?* I wondered. I always thought you coped with failure or you didn't cope with failure. I never thought anyone *loved* failure. Were these alien children or were they on to something? (Dweck, 2006, p. 3, emphasis in the original).

These boys confronted Dweck with an entirely new way of thinking, one focused more on growing abilities than on demonstrating competence. Over time, research has shown that students can take on either of two different types of mindsets when facing a learning activity. When students adopt a *growth mindset*, they view some aspect of their ability, competence, or personality as something that can be cultivated and developed. Students building from a growth mindset are more likely to welcome challenging tasks, persist through difficulty, and dive into rich, active forms of learning. The students enthused by the challenging puzzles in Dweck's early observations were bringing a growth mindset to that task. In contrast, students who work from a *fixed mindset* are more likely to focus on proving their intelligence or talent rather than on taking risks necessary to develop them. Dweck (2006) provides a compelling description of the focus taken up by these learners:

> Believing that your qualities are carved in stone—the fixed mindset—creates an urgency to prove yourself over and over. If you have only a certain amount of intelligence, a certain personality, and a certain moral character—well, then you'd better prove that you have a healthy dose of them. It simply wouldn't do to look or feel deficient in these most basic characteristics . . . Every situation is evaluated: *Will I succeed or fail? Will I look smart or dumb? Will I be accepted or rejected? Will I feel like a winner or a loser?* (p. 6, emphasis in the original).

Can you imagine how learners who bring a fixed mindset to a classroom might be reluctant to take on more challenging tasks, which might reveal gaps in their knowledge or skill? How easily discouraged are learners who think errors reflect low ability? Learners' motivation to take up and persist in active forms of learning and SRL depends on the mindsets they bring to, and develop within, learning environments.

> Learners' motivation to take up and persist in active forms of learning and SRL depends on the mindsets they bring to, and develop within, learning environments.

What Educators Can Do: Nurturing Growth Mindsets
How can educators support students' development of growth mindsets? In previous chapters, we described how educators foster growth mindsets when they:

- create positive, non-threatening *learning environments* in which all learners feel welcome, differences are celebrated, social comparisons are de-emphasized, and errors are framed as opportunities to learn (Chapter 5);

- design *activities* that extend over time and enable students to experience and observe growth in their progressive development of knowledge and skills (Chapter 7); and

- provide *supports* for students to engage in full cycles of strategic action, and in that context, observe dynamic connections between goals, actions taken, and personal progress (Chapter 8).

In addition, *assessment* and *feedback* practices have a powerful influence on students' mindsets. As Carol Dweck (2010) explains, "Praising students for the process they have engaged in—the effort they applied, the strategies they used, the choices they made, the persistence they displayed, and so on—yields more long-term benefits than telling them they are 'smart' when they succeed" (p. 18). Dweck's recommendations are to:

- praise process and growth when students succeed;
- give students constructive feedback when they struggle;
- consistently emphasize the value of challenge, not success;
- create opportunities for students to experience and reflect on their progress; and
- grade for growth.

Finally, when students say they cannot do something, Dweck recommends adding "yet." For example, if a student exclaims, "I can't understand this!" a growth-oriented response might be to reply, "You don't understand this *yet*."

Fostering Growth Mindsets: Examples

How might you get started, if you want to support students to develop growth mindsets? One excellent example is provided in SR Vignette 11-1. You might recall that, in this case, Greg was struggling with writing, but believed he could get better if he tried hard to do so. Before moving forward, we recommend you re-read that example. What do you notice about Greg's mindset in this case?

What did Mrs. Madelay do to foster growth mindsets among learners in her classroom (see Perry & Winne, 2004 for a fuller description)? Ms. Madelay created an SRL–promoting learning community. She engaged her students in complex reading and writing activities that included opportunities for choice-making, wove in opportunities and supports for SRL, and extended over time. Within that context, she consistently communicated that learning develops over time through effortful, strategic action. For example, she engaged Greg and his peers in thinking and learning about reading and writing strategies *as part of* activities, so they could recognize and experience links between strategies and progress. She explicitly spoke with students about how they were self-regulating their reading and writing processes (e.g., what tasks were asking them to do, where they would write, what strategies they might use and why, what they would do if they were "stuck"). She continually asked them questions about what they were choosing to do and why (e.g., what could you do? where could you look?).

Ms. Madelay also made sure learners who were struggling, like Greg, had access to supports from herself and peers that enabled them to participate productively in classroom-based activities as valued, full members of their learning community, all of whom make mistakes and are in the process of learning. She wove assessment practices into activities, and, in that context, engaged students in dialogue as they self-assessed progress, gave and interpreted constructive feedback, and built from errors to identify next steps.

What impact did these kinds of practices have on Greg's motivation and engagement? Even as a kindergartener Greg was developing motivationally charged beliefs, values, and expectations. Although Greg perceived his writing to be "bad," he believed that writing is hard for everyone (an *epistemological belief*). He also believed that writing competence develops over time (a *growth mindset*). The result was that Greg focused on improving his writing rather than proving his competence or avoiding embarrassment. Greg valued feedback because he thought it could help him improve. He was willing to work hard because, through his efforts, he believed his writing could and would get better.

As a second example, in Figure 11-2, we recreate a poster developed by Jennifer Ross to foster growth mindsets in her kindergarten classroom. Jenn developed this poster by adding to and modifying resources she found on Pinterest (see https://www.pinterest.com). She used this poster to help her students shift their thinking while working through activities in her classroom.

Instead of. . .	Try Thinking. . .
I'm not good at this	What am I missing?
I'm the best	I'm on the right track
I give up	I'll use some of the strategies we've learned
This is too hard	This will take some time and effort
I can't make this any better	I can always improve so I'll keep trying
I just can't do math	I'm going to train my brain in math
I made a mistake	Mistakes help me learn better
She's so smart; I will never be that smart	I'm going to figure out how she does it so I can try it!
It's good enough	It is really my best work?
Plan A didn't work	Good thing the alphabet has 25 more letters!

Figure 11-2 Fostering Growth Mindsets in a Kindergarten Classroom, by Jennifer Ross

Finding and Developing Interest

When you think of your own experience, you will likely recognize that there are some activities that you just like to do. These are activities that really *interest* you. You pursue them repeatedly because you enjoy them.

Interest is an important driver of motivation. Students who are interested in learning activities are more motivated to invest effort and energy in them (Hidi & Renninger, 2006). But, as educators know, students are not always intrinsically interested in learning activities assigned to them in school. Fortunately, as we discuss below, there are strategies educators can use to find and nurture students' development of interest (see Hidi & Renninger, 2006).

What Educators Can Do: Finding and Developing Interest   To ground our upcoming discussion, consider Renninger and Hidi's (2002) case of Sam, summarized briefly in SR Vignette 11-2. What do you notice about Sam's interests in this science project, both at the outset and over time?

What can educators do to incorporate and/or develop students' interests? First, educators can build opportunities for students to build their interests into activities. According to Renninger and Hidi (2002), educators need to establish tasks that are open-ended enough to both inspire motivation and invite substantial learning. Activities that are "complex by design" fit this bill perfectly (see Chapter 7). In complex tasks, learners have opportunities to find *something* intrinsically interesting, whether that be some aspect of content (e.g., when activities bridge content areas and focus on large chunks of meaning), some kind of process they might find enjoyable (e.g., if they have opportunities to represent their

> **SR Vignette 11-2**
> ## Finding and Developing Interest

Sam was a Grade 7 student working on a science project. He really enjoyed reading, but was not so interested in science. That said, he liked to explore "how things work." One day he was asked to work as a group in a science project with peers. He and his group had to care for an animal, write daily observations, conduct an experiment, and write a report. Sam ended up taking his group's turtle home on weekends because no one else could. At first he wasn't interested in the turtle, but over time, as he observed the turtle in various contexts (e.g., interacting with his cat, struggling to get to a water source), he warmed up to the project. For example, he brought soil in from his garden to build a ramp for the turtle. He even took the lead on writing the report (from Renninger & Hidi, 2002).

learning in different ways), or a particular way of working (e.g., when they have opportunities to work alone or with peers). In Sam's case, the project his teacher assigned enabled him to find interests within it (e.g., in how things work).

How can educators set the stage for interest development to unfold? Renninger and Hidi (2002) describe how his relatively complex science project created conditions that nurtured development of Sam's interest. Consistent with the SRL–promoting practices we have described, in this learning activity we see the following:

- Sam and his peers were provided with clear expectations but also considerable flexibility (e.g., in how to demonstrate their achievement of criteria in their report).
- Sam and his peers had opportunities to make choices (e.g., what animal to study, who to work with, how to design their experiment).
- Sam was encouraged and supported to follow his emerging curiosities.
- The activity sustained Sam's attention long enough for his interest in science to develop.
- Sam had opportunities to engage in both individual and social forms of learning.

Renninger and Hidi (2002) suggested that it was, "the combination of autonomy, opportunities to build knowledge, and interaction with peers and expert others that provided support for [Sam's] changed perception of science and may have paved the way for him to develop another individual interest" (p. 187).

Taking Up Autonomous Forms of Motivation

Students are more likely to willingly participate actively in activities if they feel that they are freely making choices about their engagement. In other words, it helps if they take up *autonomous forms of motivation* (Zimmerman, 2011).

What Are Autonomous Forms of Motivation?
According to *self-determination theory*, learners' motivation to engage in any given activity can be *intrinsic* or *extrinsic* (Deci et al., 1991; Ryan & Deci, 2000). When intrinsically motivated students take up actions because they are interesting or enjoyable. In this respect, intrinsic motivation is linked to *interest*. In contrast, when *extrinsically* motivated, students take up actions, not out of interest, but because they are necessary in achieving particular outcomes.

Whether motivation is intrinsic or extrinsic, what matters most is whether individuals perceive that they have some control over their thoughts and actions. When learners feel they are acting because they willing choose to do so, they are taking up **autonomous forms of motivation**. For example, when students are intrinsically motivated, they are choosing willingly to engage in activities out of interest or enjoyment.

Autonomous forms of motivation can be intrinsic or extrinsic. In either case, they reflect the extent to which individuals perceive that they have control over their thoughts and actions (i.e., whether they are willingly chosen).

But extrinsic motivations can vary in locus of control. For example, when reflecting on your own motivation, you may have noted times when you engage willingly (even whole-heartedly) in activities, not because they are inherently interesting or enjoyable, but because you genuinely believe they are important to achieving a goal (e.g., taking a less-than-interesting course required to gain knowledge you will need later). There are many goals and actions we choose to take up in day-to-day life because we want to live up to responsibilities we willingly assume; for example, as students, partners, parents, educators, or community members. Thus, according to self-determination theory, extrinsically motivated actions can range from *controlled* (e.g., compliance with external demands) to more *autonomous* (e.g., when individuals choose to take up goals or actions willingly).

The degree to which motivation is controlled or autonomous has an important influence on how individuals engage with any given activity. Individuals engage more enthusiastically in activities when motivation is intrinsic or autonomous (i.e., freely chosen). But when individuals perceive their actions as being *controlled* by others

Intrinsic Motivation and Rewards

When Angie was 7 years old, she went to visit her grandparents who lived across the country. She hadn't seen them since she was a toddler. She fell in love with them again right away and decided to write to them when she got home. When her grandparents wrote back, they sent Angie five dollars in their letter. Angie wrote once more, but when her grandparents again sent five dollars with their reply, she stopped writing to them. She didn't want her grandparents to think she was just writing them for the money.

(e.g., through external rewards or consequences), they are less likely to engage in those behaviours once external contingencies are removed. Thus, in educational contexts we need to attend carefully to how students perceive the *locus of control* for the actions they are taking.

How Do Rewards Fit In? Self-determination theory has sparked heated debates about the role of external contingencies, such as rewards or aversive consequences, in students' motivation and engagement (Deci et al., 1991; Ryan & Deci, 2000; Zimmerman, 2011). So, how do rewards fit in? To start thinking through that question, consider Angie's experiences as described in SR Vignette 11-3.

What does research say about the impact rewards have on learning and motivation? It seems that rewards can be useful in some situations, but only if used very carefully with close attention to both how students interpret them and, correspondingly, their short- and long-term influences on motivation and behaviour.

When can rewards be helpful? Research suggests that external rewards (e.g., praise, stickers, stamps) can support motivation and learning if students perceive them as supporting their learning or autonomy (Zimmerman, 2011). For example, consistent with our discussion of feedback in Chapter 9, if rewards direct learners' attention to important goals, their progress, or possible ways forward, then they can support their developing capacities as learners. Rewards can also help in jumpstarting students' interest in an activity, to get them going until a more enduring interest in or commitment to the activity develops.

However, research suggests that rewards can undermine intrinsic motivation (see Ryan & Deci, 2000). In other words, if individuals are engaging in an activity because they find it interesting or enjoyable, providing rewards can actually *reduce* the likelihood of their continuing in that activity. This happened in Angie's case, when her grandparents included money in their return correspondence. A simple act intended by her grandparents to thank Angie for writing had unanticipated consequences (i.e., Angie stopped writing). Thus, if educators set up rewards in classrooms, they need to be mindful of how learners might interpret them, and of the potential effect on their intrinsic motivation.

Finally, if students interpret rewards as aimed at *controlling* their behaviour, then rewards can have negative long-term consequences on learning, motivation, empowerment, and *self-regulation*. When students perceive rewards as controlling, they may comply, but they might also choose to rebel (Deci et al., 1991). Either way, individuals are not likely to maintain behaviours when rewards are removed. Thus, if the goal is to help students learn to *self-regulate* their learning, putting rewards in place is not likely to be helpful. It is better to support students to develop interest in or perceive the value of an activity (e.g., for achieving a longer-term goal). It is also important to help them *learn how to* self-regulate their thoughts and actions, building from more autonomous forms of motivation (Zimmerman, 2011).

In Starting Small 11-1, we describe how April Chan shifted her practice in order to nurture more autonomous forms of motivation in her young learners. Notice in this case how her students were taking ownership over their class goals and felt proud when they succeeded in helping others.

Rethinking Rewards by April Chan

This week in my [Grade 1] class, I thought a little bit about motivation (where does it come from? Internal versus external motivation? Does it have anything to do with one's locus of control?). As a class, we discussed the purpose of having a class goal. Two of my students said, "So we can learn," and "So that we can be better people." (It almost made me cry happy tears.) After having a class discussion about the purpose of goals and how we can become better by setting them, we decided to try one week without a class prize. We talked about how full our "buckets" would be, how full others' buckets would be, and how it would make us feel. At the end of each day, we had a short reflection time about how well we had accomplished our class goal. This week, our goal was to "do ground clean up and clean up the school for planet earth." At the end of the week, we had a class meeting to talk about how it made us feel when we worked toward our goal. Students generally responded positively, and were excited to tell their parents about how they had filled other people's buckets.

Building a Sense of Competence, Confidence, and Control over Learning

Students' sense of competence, confidence, and control over outcomes underlies many of the motivationally charged beliefs, values, and expectations so important to motivation and SRL, including *growth mindsets, outcome expectations, self-efficacy beliefs*, and *causal attributions* (Bandura, 1989, 1993; Borkowski, 1992; Wigfield & Eccles, 2002; Zimmerman, 2011). Students' beliefs that they can achieve valued goals are foundational to motivation and SRL. Why would learners invest time and energy in an activity if they have little faith in their capacity to achieve their goals? To foster motivation, educators need to help learners believe they can achieve valued outcomes through effortful, strategic action.

To foster motivation, educators need to help learners believe they can achieve valued outcomes through effortful, strategic action.

Thus, to foster motivation and SRL, it is critical for educators to nurture students' beliefs in their own capabilities to be successful (Bandura, 1993; Schunk & Zimmerman, 2006). Fortunately, there are many strategies educators can use to achieve this goal. In this section, we give just two important examples.

Supporting Choice-Making and Control over Challenge   Research suggests that when students can control the amount of challenge they are facing within activities, they feel more capable of achieving positive outcomes. Indeed, one of the benefits of offering choices within complex activities is that learners can make choices in ways that control the amount of challenge they experience (Perry, 2013). That said, students may require support to make good choices based on their particular strengths and needs. Thus, a first, powerful way to foster students' sense of competence, confidence, and control over learning is to provide *opportunities* and *supports* for students to *learn how to make choices* that enable them to learn effectively and control the amount of challenge they experience within activities.

Fostering Self-Efficacy   One of the most heavily researched motivational beliefs, particularly in relation to SRL, is *self-efficacy*. Bandura (1989) defined *self-efficacy* as "people's beliefs about their capabilities to exercise control over events that effect their own lives" (p. 1175). Self-efficacy is context dependent. Self-efficacy perceptions reflect a learner's belief that, "I can do this task in this situation" (Linnenbrink & Pintrich, 2003).

Research has consistently documented links between self-efficacy and learners' motivation, SRL, and achievement (Chen & Usher, 2012). Students who perceive themselves as capable of achieving a goal are more likely to take on tasks and persist through challenges. They work harder, use more cognitive and metacognitive strategies, and engage more effectively in monitoring progress and adapting outcomes (e.g., Borkowski & Muthukrishna, 1992; Schunk, 1994, 2008; Zimmerman, 2000). Thus, a second powerful way to nurture students' sense of competence, confidence, and control over outcomes is to foster their development of productive self-efficacy perceptions.

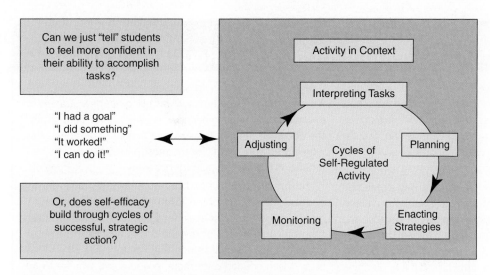

Figure 11-3 Where Does Self-Efficacy Come from?

How can educators support students' development of positive self-efficacy perceptions (e.g., see Bandura, 1997; Chen & Usher, 2012; Pajares, Johnson, & Usher, 2007; Zimmerman, 2000)? In cases when learners are relatively inexperienced or uncertain, then *verbal persuasion* or *vicarious experiences* can be influential. For example, when students are first learning a skill, educators can foster self-efficacy by offering growth-oriented encouragement (e.g., "you can learn to do this"). This kind of *verbal persuasion* can support learners' beliefs in their capacities to be successful. Furthermore, having opportunities to view someone else being successful in an activity can bolster learners' beliefs in their own capacities to succeed. This kind of *vicarious experience* is particularly helpful when students observe a "coping" model (ideally someone they perceive is like them), who successfully overcomes obstacles, rather than someone who performs the activity more expertly (i.e., a mastery model).

But research has consistently shown that the most powerful approach to fostering students' self-efficacy is through their own *enactive experiences*. That is, they need to develop self-efficacy based on their own experiences in activities. For example, Figure 11-3 depicts the conclusion Butler drew from more than 100 case studies (see Butler 1995, 1998, 2002). Butler found that, at least for learners who were struggling, verbal persuasion was insufficient in making them feel better about themselves as learners. They *knew* they were not achieving as they hoped. They were demoralized and pessimistic about their capabilities to do any better. Butler realized she needed to help them *experience* success to see and believe that they *could* achieve it.

Research has consistently found that individuals' personal experiences have the largest impact on the development of self-efficacy.

Thus, to help students develop self-efficacy, Butler put into place SRL–promoting practices of the sort we have described through this book. She worked side by side with students as they completed actual classroom work. In that context, she provided *supports* that guided their successful engagement in cycles of strategic action (e.g., using more or less direct forms of strategic questioning). Whenever students achieved a goal or improved, she supported them to explicitly notice the gain and account for why it occurred. In this way, across activities, she supported students to engage in cycles of strategic action, *experience success*, and then recognize how the outcomes resulted from the *actions they had selected and enacted to achieve them*. Encouragingly, one of the most powerful and consistent outcomes from Butler's sequence of studies was gains for students in self-efficacy perceptions.

Fostering Learners' Self-Efficacy: An Extended Example   To close this section, in SR Vignette 11-4 we provide an illustrative example drawn from one of Butler's first studies (Butler, 1995). As you read this example, what do you notice? What enabled Jennifer to more effectively mobilize her knowledge and skills, and ultimately, to be and feel more capable of being successful?

Fostering Jennifer's Development as a Self-Regulating Writer

Jennifer was an 18-year-old first-year university student who had been identified as having a learning disability during her school years. Although she had done well enough to get into university, Jennifer had consistently struggled with writing. So, she sought help from Deb just as she was starting at her new school.

In their first meeting, Jennifer described her writing as, "unorganized . . . choppy would be the best way to describe it." She said that, when getting ready to come to university, she had given up on a scholarship application because she couldn't "get her organization going." When Deb asked about writing strategies she drew on, Jennifer replied, "I write down my point and in the end I have a mess." Jennifer added that she had been taught "outlining" in school, but didn't find that helpful. She complained emphatically, "Outlining . . . outlining is stupid. I don't get outlining at all!"

Over the course of a year, Deb worked with Jennifer through a series of writing assignments, gradually fading her support across assignments as Jennifer became more independent. For each, Deb started by asking Jennifer to "interpret the assignment" so they were both crystal clear on what was expected. Deb noticed that Jennifer was adept at reading and interpreting available instructions to figure out what she needed to do in any given essay (e.g., the topic, how long, what audience, what kind of research, etc.). Jennifer also needed little support to gather, read, and make sense of information needed for each paper.

It was when she came to the actual writing process that Jennifer was paralyzed. Jennifer came to one session with a pile of notes from her research. She said she had no idea what she should do from there. So, Deb sat down with Jennifer to talk through how she might approach her writing. Jennifer relaxed when she realized that Deb was prepared to walk through the first assignment with her. To get going, Deb asked, "So, what do you think you could do?" Jennifer replied quickly, "Maybe I'll make a plan." Deb asked Jennifer how she might do that. Jennifer replied, "Well, I could start by writing down my main points." Deb nodded her head, suggesting that sounded like a good idea. Deb prompted Jennifer to try out her strategy to see if it could work. Jennifer started working while Deb watched, asking questions now and then to make sure Jennifer was thinking through her planning effectively (e.g., thinking back to the goals for the essay, linking to the research she was doing). Deb observed that Jennifer really needed very little assistance to identify well-targeted main ideas.

Once Jennifer had listed all of her main ideas, Deb asked, "What next?" Jennifer thought for a bit, then suggested, "Maybe I could take all my main points and break those down into a series of sub-points." Deb nodded again, agreeing that might be a reasonable approach to try. Once again, Jennifer got to work as Deb observed. Every now and then

Deb asked a question to surface Jennifer's thinking. She wanted to make sure Jennifer was using her new strategy in a way that was helping her to achieve her goals. Periodically, she also cued Jennifer to assess her actions (e.g., how is this working for you?). But, for the most part, Deb just watched Jennifer elaborate the plan for her essay.

Finally, once Jennifer had created a plan with main points and associated sub-points, Deb asked Jennifer, "What's next?" Jennifer thought again for some time, then suggested, "Maybe I'll take each of my sub-points and flesh them out into sentences. Then, if I string them all together, I'll have an essay." Deb nodded once more, encouraging Jennifer to try out her idea. Again, Deb mostly watched as Jennifer started working through her plan, asking questions intermittently to ensure that her approach was being effective.

Over time, as Jennifer developed and field-tested her new approach to writing, she articulated what she was doing, in her own words, on a personalized "strategy sheet." Deb explained that the purpose of the strategy sheet was for Jennifer to develop, try out, and keep a record of approaches *that were working for her*, that she could take forward to help her with writing into the future.

Jennifer started developing her planning strategy while working with Deb on her first essay. She refined her strategies with Deb through a couple of additional essays, and then wrote the rest of her assignments on her own. As the year unfolded, Jennifer was enormously pleased with the gains she was making. She was achieving B's and A's on writing assignments. She also reflected on gains she was making in her confidence as a writer:

> And then just the marks are a lot different. That, I feel like, you know, like, when you're walking around the class and we're getting our essays back, my marks are average or above average. So I feel better about it. Like, I don't feel like I'm such a dunce. (Butler, 1995, p. 186).

As she latched on to the value of her personalized strategies, Jennifer announced to Deb that she was getting better at other kinds of tasks, not just writing. For example, Jennifer found that, building from her new more-focused approach to writing, she was now also better at taking notes:

> I'm concentrating on flow, I can pick up on other people's flow now. So like, you know, the teacher's going on, I no longer write down like, scribbling madly about every single point he makes, but I can almost summarize . . . my note-taking is better now.

By the end of the year, Jennifer was just thrilled with the planning strategy she had developed to address her long-standing problems with writing. In their last meeting, she proclaimed, "Outlining . . . Outlining is stupid! But I don't know what I would do without my plans!"

Fostering Jennifer's Development as a Self-Regulating Writer

What do you notice in SR Vignette 11-4 about how Deb supported Jennifer's development as a self-regulating writer, and in that context, her construction of positive self-perceptions of competence and control? What kinds of knowledge and beliefs did Jennifer bring to this context? How did Deb support Jennifer to draw on her knowledge and skills more strategically and adaptively? How did Jennifer's thinking about herself as a learner and writer change over time?

MOTIVATING AND ENGAGING LEARNERS: NEXT STEPS

In this chapter, we have defined a wide range of beliefs, values, and expectations that learners bring to classrooms that influence motivation and engagement. While motivation is complex and multidimensional, hopefully you can start to see some common themes that underlie various concepts and theories. We pulled out five themes here for more in-depth exploration. Perhaps you noticed other important themes underlying our discussion of motivation and engagement.

One thing you might have realized through our discussion in this chapter is that SRL–promoting practices have great potential to achieve multiple positive outcomes all at once. For example, safe, supportive learning environments create conditions for nurturing productive *epistemological beliefs* and *growth mindsets*. When educators design activities that are complex by design, they provide opportunities for learners to find or develop their interests with them. When they engage students in talking about the purpose of learning, especially if that purpose is authentic and meaningful, then educators also foster learners' *autonomous motivation*. Finally, by supporting learners' engagement in cycles of strategic action, educators foster learners' construction of all sorts of valuable knowledge, beliefs, and expectations, including a growing sense of competence and control as learners.

To close this discussion, we invite you to think about motivation in your own experience or practice. Have you seen the kinds of beliefs, values, and expectations we discussed in this chapter in your own work with students? Have you observed their influence on motivation and engagement? What approaches are you using already to create environments and activities that motivate and engage learners? What more might you try? What more do you want to know?

Recommended Resources

Bandura, A. (1989). Human agency in social cognitive theory. *American Psychologist, 44*(9), 1175–1184.

Bandura, A. (1993). Perceived self-efficacy in cognitive development and functioning. *Educational Psychologist, 28*, 117–148.

Bandura, A. (1997). *Self-efficacy: The exercise of control*. New York: Freeman.

Borkowski, J. G. (1992). Metacognitive theory: A framework for teaching literacy, writing and math skills. *Journal of Learning Disabilities, 25*, 254–257.

Borkowski, J. G., & Muthukrishna, N. (1992). Moving metacognition into the classroom: "Working models" and effective strategy teaching. In M. Pressley, K. R. Harris, & J. T. Guthrie (Eds.), *Promoting academic competence and literacy in school* (pp. 477–501). Toronto: Academic Press.

Butler, D. L. (1995). Promoting strategic learning by postsecondary students with learning disabilities. *Journal of Learning Disabilities, 28*, 170–190.

Butler, D. L. (1998). The Strategic Content Learning approach to promoting self-regulated learning: A summary of three studies. *Journal of Educational Psychology*, *90*, 682–697.

Butler, D. L. (2002). Individualizing instruction in self-regulated learning. *Theory into Practice*, *41*(2), 81–92.

Chen, J. A., & Usher, E. L. (2012). Profiles of the sources of science self-efficacy. *Learning and Individual Differences*, *24*, 11–21.

Deci, E. L., Vallerand, R. J., Pelletier, L. G., & Ryan, R. M. (1991). Motivation and education: The self-determination perspective. *Educational Psychologist*, *26*(3&4), 325–346.

Duell, O. K., & Schommer-Aikins, M. (2001). Measures of people's beliefs about knowledge and learning. *Educational Psychology Review*, *13*(4), 419–449.

Dweck, C. S. (2006). *Mindset: The new psychology of success*. New York: Random House.

Dweck, C. S. (2010). Even geniuses work hard. *Educational Leadership, 68*(1), 16–20.

Dweck, C. S., & Leggett, E. L. (1988). A social-cognitive approach to motivation and personality. *Psychological Review*, *95*(2), 256–273.

Eccles, J. (2009). Who am I and what am I going to do with my life? Personal and collective identities as motivators of action. *Educational Psychologist*, *44*(2), 78–89.

Hidi, S., & Renninger, K. A. (2006). The four-phase model of interest development. *Educational Psychologist, 41*(2), 111–127.

Linnenbrink, E. A., & Pintrich, P. R. (2003). The role of self-efficacy beliefs in student engagement and learning in the classroom. *Reading and Writing Quarterly*, *19*, 119–137.

Pajares, F., Johnson, M. T., & Usher, E. L. (2007). Sources of writing self-efficacy beliefs of elementary, middle, and high school students. *Research in the Teaching of English*, *42*(1), 104–120.

Paris, S. G., Byrnes, J. P., & Paris, A. H. (2001). Constructing theories, identities, and actions of self-regulated learners. In B. Zimmerman and D. Schunk (Eds.), *Self-regulated learning and academic achievement: Theoretical perspectives* (2nd ed.) (pp. 253–287). Mahwah, NJ: Erlbaum.

Perry, N. E. (2004). Fostering self-regulated learning in exceptional students in general education classrooms. *Exceptionality Education Canada, 14*, 65–87.

Perry, N. E. (2013). Classroom processes that support self-regulation in young children [Monograph]. *British Journal of Educational Psychology, Monograph Series II: Psychological Aspects of Education—Current Trends, 10*, 45–68.

Perry, N. E., & Winne, P. H. (2004). Motivational messages from home and school: How do they influence young children's engagement in learning? In D. McInerney & S. Van Etten (Eds.), *Big theories revisited: Vol. IV: Research on sociocultural influences on motivation and learning* (pp. 199–222). Greenwich, CT: Information Age.

Pintrich, P. R. (1999). The role of motivation in promoting and sustaining self-regulated learning. *International Journal of Educational Research*, *31*, 459–470.

Renninger, K. A., & Hidi, S. (2002). Student interest and achievement: Developmental issues raised by a case study. In A. Wigfield & J. S. Eccles (Eds.), *Development of achievement motivation* (pp. 173–195). New York: Academic Press.

Ryan, R. M., & Deci, E. L. (2000). Self-determination theory and the facilitation of intrinsic motivation, social development, and well-being. *American Psychologist*, *55*(1), 68–78.

Schommer, M. (1990). The effects of beliefs about the nature of knowledge on comprehension. *Journal of Education Psychology*, *82*, 498–504.

Schommer, M. (1993). Epistemological development and academic performance among secondary students. *Journal of Education Psychology, 85*, 406–411.

Schommer, M., Crouse, A., & Rhodes, N. (1992). Epistemological beliefs and mathematical text comprehension: Believing it is simple does not make it so. *Journal of Educational Psychology*, *84*, 435–443.

Schunk, D. H. (1994). Self-regulation of self-efficacy and attributions in academic settings. In D. H. Schunk & B. J. Zimmerman (Eds.), *Self-regulation of learning and performance: Issues and educational applications* (pp. 75–99). Hillsdale, NJ: Erlbaum.

Schunk, D. (2008). Metacognition, self-regulation, and self-regulated learning: Research recommendations. *Educational Psychology Review*, *20*, 463–467.

Schunk, D. H., & Zimmerman, B. J. (2006). Competence and control beliefs: Distinguishing the means and ends. In P. A. Alexander & P. H. Winne (Eds.), *Handbook of educational psychology* (2nd ed.) (pp. 349–367). Mahwah, NJ: Erlbaum.

Turner, J. C., & Patrick, H. (2008). How does motivation develop and why does it change? Reframing motivational research. *Educational Psychologist*, *43*(3), 119–131.

Wigfield, A., & Eccles, J. S. (2000). Expectancy-value theory of motivation. *Contemporary Educational Psychology*, *25*, 68–81.

Wigfield, A., & Eccles, J. S. (2002). The development of competence beliefs, expectancies for success, and achievement values from childhood through adolescence. In A. Wigfield & J. S. Eccles (Eds.), *Development of achievement motivation* (pp. 91–120). San Diego, CA: Academic Press.

Zimmerman, B. J. (2000). Self-efficacy: An essential motive to learn. *Contemporary Educational Psychology*, *25*, 82–91.

Zimmerman, B. J. (2011). Motivational sources and outcomes of self-regulated learning and performance. In B. J. Zimmerman and D. H. Schunk (Eds.), *Handbook of self-regulation of learning and performance* (pp. 49–64). New York: Routledge.

Chapter 12
Empowering 21st-Century Learning

INTRODUCTION

In Part Three of this book, we are explaining how, by fostering the development of self-regulating learners, educators can effectively take up three key challenges facing them today. In Chapter 10, we started by explaining how nurturing SRL enables teachers to *meet the diverse needs of learners*. In Chapter 11, we described how SRL–promoting practices can help in *motivating and engaging learners*. In this final chapter, we consider how, by using SRL–promoting practices, educators can *empower 21st-century learning*.

Learning Intentions

After reading this chapter, you should be able to do the following:

LI 1 Describe how a focus on SRL can *empower* individuals to understand and navigate environments successfully, both while learning in classrooms and throughout their lives.

LI 2 Imagine how, by designing SRL–promoting environments and practices, educators can empower all students' development as *21st-century* learners.

The Promise of SRL in Empowering 21st-Century Learning

How can SRL–promoting environments and practices empower learners? What does empowerment look like? Why is it so important to empower learners to engage in the kinds of lifelong learning, critical thinking, creativity, and innovation associated with 21st-century learning? What kinds of practices are more or less likely to achieve that aim?

ANCHORING OUR DISCUSSION

In this last chapter, we consider how nurturing effective forms of SRL has great potential to empower 21st-century learning. Thus, to anchor our discussion, it will be helpful to link back to themes we have introduced related to both *empowerment* and *21st-century* learning.

What does SRL have to do with *empowerment*? Starting in Chapter 1, and throughout this book, we have framed our overarching goal as ensuring students understand how to navigate environments successfully *and* feel empowered to do so. For example, in Chapter 1, we emphasized that individuals can take and feel in control over success if they deliberately and reflectively self-regulate their engagement in activities.

In this chapter, we cycle back to this foundational idea. What does empowerment look like? How might SRL–promoting practices enable students to be, and feel, in control over their learning and performance, in and beyond school, both now and into the future? To address these questions, we consider empowerment from two perspectives. First, we describe relationships between *agency* and empowerment. Second, we explain how calls to enable *self-determination* fit with our goals to empower learning.

How might promoting SRL help in empowering *21st-century* learners? In Chapter 4 we argued that competencies associated with 21st-century learning comprise important goals we need to pursue as educators, given what learners today need to know to thrive in their lives post-school. In that context, we defined *21st-century learning* as "a constellation of knowledge and competencies required to thrive in today's rapidly-evolving, information-rich societies." We concluded that:

> Fostering 21st-century learning during the school years is necessary to prepare students to act as *lifelong, self-regulating* learners with adaptive expertise who can contribute to shaping the worlds in which they will live and work.

In this chapter, we illustrate the power of SRL–promoting environments and practices to empower 21st-century learning. We emphasize how supports for SRL not only enable students to navigate expectations in classrooms; they also empower individuals to take control over and push their learning forward in new and ever-emerging directions. By creating SRL–promoting environments, educators not only foster academic achievement in activities we imagine; they also inspire students' curiosity, creativity, critical thinking, and innovation.

WHAT DOES EMPOWERMENT LOOK LIKE?

What does empowerment "look like"? To address that question, we start by describing Tanya's experiences in high school. As you read SR Vignette 12-1, what do you notice about Tanya's *(dis)empowerment* as a 21st-century learner?

When Deb first met Tanya, she uncovered considerable strengths but also daunting challenges. Tanya was an exceptionally strong visual and conceptual learner. But Tanya had difficulties with phonological processing, "sounding out" words, and spelling. In fact, Deb realized that Tanya had learned to read by "brute force," relying almost completely on an extensive sight vocabulary coupled with her strong conceptual understanding. Tanya was very physical. Her one positive outlet in high school had been that she was on almost every sports team. But she had trouble sitting still for long periods, particularly when stressed or agitated, which was

What Does Empowerment Look Like?

Tanya[1] desperately wanted to go back to school. She had enrolled in a psychology course (on brain and behaviour) at a local college but was convinced she was going to fail. She was told she had "dyslexia" in Grade 10, but by that time she was so far behind that catching up seemed insurmountable. She only stuck it out through high school because one hugely supportive teacher had convinced her not to drop out. In that teacher's English class, Tanya had been given the opportunity to present her ideas visually and so actually got an "A" on an assignment. Tanya still carried that dog-eared assignment around with her. It helped her remember that she could succeed, if she were given a chance to show what she could do.

Tanya looked down at the chapter she was supposed to read in preparation for an upcoming test. She flipped through a couple of pages, sampled a paragraph full of complicated jargon, then flipped ahead to the end. As she did so, her mind wandered back to her experiences in high school. Tanya was excited about the chance to learn about neuropsychology. She had always been interested in science. In fact, she had always wanted to be a paediatrician. She still resented that she had always been excluded from science classes during high school because she couldn't read or spell well. She took years of wood working instead, which she liked, but did not help her in achieving her goals.

Tanya was actually surprised that she had even stuck it out through high school. Sure, she had loved playing on the basketball, volleyball, and softball teams, even if her school's uniforms were tattered compared to the carefully matched outfits worn by kids from the "right" part of town. In some courses she had made herself enough of a nuisance (i.e., as a class clown) for teachers to "push her through" rather than risk her coming back for a repeat of their class. For example, she had "gamed" her way through her French class without learning anything. By the end of the term, she and her teacher had come to a tacit agreement. He would give her a barely passing mark if she agreed never to take French again. But, overall, she thought she had encountered nothing but obstacles. As she sat there facing her textbook, she deeply regretted all that "prior learning loss" that was hampering her now.

Tanya so wished that her mother had helped her, or at least stood up for her. But when Tanya brought home less than stellar report cards, her mother's typical response had been, "Well, I guess there are no Einsteins in our family." Tanya tried to squash her recurring frustration on that point. She reminded herself that her mother worked long hours, late into the night, to support three children as a single parent. She had only completed up to Grade 8 herself in a one-room schoolhouse in a very small, rural community. She had been much too intimidated to step foot in a school, much less speak to Tanya's teachers.

Still, Tanya became increasingly agitated as she looked at the thick textbook in front of her. In a flash, she stood up and twisted her course textbook as if she were trying to tear it apart at the seams. When she couldn't rip through a large chunk of pages, she hurled the book across the room. She collapsed back into her chair, starting to shake. Eventually, after several minutes, she stood up, retrieved her book, and turned again to the first page.

[1]Tanya is a pseudonym.

pretty much any time she was asked to read or study. As Deb "watched her learn," she was frankly impressed by Tanya's creativity, quick wit, and analytic skills. But Tanya was adamant that she wasn't "smart." During school, she had found her classes to be slow and boring, thinking she understood everything that was said. But when it came to tests and assignments, she had never done well. So, Tanya didn't believe that she understood anything.

Deb reflected on why Tanya responded so strongly and emotionally to her reading assignment. Deb noticed that Tanya's assignments in college were very similar to ones she had struggled with during her school years (e.g., read and answer multiple choice or short answer questions on the material). Deb realized that Tanya cared deeply about going back to school and pursuing her dream to become a paediatrician or scientist, but was petrified she would fail

What Does Empowerment Look Like?

What are your first impressions of Tanya? Is Tanya motivated? How do you know? What do you notice about Tanya's sense of control over her life and learning? What do you think might be getting in the way of her success now? How might her experiences in school have better prepared her to be, and feel, empowered as a lifelong, 21st-century learner?

yet again. Tanya seemed to be hanging on to the one positive influence she had experienced during her school years—a teacher-turned-friend who had believed in her abilities and given her a faint ray of hope that there could be a "way out" from her repeated experiences of failure. Deb decided that she needed to help Tanya, not by solving problems for her but by *empowering* Tanya to learn how to fulfill and "see" her very real potential. Tanya needed to learn how to build from her considerable strengths to develop as an empowered 21st-century learner.

EMPOWERING LEARNERS

So, how can we understand dimensions of empowerment and how to support it? In this section, we take up that question from two perspectives. First we describe relationships between *agency* and empowerment. Second, we highlight insights from *self-determination theory* that can assist us in creating environments and practices that both motivate and empower learners.

Agency and Empowerment

What does empowerment look like? Our first answer is that learners are empowered when they have opportunities to exercise *agency* in their lives and learning. Bandura (1989) defined **agency** as, "the capacity to exercise control over one's own thought processes, motivation, and action" (p. 1175). When students exercise agency, they are "proactively engaged in their own development and can make things happen by their actions" (Pajares, Johnson, & Usher, 2007, p. 105). Individuals who exercise agency take control over their lives and learning. SRL–promoting practices help students learn how to exercise agency in productive ways.

> **Agency** refers to individuals' capacities to exercise control over their thoughts and actions in a particular situation.

Self-Efficacy   There are two complementary aspects to individuals' experience of agency in a given activity. First, according to Bandura (1989, 2006), an individual's experience of agency is strongly connected to their perceptions of *self-efficacy*. As we explained in Chapter 11, self-efficacy reflects individuals' beliefs in their capacity to achieve outcomes in particular situations (Zimmerman, 2011). When individuals believe in their personal capacities, they feel more empowered to achieve valued goals in real situations and activities. They are also more likely to take up activities, invest effort, and persist through challenges.

For example, in SR Vignette 12-1, Tanya had low perceptions of self-efficacy. To help her be and feel more successful, Deb used the kinds of SRL–promoting practices we have discussed throughout this book (e.g., see Chapter 8). What happened? Tanya started to see that she could achieve goals through the actions she was taking (i.e., she developed positive self-efficacy beliefs). She started taking on more challenging activities (e.g., a course on Shakespeare), investing time and energy in developing better learning strategies (e.g., when preparing for tests), and persevering through challenges (e.g., navigating complex ideas and terminology in her textbook on the brain and behaviour). As Tanya's belief in her ability to control outcomes strengthened, her stress levels also lowered and her anxiety was reduced.

Having a Voice   Second, agency also depends on an individual's sense of control, not just over their capacity to achieve goals (i.e., *self-efficacy* beliefs), but also on their perception that they have a *voice* in the direction their lives are taking (Butler, Schnellert, & MacNeil, 2015). For example, Tanya's sense of empowerment during high school was undermined when she was not allowed to take science classes, and, more generally, when she was excluded from opportunities to participate in rich, challenging forms of learning (e.g., in more advanced English classes). Unfortunately, although Tanya achieved an A grade in her college-level courses (psychology and English), she ultimately gave up on her dream of achieving a college degree. She just didn't believe that post-secondary environments, as designed at the time, created conditions supportive of her learning in ways that she *wanted* and needed.

What Educators Can Do: Empowering Learners   In sum, from an agency perspective, there are two layers to students' empowerment within learning environments. Students' perceptions of *self-efficacy* are among the most powerful engines underlying

> Learners are empowered when they have a voice in what they are learning, how they are learning, and how their learning is assessed.

motivation and engagement. But learners also benefit from having a *voice* in what they are learning, how they are learning, and how their learning is assessed.

The SRL–promoting practices we have outlined in this book are ideal for empowering learners in both of these ways. For example, as we have described throughout this book (e.g., see Chapter 11), SRL–promoting practices have a strong influence on learners' construction of *self-efficacy*, and, more generally, on their sense of control and competence as learners.

In addition, SRL–promoting practices create opportunities and supports for students to have a meaningful *voice* in what and how they are learning. Educators can do this by

- including students in co-constructing classroom norms, learning goals, and activities (see Chapter 5);

- engaging students in activities that are complex by design, especially those that include more open-ended, self-directed or experiential forms of learning (see Chapter 7; Dumont, Istance, & Benavides, 2012; Perry, 2013);

- providing opportunities and supports for students to make productive, meaningful choices (e.g., in topics, processes, how to represent learning) (see Chapters 6 and 7);

- supporting students to *learn how to* take deliberate, strategic control over learning across different kinds of activities and environments (see Chapter 8); and

- engaging students in on-going, dynamic forms of peer- and self-assessment (see Chapter 9).

Self-Determination Theory

Self-determination theory provides a second powerful lens for considering what it means to *empower* learners in classrooms (see Deci, Vallerand, Pelletier, & Ryan, 1991; Ryan & Deci, 2000; Zimmerman, 2011). Broadly speaking, there are two ways in which our thinking about empowerment can be informed by self-determination theory (see Figure 12-1). From different angles, researchers and educators have been drawing on self-determination theory to consider what it takes for students to take control over their lives and learning (i.e., so they are enabled to exercise *agency*), as well as the importance of students having a sense of control over the pathways their lives are taking (i.e., building *self-efficacy*, having a *voice* in their lives and learning).

Self-Determination Theory as a Theory of Motivation   First, as we described in Chapter 11, self-determination theory is often positioned as a theory of motivation (Deci et al., 1991). From that perspective, the theory suggests that, to empower learners, we need to *nurture autonomous forms of motivation* and create environments and activities in ways that *satisfy individuals' basic psychological needs* (see Figure 12-1).

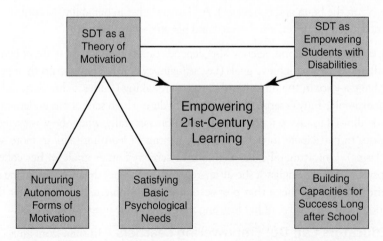

Figure 12-1 Self-Determination Theory (SDT) and Empowering Learners

Nurturing Autonomous Motivation. In Chapter 11 we explained how self-determination theorists differentiate between intrinsic and extrinsic motivation. To review, individuals who are intrinsically motivated choose to take up activities for their own sake, because they are interesting and enjoyable. Individuals who are extrinsically motivated take up actions to achieve some end. That end could be something that they feel is very important themselves, given their goals or the situation, or it could be something they feel compelled to do by others (or something in between). Whether intrinsically or extrinsically motivated, what matters is what learners perceive to be the *locus of control* for their actions. In more autonomous forms of motivation, students perceive themselves as willingly making the choice to engage in an activity because they believe it is important to do so. In these situations, students perceive themselves as having a *voice* or *agency* in their lives and learning.

In Chapter 11 we concluded that as educators, our task is not to compel learners to comply with expectations. Instead, our goal is to nurture agency and self-determination by inviting students to create, co-create, or at least make personally valued or relevant choices. We empower learners when we encourage and enable them to take up learning activities willingly, because *they* perceive them to be interesting, important, or valuable.

> We empower learners when we encourage and enable them to take up learning activities willingly, because they perceive them to be interesting, important, or valuable.

Satisfying Students' Basic Personal Needs. According to self-determination theory, we also motivate, engage, and empower learners when we create environments and use practices that help satisfy their three **basic psychological needs**; namely, for *competence*, *belonging*, and *autonomy*. According to Deci et al. (1991), individuals can only be fully self-determining to the extent that these three psychological needs are satisfied. Fortunately, the kinds of SRL–promoting practices we have described throughout this book have great potential to meet all of these requirements.

> **Basic psychological needs,** according to self-determination theory, include needs for competence, belonging, and autonomy. Individuals can only be fully self-determining to the extent that these three basic psychological needs are fulfilled.

First, SRL–promoting practices have outstanding potential to support learners' sense of *competence*. For example, linking back to our discussion of motivation (see Chapter 11), by fostering SRL educators can nurture learners' construction of the following:

- *growth mindsets*, as students start to believe their abilities can be improved;
- *self-efficacy*, as students see they can succeed through effortful, strategic action;
- *positive outcome expectations*, as students associate actions with outcomes;
- *productive attributions*, when students link success to factors within their control.

Overall, SRL–promoting practices consistently enhance not only achievement but also learners' self-perceptions of *competence* and control over their lives and learning.

Second, SRL–promoting environments are ideal for supporting learners' needs for *belonging*. In Chapter 5 we explained in detail how SRL–promoting environments create safe, supportive, non-threatening spaces for learning. They do that in part by nurturing the development of communities of learners in which all students feel welcome, differences are recognized and celebrated, learning is social, and members feel comfortable taking risks. Students can satisfy their needs for belonging in these kinds of positive learning environments.

Finally, and key in terms of empowering learners, SRL–promoting practices work particularly well in satisfying learners' need for *autonomy*. Not only do they provide *opportunities* for autonomy as a basic human need, but they also provide *supports* for students to *learn how to* exercise agency and autonomy productively within different kinds of activities. For example, building on SRL–promoting practices, educators can foster autonomy by the following:

- positioning students as owners of their learning;
- providing opportunities and supports for students to make good choices and decisions;
- deliberately bridging from guiding learning to fostering independence; and
- including learners in co-constructing learning goals and self-assessment.

Self-Determination Theory and Empowering Students with Disabilities

Above, we drew on self-determination theory as a theory of motivation in identifying the importance of nurturing *autonomous forms of motivation* and creating conditions through which learners' *basic psychological needs* can be met (see Figure 12-1). In this section, we build on self-determination theory from a second perspective, drawn from the special education literature.

As we described in Chapter 4, special educators have long drawn on self-determination theory to describe important competencies needed for lifelong success by individuals with disabilities. These capacities are essential for individuals to exercise agency and autonomy as lifelong, 21st-century learners both within and outside of schools. From a self-determination perspective, the following component skills are required to do that (see Figure 4-1):

- capacities to make decisions and solve problems (i.e., choice-making, decision-making, problem solving);

- knowledge, skills, and strategies needed to manage one's own performance (i.e., goal setting and attainment, self-instruction, self-observation and evaluation);

- self-awareness and self-advocacy (i.e., self-awareness, self-knowledge, self-advocacy, and leadership); and

- belief in one's own capacities to succeed (i.e., reflected in one's independence, risk taking and safety skills, personal sense of efficacy, and internal sense of control).

Students' development of competencies associated with self-determination is critically important, not only for students with disabilities, but for all of our students. All students need to know how to take deliberate control over their lives and learning.

In Chapter 4, we defined these, alongside a focus on 21st-century learning capacities, as among our big picture goals for learners in our classrooms. We also identified important connections with our focus on SRL. Finally, we stressed that students' development of these competencies is critically important, not only for students with disabilities, but for *all* of our students. All students need to know how to take deliberate control over their lives and learning.

Pulling It All Together: Empowering Learners

In this first part of Chapter 12, we have considered what empowerment looks like in classrooms from two broad perspectives. First, we have suggested that empowering learners requires that they have opportunities and supports to exercise agency, both by developing a belief in their capacity to control outcomes (i.e., *self-efficacy*) and by perceiving themselves as having a *voice* in how their lives and learning are unfolding. Second, we drew on self-determination theory to suggest that, to be empowered, learners need to be supported in taking up more *autonomous* forms of motivation, to live and work in environments in which their *basic psychological needs* can be met, and to develop the competencies necessary to be self-determining into their lives both within and outside of school.

The pedagogies we employ in classrooms can enable, or inadvertently constrain, learners' development as lifelong, empowered, 21st-century learners. For example, Tanya's experiences in her home, school, and college limited her opportunities to achieve her very real potential. In contrast, throughout this section and this book, we have described ways in which SRL–promoting environments and practices are ideal for empowering learners from both of these perspectives.

>> Food for Thought 12-3
Empowering Learners

Based on our discussion in this section, what are key dimensions of *empowerment*? What do you think it looks like for students to be "empowered"? How and why can designing SRL–promoting environments and practices help in fostering agency, self-determination, and empowerment? What kinds of classroom practices do you think would be less empowering, from students' perspectives? Why might empowering students be essential if our goal is to foster the development of 21st-century, lifelong learners?

EMPOWERING 21ST-CENTURY LEARNING

To succeed in the 21st-century, all individuals will face shifting conditions in workplaces and daily life that demand continual learning and adaptive expertise. The challenge for educators is to empower all students to reach their full potential as 21st-century learners (Chapter 4).

So far in this chapter, we have argued that empowered learners believe in their capacity to achieve valued outcomes (i.e., *self-efficacy*), perceive themselves as having a *voice* in their lives and learning, experience opportunities for all of their psychological needs to be met (e.g., for *competence, belonging,* and *autonomy*), and have developed the beliefs and capacities needed to be *self-determining* into adulthood. But, to thrive both inside and outside of schools, these empowered individuals also need to develop capacities required of *21st-century learners.* What is 21st-century learning? As we described in Chapter 4, 21st-century learning is typically associated with lifelong learning and self-direction; critical thinking and problem solving; effective communication, collaboration, and leadership; technological literacy; and creativity and innovation. You might notice in this list considerable overlap with capacities associated with self-determination (e.g., problem solving, managing one's own performance, leadership).

In the second half of this chapter, we illustrate how educators can build from the kinds of SRL–promoting practices we described throughout this book to foster learners' development of these important capacities. To ground that discussion, in Activity 12-1, we invite you to imagine how SRL–promoting practices can help in nurturing 21st-century learning.

⟩ Activity 12-1
Imagining How SRL–promoting Practices Can Nurture 21st-Century Learning

If you wanted to foster learners' development as 21st-century learners, what could you do? In this activity, we invite you to consider how the kinds of SRL–promoting practices we have identified throughout this book might help you in that regard. To that end, see if you can fill in the last column in Table 12-1.

How could you take up the SRL–promoting practices you have been learning about in order to nurture (a) *lifelong learning* and *self-direction*; (b) *critical thinking* and *problem solving*; (c) *effective communication, collaboration,* and *leadership*; (d) *technological literacy*; and/or (e) *creativity* and *innovation*?

Table 12-1 The Potential of SRL–Promoting Practices in Fostering 21st-Century Learning

SRL–Promoting Practices	What does that look like?	21st-Century Capacities Supported? How?
Creating safe and supportive learning environments	In *communities of learners* students are supported to engage in both individual and social forms of learning. They grapple with big ideas, both on their own and with others (Chapter 5).	
Designing activities that are complex by design	Educators can design *complex activities*; for example, by creating cross-curricular units, offering choices, requiring multiple kinds of processes, and encouraging learners to represent learning in multiple ways. These activities create rich opportunities for active learning and SRL (Chapter 7).	
Building supports for SRL into activities	Educators can build supports into activities for students to *learn how to learn*, and, more specifically, how to engage in more-effective forms of SRL. For example, they do this when they focus explicitly on learning processes and deliberately bridge from guided learning to fostering independence (Chapter 8).	
Designing SRL–promoting assessment and feedback practices	Educators can support students' engagement in all aspects of the assessment cycle, from defining goals and learning intentions, to peer and self-assessment and feedback, to deciding what's "next" (Chapter 9).	

Empowering Learning by Christy Catton

Once you start allowing the kids to question and to direct their own learning, it is amazing how they will take you in totally unexpected directions, if you let them go. I've often found the best and most insightful conversations in our class come from a student asking an unexpected question, something I hadn't thought of. I think it is more meaningful because the question stems from genuine interest and curiosity, not just a desire to get the answer the teacher was looking for.

SRL and Inquiry by Briana Adams

Overall, I was surprised that my young students were able to engage in inquiry but have realized that anything is possible with the right structure and level of instrumental support. The projects are now on display and I have had many other teachers ask if we did the projects with our big buddies. When I tell them that the students did them on their own, they can't believe it. What amazes me is the amount of learning, across subject areas, that I got out of my students without even trying. Since, they were so excited and motivated to act like scientists, and the amount of choice provided in the activity allowed them to be optimally challenged, they pushed themselves beyond what they would have done in any other, typical activity in my classroom.

Empowering 21st-Century Learning: Extended Examples

In the rest of this chapter, we give examples of how teachers have been using promising practices to empower 21st-century learning. While they may not have thought about or described their practice in those terms, in each example, see if you can identify *how* these educators are fostering 21st-century learning.

For example, in Starting Small 12-1, we offer two examples from our recent professional development projects. In each, a teacher was reflecting on what she had learned through her efforts to foster SRL in her classroom. In the first example, Christy Catton, an elementary school teacher, reflects on her experiences in supporting learners in her various classes. In the second, Briana Adams, a kindergarten teacher, describes what she observed when engaging her young kindergarten students in inquiry-based learning. As you read these brief reflections, what SRL–promoting practices do you see? What kinds of 21st-century capacities are these teachers noticing or developing in their young students?

A Classroom-Level Example: The Animal Adaptations Inquiry Project

In our next example, Dave Dunnigan describes how he involved his Grade 6/7 students in a complex activity in ways that pulled together the range of SRL–promoting practices we have identified in this book. As you read SR Vignette 12-2, what do you notice about the practices Dave was using? How was Dave fostering his students' sense of agency and self-determination? How were his students also developing capacities as 21st-century learners?

by Dave Dunnigan

This project was developed in conjunction with my then–teaching partner Terry Argotow. We began with a video provocation in which our two classes of students were shown a short video on the ways in which polar bears adapted to survive in an extreme environment. Following a group discussion, the project was presented to the students in a two-page handout (see Figure 12-2). Choice was provided within the structure of the project; four topics were provided to students, with the option to create their own topic should they so wish. Students also had the choice as to who to learn with (from either class), and also how they wished to present their learning. The most popular choice was a PowerPoint presentation, although some groups chose to use Prezi and others to create poster boards of their learning.

Part way through the research, we got the two classes together again to develop criteria for evaluation. Students were asked to contribute their ideas as to what would

NOVEMBER 5, 2013

SCIENCE 6/7

WEIRD AND WONDERFUL ADAPTATIONS	SURVIVING IN EXTREME ENVIRONMENTS	BIOLOGICAL BEHAVIOURS FOR SURVIVAL	HIDING IN PLAIN SIGHT
 Damian Ryszawy/Shutterstock	 outdoorsman/Shutterstock	 TessarTheTegu/Shutterstock	berdoulat jerome/Fotolia

ANIMAL ADAPTATIONS INQUIRY

Cathy Keifer/Fotolia

Welcome. . . to the amazing world of adaptations!

Living things are all adapted to surviving in the habitat and environment in which they live. These adaptations could be physical: body or plant parts, skin, fur, limbs, claws, thorns, etc. They could also be behavioural: the ways in which the animal has learned to behave in order to survive. Your task: to choose one of the titles above to prepare a presentation to your peers on the science of biological adaptation.

Don't forget that plants are also adapted to survive in their environments—you don't need to report only on animals!

Figure 12-2 The Animal Adaptations Inquiry Project

NOVEMBER 5, 2013   **SCIENCE 6/7**

How to Present Your Learning

You have a choice as to how your learning is presented to your
classmates. You may use a slideshow with explanations, PowerPoint,
poster or poster-board with pictures, or another method you think will
work: Let your teacher know.

Timeline for Completion

• Research completed and pictures printed by

_____

• Rough draft of text due by

_____

• Final copy typed or printed by

_____

• Presentation ready by

_____

Criteria for Success

As a group, we brainstormed the following criteria for a successful
project:

1. Information:

A. should have some depth and detail to explain the
adaptation, beyond a "one-liner." You should have 7–10 examples.

B. should have variety and originality. Something that surprises us in
some way, a unique adaptation or creature.

C. Visuals present the animal and adaptation in a clear way, which
may be in colour where necessary and effective.

2. Presentation:

D. Is engaging to the audience

E. In words the presenters and audience understand, clearly stated

F. Organized to make it easy for the audience to follow.

Your project must include the
following: the "Givens"

Key visuals

Several examples

Organized in a way that makes
sense

Your name(s)

Jon Berkeley/Alamy

kyslynskyy/Fotolia

BorisVian/Shutterstock

dg/Fotolia

Figure 12-2   (*continued*)

Science 6/7: Animal Adaptations

Names: _____ *Topic:* _____

PLO: Analyze how different organisms adapt to their environments

	Fully Meeting Expectations/Exceeding Expectations	Meeting	Minimally Meeting	Approaching
Analysis of Adaptations	• 7–10 adaptations identified and analyzed in a way that shows deep understanding of how the adaptation helps the organism survive	• 7–10 adaptations identified and analyzed in a clear way connected to the survival of the organism	• 7–10 adaptations with some analysis and connection to survival	• Fewer than 7 organisms, may have difficulty identifying and connecting adaptations to survival
Visual Impact	• Visuals present the adaptation in a powerful way that adds to the analysis	• Visuals are clear and connected to the analysis	• Visuals connect to the analysis in most cases	• Visuals reflect the organism, may not be clear how they connect to analysis
Engaging Presentation	• Engages audience throughout presentation; may use props, humour, and other effective presentation techniques to maintain interest	• Engages audience through most of presentation, uses presentation techniques to maintain interest	• Generally engaging, attempts to use presentation techniques to engage with some success	• Some attempt to engage audience, effective in part

Note: PLO = prescribed learning outcome from the provincial curricula in British Columbia.

Figure 12-3   Co-Constructed Criteria for the Animal Adaptations Project

constitute an excellent or deep understanding of the topic they had chosen; from this list, we categorized their ideas into two categories with supporting details. Presentations were then evaluated both by peers and teachers using rubrics based on the student-generated criteria (see Figure 12-3).

Not only was student engagement and motivation very high in both classes, Terry and I both noted how successful a learning experience the project was for our students, particularly those who have struggled with maintaining their engagement with other school assignments.

In Activity 12-2 we invite you to identify ways in which Dave Dunnigan's animal adaptations inquiry project created opportunities, and supports, for his Grade 6/7 students' development as empowered, 21st-century learners.

A School-Level Example: Creating a New Learning Environment for Grade 8 Students   In SR Vignette 12-3, we give a more ambitious example. Here we describe how a team of teachers worked to reshape structures and practices within their school. Again, as you read we invite you to consider how the practices they put in place created opportunities and supports for students' development as empowered, 21st-century learners. As you read through this example, it might help to refer back to the goals we summarized in Table 12-2 (see Activity 12-2).

>Activity 12-2
The Animal Adaptations Inquiry Project

To help you "see" the promising practices integrated into Dave Dunnigan's animal adaptations inquiry project, we invite you to fill in column two in Table 12-2. As you consider goals associated with empowering 21st-century learning (in column 1), can you see connections and overlaps across ideas being discussed from varying perspectives (e.g., about agency, self-determination, and 21st-century learning)? What do you notice about how practices Dave is using can help in achieving multiple key goals simultaneously?

Table 12-2 Fostering the Development of Empowered, 21st-Century Learners	
To empower 21st-century learning. . .	**What do you notice in this example?**
Create opportunities and supports for learners to build *self-efficacy* and exercise *agency*	
Foster *autonomous forms of motivation*	
Enable students to meet three psychological needs (*competence, belonging, autonomy*)	
Create opportunities for students to build capacities associated with *self-determination* (making decisions and solving problems; constructing knowledge, skills, and strategies needed to manage one's own performance; self-awareness and self-advocacy; belief in one's own capacities to succeed)	
Create opportunities for students to build capacities associated with *21st-century learning* (e.g., *lifelong learning, self-direction, critical thinking, problem solving, communication, collaboration, leadership, technological literacy, creativity, innovation*)	

Creating a New Learning Environment for Students as They Transition into Secondary Schools

Paul Britton and his colleagues wanted to create richer learning experiences for students transitioning from elementary schools into their Grade 8–12 secondary school. They recognized a need to make significant changes if they wanted to better meet the needs of their very diverse learners. Most troubling was that an increasing number of their students were failing courses in their Grade 8 year. New students were clearly finding it difficult to navigate expectations in their secondary-level learning environment.

Overall, the student body at Paul's school was very diverse—socioeconomically, culturally, linguistically, and academically. Their expanding French immersion program had grown to include 60 percent of their Grade 8 student population. At the same time, their English language program was shrinking. The school staff was struggling to assess and accommodate the substantial differences in experience, strengths, challenges, interests, and skills their entering Grade 8 students were bringing to the school. Too many students were failing to thrive, feeling disconnected, and questioning their ability to succeed in secondary school. The school staff feared that these students were vulnerable, both for taking up risky behaviours and for disengaging from formal education.

Creating a New Learning Environment for Grade 8 Students

Paul and his colleagues wanted to disrupt these trends and create more positive learning pathways for their very diverse students. Their goals were to ease students' transition into the high school learning environment, better assess and address their students' wide-ranging needs, increase learners' motivation and engagement, foster students' sense of competence and control over learning, and engage students in richer forms of learning.

At the time they started this change initiative, their school was structured in a relatively "traditional" block system in which students attended eight different classes with eight different teachers. In the spring of 2012, the school decided to replace this traditional structure with a newly envisioned junior academy for just their Grade 8 students. To design the new academy, the school's vice principal, Jackie Kersey, called on department heads to be part of a visioning exercise led by Paul, the science department head and professional development chair. The team was given time to develop a foundational model and associated philosophy.

Together they envisioned creating a community of learners within which entering Grade 8 students could take up all of their core subjects (English, social studies, science, and math) using an integrated project-based model. With this vision in mind, they started to imagine how to make the new junior academy work as a flexible, responsive, dynamic, and integrated learning opportunity within the school's rigid block-oriented system. In Figure 12-4 we summarize the structure that the school team decided to try out. Eventually, they decided to start small by revising the program just for the incoming cohort of 66 English-language program students.

Designing New Practices Once the overall structure was in place, the team started to plan activities through which they could coordinate and integrate across curricular areas using a project-based model. To that end, they created thematic units that would allow teachers to cover multiple learning outcomes related to a big idea. They then worked to design activities and explorations that would (1) encourage the formation of a learning community, (2) enable them to assess students' strengths and needs, and (3) foster students' development of both content knowledge and foundational inquiry skills.

In this vignette, we describe the teachers' first attempt at curricular integration in a project that brought together goals from across science, math, social studies, and language arts

Semester 1

Period	Programming	
1	Jr. Academy	Core (English, Math, Science, Socials + Health and Careers)
2		
3		
4	Language course **Jr. Acad. Teacher common prep.**	French, Okanagan Language, Learning Skills

Semester 2

Period	Programming	
1	Jr. Academy	Core (English, Math, Science, Social)
2	Gr. 8 Elective	
3	Gr. 8 Elective	
4	Gr. 8 Elective	

Figure 12-4 An Infrastructure for Co-Planning an Integrated Curriculum

curricula. They were inspired by a British Columbia Institute of Technology (BCIT) project that had encouraged teams to build basic submersible remotely operated vehicles (ROVs) as part of an extracurricular program for high school students. With permission from BCIT, Paul and his colleagues adapted the BCIT project to design an activity that would engage their Grade 8 students in inquiry processes while designing, building, and field-testing ROVs. To complement the math–science focus in the original BCIT project, the team added curricular objectives from social studies (e.g., by adding in societal and geographic considerations) and language arts (e.g., by engaging students in intensive reading and writing of informational texts).

In Figure 12-5 we present the activity as it was initially assigned to students. Notice that an "authentic" problem was framed within the context of a BC company on the cutting edge of underwater investigation (Nuytco); that students were charged with creating an affordable method of underwater exploration for the developing world, for this company; and that, for this first inquiry project, students were provided with

a procedural facilitator to support their engagement in inquiry processes (see Chapter 8). Because students were likely new to inquiry, the teachers wanted to help them learn how to engage creatively and flexibly in strategic action cycles as they engaged with an authentic design problem. Furthermore, as students made plans and designed their submarines, the teachers supported them to seek out, co-construct, coordinate, and adaptively mobilize knowledge about density, buoyancy, and pressure (from the science curriculum) and about scale, ratios, and 3-D drawings (from the math curriculum).

Students' Engagement in Learning How were students engaged in new ways of learning through this inquiry-oriented activity? Students started by working in small groups to interpret the project and brainstorm what they might need (e.g., to learn, to do), building on their combined knowledge and experience. In subsequent weeks, students were supported to build and mobilize their learning about science and math through an "engineering design" process.

Submarine Project

Phil Nuytten and Nuytco has recently asked you to submit a proposal for the design and build of a low budget Submersible ROV to be used by the developing world for exploration of underwater environments. These may be used for a variety of jobs (mining exploration, oil discovery, scientific research, repair and maintenance of ships and underwater equipment.)

Nuytco will pay close attention to all aspects of your work and will expect a prototype to be built and operational by September 27.

Constraints for project:
- Equipment:
- 8 elbows
- 6 T's
- ½ inch PVC pipe
- light diffuser (grid material)
- 3 modified bilge pumps and wiring harness
- zap straps
- foam (buoyancy)
- Washers for weight
- Any extra materials must be recycled or not cost anything
- Size: must fit in provided tubs
- Must be able to move forward, turn, and go up and down
- Must be able to attach equipment/payload (camera)

Please complete the following steps:

1. What types of tasks can our submarine do? (collect samples?, collect temperature?, find depth?, observe aquatic life?...)

   _____

   _____

2. Is the data quantitative (a measurement) or qualitative (an observation)?

   _____

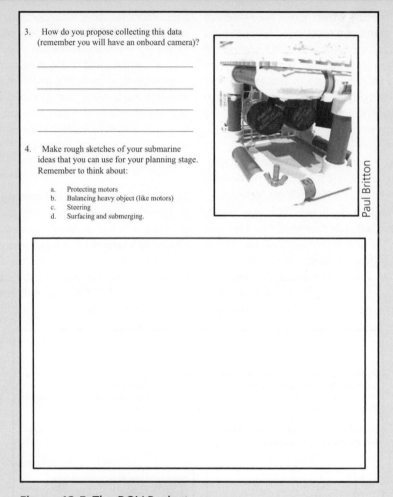

Figure 12-5 The ROV Project

In some lessons, students were assisted to think through the requirements of the problem (planning and engineering). In other lessons, students were assisted to gather and digest information they would need en route to creating and testing solutions. As students worked recursively through these processes, they discovered new dimensions of the project that they had to consider in their design process.

Across lessons, all student groups were supported to build, test, and refine ROVs. However, Paul and his colleagues noticed that students preferred to work through the project in different ways. Some worked through a more linear process by collecting ideas, formulating a plan, and then acting on that plan. Others liked to start by creating a rough design and then honing it over time. The teachers also noticed that many students were more comfortable with straightforward, structured, and heavily guided approaches for learning and assessment. These students were reluctant to express themselves in more creative ways or to take risks during classroom activities. Thus, Paul and his colleagues

realized that they needed to work hard to create a safe environment within which challenges and mistakes were framed as a natural and important part of exploration, inquiry, and learning.

Once student groups had prototypes of their ROVs in hand, they tested them in the back of a pickup truck where the bed had been lined with a tarp and filled with water. Paul and his colleagues noticed that many initially reluctant students joined in quite actively when it came time to test their designs for the first time. Furthermore, as students observed their ROVs working, with varying degrees of success, they seemed inspired to debug design flaws and create refinements. By the time students were ready for their maiden voyage of their ROVs in a lake, all student groups had created plans and a functional ROV that combined to demonstrate their knowledge of key concepts in science and math. Students also had a thorough understanding about how their ROVs operated. They were able to undertake very creative onsite repairs and adjustments. The teachers were also delighted when students decided to extend their learning in small groups when asked, "Now what?" As a follow-up to their ROV project, the class initiated and co-designed a new, independent project on water.

Reflections on the Promise of Integrated, Problem-Based Learning Paul and his colleagues experienced some challenges when designing and enacting their open-ended, inquiry-based project, particularly because students were given a great deal of choice. For example, logistical challenges arose when students preferred different amounts of structure or chose to work through the project in different sequences (e.g., in when and how to make water-based ROV trials available as students wanted or needed them). Building from what they learned through this first activity, in subsequent open-ended projects the teachers ensured that options were available for students to proceed through projects in different ways and with more or less structure and scaffolding. They also worked carefully to assist students in making productive choices about how much independence or support they might need (i.e., to control the level of challenge they were experiencing). For example, if students seemed to be avoiding risks, they were encouraged to take on more independent forms of learning. In other cases, students were encouraged to access support if they were floundering. Over time, they also found ways to help students understand and navigate their own learning, comfort, and frustration "zones" (see Kuypers, 2011).

The changes that Paul and his colleagues are making are clearly still "works in progress." Yet, Paul and his colleagues have already learned a great deal from their experiences in this change initiative, particularly about the potential of integrated, project-based learning frameworks for empowering rich forms of engagement and learning. Some of their early conclusions have been as follows:

- Project-based learning can be an invaluable tool for meeting the needs of diverse learners. The choices and opportunities for self-discovery created in these kinds of open-ended learning environments allow students to work on similar content at the level they are capable of while pushing them to learn in new and dynamic ways. Having choices enables students to learn to the best of their abilities and to celebrate their strengths.

- Learning in open-ended activities is enhanced when students are asked to communicate their learning in some kind of public forum. Being required to share projects (formatively and at the end) both encourages accountability and creates an opportunity for students to learn from one another and further their understanding.

- Students need opportunities to access different levels of support, dynamically, within project-based learning activities. Paul and his colleagues observed that some students were reassured by more-structured teaching approaches. When they could access predictable, structured forms of teaching, these students became more confident in their discoveries, which bolstered their confidence to explore further.

- Engaging students in collaborative, project-based learning can also support students' social-emotional needs in times of transition. In this project, Paul and his colleagues observed a notable reduction in office referrals and unexcused absences among their Grade 8 students. Furthermore, by working as a collaborative team, teachers were better able to get to know students, provide positive behaviour support, and scaffold supports for students' development of effective forms of SRL.

Empowering 21st-Century Learning: Reflections

In SR Vignette 12-3, Paul and his team had the opportunity not only to embed SRL–promoting activities into their classrooms but also to reshape the entire way in which curricula were presented to their Grade 8 students. Paul and his colleagues seized the opportunity to completely redesign students' learning environments and experiences. In so doing, they created opportunities to foster students' development as empowered, 21st-century learners.

> Food for Thought 12-4
> # Empowering 21st-Century Learning

What struck you as you read about the efforts of Paul and his team to restructure students' learning experiences at his school? How might the changes they made help them to achieve their goal to motivate, engage, and empower learners? Do you think their approaches had promise to nurture learners' development of capacities necessary to empower 21st-century learning (see Activity 12-2)? What do you wonder? What might you try?

First, consider how the incoming Grade 8 students might start to feel empowered in this new learning context. Paul and his team deliberately created opportunities for students to exercise agency. For example, they deliberately fostered students' sense of competence and control over learning (e.g., perceptions of *self-efficacy*). To that end, they built in supports so that students could be successful in visioning, planning, building, testing, and adaptively refining actual ROVs that they tested in water (a pickup truck, a lake). When students could experience and "see" their own success in what was clearly a challenging task, one that required adaptive mobilization of knowledge in both science and math, imagine how their sense of their own capabilities grew. Also, students clearly had a *voice* in how their learning unfolded. While in this first activity all students shared a common goal of building ROVs, many choices were built into the activity, enabling students to control their learning through that experience. Over time, as students further built their inquiry skills, Paul and his team bridged to more open-ended, project-based activities through which students could also choose their own learning goals (e.g., as students did when they decided they wanted to develop and engage in a new water-based project as a follow-up to the ROV project).

Furthermore, Paul and his colleagues created an environment that encouraged self-determination and autonomous forms of motivation. For example, they nurtured students' interest in the activity (i.e., to foster intrinsic motivation). They did this by providing choices, supporting students to work with peers, and engaging them in field testing and refining actual ROVs. Paul and his team encouraged students to see the value and meaning in the activity by linking it to a real-world problem. They also helped students experience the real-world value of science and math concepts as they mobilized those concepts adaptively in a practical application.

Students could also engage more comfortably in self-determined forms of action, because Paul and his colleagues carefully defined and nurtured their ability to fulfill basic personal needs. To meet students' needs for *belonging*, they created a collaborative classroom community in which students learned together; shared and built from each other's knowledge, strengths, and skills; could feel free to be themselves and learn in their own ways; and where mistakes were framed as a necessary part of learning. To help students develop and witness their own *competence* as learners, they enabled students to experience and reflect on progress in relation to the actions they were taking (e.g., as their ROV designs improved over time). Finally, they empowered learners by offering opportunities for, and supporting, *autonomy* (e.g., choices, decision-making).

Second, we also observe great potential in Paul and his colleagues' practices in terms of fostering students' development of key competencies associated with both *self-determination* and *21st-century learning*. For example, consider the potential of the practices Paul and his colleagues developed to foster rich forms of problem solving, critical thinking, creativity, and innovation. As they grappled with a real design problem, even in this very first, more-guided activity, students had to engage in goal directed problem solving. They had to interpret the design problem; assess their existing knowledge and what more they needed to know; mobilize knowledge to plan, enact, and refine their designs and prototypes; and think on their feet when problems arose. Students also developed *adaptive expertise* as they had to mobilize knowledge flexibly and adaptively through iterative cycles of goal setting, planning/designing, building and testing, and refining. By supporting students' engagement in these rich forms of learning and thinking, Paul and his colleagues contributed to their students' development as self-regulating, self-determining, lifelong learners.

Of course, as is the case when trying any new initiative, Paul and his team encountered some very real obstacles when trying to make such a substantial change to how teaching and learning was structured at their school. For example, they were challenged to fit a more-integrated model into their school's restrictive block scheduling (of classes, of teaching assignments). They were challenged to build activities that accommodated students' needs for both flexibility and structure. Over time, they have been working to refine their goals and practices so as to better achieve their goals and meet students' needs. But, by starting out with a smaller pilot, they gave themselves the space to try out new ideas and explore possibilities. By treating setbacks as an integral part of innovation, they too are treating their challenges as "opportunities to improve and learn."

EMPOWERING 21ST-CENTURY LEARNING: NEXT STEPS

In this chapter, we have described and illustrated how educators can design SRL–promoting environments and practices so as to empower students and nurture 21st-century learning. As we close this section, and Part Three of this book, we invite you to reflect on what you have learned by engaging with the ideas and examples in this chapter. What can you take away that you might draw on for your further learning or practice? What could you do to empower 21st-century learning in your context? What are you doing already? What do you wonder?

Finally, what is next for you? As you contemplate that final question, we encourage you to turn to the Epilogue, where we describe possible next steps for you, should you be interested in taking up ideas you've been working with throughout this book in your own work with students.

Recommended Resources

Bandura, A. (1989). Human agency in social cognitive theory. *American Psychologist, 44*(9), 1175–1184.

Bandura, A. (2006). Toward a psychology of human agency. *Perspectives on Psychological Science, 1*(2), 164–180.

Butler, D. L., Schnellert, L., & MacNeil, K. (2015). Collaborative inquiry and distributed agency in educational change: A case study of a multi-level community of inquiry. *Journal of Educational Change*, 16(1), 1–26.

Deci, E. L., Vallerand, R. J., Pelletier, L. G., & Ryan, R. M. (1991). Motivation and education: The self-determination perspective. *Educational Psychologist, 26*(3&4), 325–346.

Dumont, H., Istance, D., & Benavides, F. (Eds.) (2012). The nature of learning: Using research to inspire practice. Practitioner Guide from the Innovative Learning Environments Project. OECD: Centre for Educational Research and Innovation.

Kuypers, L. M. (2011). *The zones of regulation*. San Jose, CA: Social Thinking Publishing.

Pajares, F., Johnson, M. T., & Usher, E. L. (2007). Sources of writing self-efficacy beliefs of elementary, middle, and high school students. *Research in the Teaching of English, 42*(1), 104–120.

Perry, N. E. (2013). Classroom processes that support self-regulation in young children. *British Journal of Educational Psychology, Monograph Series II: Psychological Aspects of Education—Current Trends, 10*, 45–68.

Ryan, R. M., & Deci, E. L. (2000). Self-determination theory and the facilitation of intrinsic motivation, social development, and well-being. *American Psychologist, 55*(1), 68–78.

Zimmerman, B. J. (2011). Motivational sources and outcomes of self-regulated learning and performance. In B. J. Zimmerman and D. H. Schunk (Eds.), *Handbook of self-regulation of learning and performance* (pp. 49–64). New York: Routledge

Epilogue
Working Collaboratively to Foster the Development of Self-Regulating Learners

WHAT'S NEXT?

We wrote this book for educators who were interested in learning more about highly effective approaches to teaching and learning and wondered where *self-regulated learning* (SRL) fit into this aim. Across sections of the book, we identified why it is so important to foster SRL in schools (Part One), provided rich descriptions of guidelines and practices for *developing self-regulating learners* (Part Two), and then highlighted the promise of SRL–supportive environments and practices for *meeting the needs of diverse learners*, *motivating* and *engaging learners*, and *empowering 21st-century learning* (Part Three). We hope that by engaging with the material in this book you have constructed a rich understanding about the dimensions of self-regulated learning and how to support it in classrooms.

In this epilogue, we invite you to consider what you will do next to bring these ideas to life in the contexts in which you are living and working. Has our description of SRL mapped well onto what you see learners doing in your formal or informal learning contexts? Are there goals you have identified through this book that you might take up, for yourself or for your students? Have the activities, vignettes, or food-for-thought features inspired you to imagine new ways of teaching or learning? Have the different planning tools we offered in Chapters 4, 5, 7, 8, and 9 provided useful frameworks for thinking through how you might design SRL–supportive environments and practices? Building from all this material, what might you do now, if you are interested in taking action based on what you have been reading and thinking?

> What might you do now if you are interested in taking action based on what you have been reading and thinking?

ENGAGING IN PROFESSIONAL LEARNING AND INQUIRY

In our introduction, we suggested you consider taking up an inquiry stance as you engaged with the material in this book. We certainly hope this book will serve as a valuable resource to any educator wishing to learn more about how to nurture the development of self-regulating learners. But we also deliberately designed this book for individuals or teams of teachers engaged in *inquiry* with the goal of developing SRL–promoting policies and practices in their particular contexts.

We all know that it is hard to sustain the excitement generated when we encounter new, productive ideas once we hit the realities of classrooms, with all the attending time crunches, competing priorities, and glitches that come along with trying something new. An inquiry-based approach, especially when taken up collaboratively with colleagues, is ideal for building new practices over time and through the inevitable obstacles and challenges that arise. When teachers engage in collaborative inquiry, they are more likely to develop and implement understandings and practices that make a difference in classrooms (Ball, 1995; Borko, 2004; Cochran-Smith & Lytle, 2009). Inquiry-based professional development also helps educators make dynamic connections among the ideas derived from theory, research, policy, and practice (see Butler & Schnellert, 2012; Halbert & Kaser, 2013; Schnellert & Butler, 2014; Timperley, 2008, 2011). Teachers engaged in collaborative inquiry are and feel empowered to make a difference for students (e.g., see Butler, Schnellert, & MacNeil, 2015).

What does inquiry look like? In our introduction, we described the model of inquiry Judy Halbert and Linda Kaser put forward (2013). In their model, educators engage in dynamic, iterative cycles of inquiry by *scanning* their current context to identify pressing questions, challenges, or goals; *focusing* attention on key priorities; *developing a hunch* about what might be happening; engaging in *new professional learning* to inform their thinking, learning, and practice development; *taking action* based on what they are learning; and then reflectively *checking* on what happens and refining inquiry questions and processes based on successes and challenges (see Figure I-1). As a way forward, we encourage you to consider engaging in these processes to structure and sustain your on-going professional learning.

The SRL planning tools we have provided through this book also are designed to inspire and support your engagement in reflective cycles of inquiry. For example, you can use SRL Planning Tool 4-1 whenever you want to scan for SRL, develop a hunch about what is going on, and/or decide where to focus your practice or learning. We offer SRL Planning Tools 7-1, 8-1, and 9-1 to help you in planning for how you might take action by designing activities, supports, and assessments/feedback in order to foster active learning and SRL. You can use SRL Planning Tool 5-1 whenever you want to systematically try out ideas, monitor, and reflect on what's working, and refine your thinking, learning, or practices based on what you are seeing. You can also adapt our tools or develop a different approach to setting goals, planning, tracking, and refining your efforts, based on where you are in your professional practice and learning.

> Teachers engaged in collaborative inquiry are and feel empowered to make a difference for students.

FOSTERING SRL IN CLASSROOMS

Whether or not you choose to engage in inquiry-based professional learning, we hope that this book will serve as a resource for you to inform your thinking, learning, and practice about SRL in your own work with learners. Our observation is that, when armed with information about SRL, teachers at all stages of their career can design and take up SRL–supportive practices in ways that make an important difference for students.

For example, in her research, Nancy Perry has documented how early career teachers, including those in preservice programs, can learn to design and implement SRL–supportive practices in classrooms (see Perry, Hutchinson, & Thauberger, 2007, 2008; Perry, Phillips, & Hutchinson, 2006). With our colleagues, all three of us have documented how practising teachers can learn how to build and situate SRL–promoting practices into the contexts in which they are working (see Butler, Novak Lauscher, Jarvis-Selinger, & Beckingham, 2004; Butler & Schnellert, 2012; Cartier, Butler, & Bouchard, 2010; Perry & VandeKamp, 2000; Perry, VandeKamp, Mercer, & Nordby, 2002; Schnellert, 2011; Schnellert, Butler, & Higginson, 2008). As a result, teachers observe important gains in their students' learning and SRL (e.g., see Butler, Schnellert, & Cartier, 2013).

Through this book, we have offered explanations, figures, exercises, vignettes, and planning tools, built from over 20 years of collaborative work with many educators across grade levels, to help *you* in seeing and supporting SRL. We invite you to draw on these resources dynamically as you continue to imagine how you can foster the development of self-regulating learners in your context.

CONCLUDING COMMENTS

We wrote this book because we believe that by fostering SRL we can empower all learners in today's schools to feel and be successful to the best of their abilities. We also wrote this book because we are strongly committed to mobilizing what we know about SRL and its foundational role in learners' productive and generative engagement in learning. As you have been working with the material we have presented here, we hope you too have started to witness SRL *as a powerful way of navigating* activities both within and outside of schools. As educators, we have a crucial role to play in enabling our students' success in and beyond school, now and through their lifetimes. Ensuring their success demands that we, as educators, nurture their development as empowered, reflective, self-regulating, life-long learners.

Recommended Resources

Ball, D. L. (1995). Blurring the boundaries of research and practice. *Remedial and Special Education, 16*(6), 354–363.

Borko, H. (2004). Professional development and teacher learning: Mapping the terrain. *Educational Researcher, 33*(8), 3–15.

Butler, D. L., Novak Lauscher, H. J., Jarvis-Selinger, S., & Beckingham, B. (2004). Collaboration and self-regulation in teachers' professional development. *Teaching and Teacher Education, 20*, 435–455.

Butler, D. L., & Schnellert, L. (2012). Collaborative inquiry in teacher professional development. *Teaching and Teacher Education, 28*, 1206–1220.

Butler, D. L., Schnellert, L., & Cartier, S. C. (2013). Layers of self- and co-regulation: Teachers' co-regulating learning and practice to foster students' self-regulated learning through reading. *Education Research International*. DOI:10.1155/2013/845694

Butler, D. L., Schnellert, L., & MacNeil, K. (2014, online; 2015, in print). Collaborative inquiry and distributed agency in educational change: A case study of a multi-level community of inquiry. *Journal of Educational Change, 16*(1), 1–26.

Cartier, S. C., Butler, D. L., & Bouchard, N. (2010). Teachers working together to foster self-regulated learning through reading by students in an elementary school located in a disadvantaged area. *Psychological Test and Assessment Modeling, 52*, 382–418.

Cochran-Smith, M., & Lytle, S. L. (2009). *Inquiry as stance: Practitioner research in the next generation.* New York: Teachers College Press.

Halbert, J., & Kaser, L. (2013). *Spirals of inquiry for equity and quality.* British Columbia (BC): BC Principals' and Vice Principals' Association.

Perry, N. E., Hutchinson, L., & Thauberger, C. (2007). Mentoring student teachers to design and implement literacy tasks that support self-regulated reading and writing. *Reading & Writing Quarterly, 23*(1), 27–50.

Perry, N. E., Hutchinson, L., & Thauberger, C. (2008). Talking about teaching self-regulated learning: Scaffolding student teachers' development and use of practices that promote self-regulated learning. *International Journal of Educational Research, 47*(2), 97–108.

Perry, N. E., Phillips, L., & Hutchinson, L. (2006). Mentoring student teachers to support self-regulated learning. *The Elementary School Journal, 106*(3), 237–254.

Perry, N. E., & VandeKamp, K. O. (2000). Creating classroom contexts that support young children's development of self-regulated learning. *International Journal of Educational Research, 33*, 821–843.

Perry, N. E., VandeKamp, K. O., Mercer, L. K., & Nordby, C. J. (2002). Investigating teacher-student interactions that foster self-regulated learning. *Educational Psychologist, 37*, 5–15.

Schnellert, L. (2011). Collaborative inquiry: Teacher professional development as situated, responsive co-construction of practice and learning. (Doctoral dissertation). Retrieved from https://circle.ubc.ca/handle/2429/38245.

Schnellert, L., & Butler, D. L. (2014). Collaborative inquiry for teacher development. *Education Canada.* Available at http://www.cea-ace.ca/education-canada/article/collaborative-inquiry.

Schnellert, L., Butler, D. L., & Higginson, S. (2008). Co-constructors of data, co-constructors of meaning: Teacher professional development in an age of accountability. *Teaching and Teacher Education, 24*(3), 725–750.

Timperley, H. (2008). Teacher professional learning and development. Educational Practice Series–18. Netherlands: International Academy of Education/International Bureau of Education. Retrieved Dec 29, 2013, from http://unesdoc.unesco.org/images/0017/001791/179161e.pdf

Timperley, H. (2011). *Realizing the power of professional learning.* New York: Open University Press.

Developing Self-Regulating Learners List of Definitions

Preface

Inquiry processes in teachers' professional learning involve iterative cycles of strategic action and involve scanning, focusing, developing a hunch, engaging in new professional learning, taking action, checking on what happens, and then refining questions and inquiry processes as needed.

Chapter 1

Cognition refers to how individuals think while engaged in activities, such as reading a textbook, writing, planning a route to get from A to B, or gathering thoughts for a presentation.

Co-regulation involves giving and receiving support that is instrumental to the development of effective forms of self-regulation.

Emotion refers to individuals' affective responses when presented with or engaged in an activity (e.g., stress, excitement, pride, anger, frustration).

Metacognition refers to individuals' knowledge *about* and *orchestration of* cognition.

Metacognitive knowledge is reflected in the understandings individuals bring to activities about learning and about themselves as learners.

Motivation is a broad term used to describe what drives individuals' willingness to invest and engage in activities.

Self-regulated learning (SRL) unfolds within activities when individuals are focused on deliberately self-regulating their *learning*.

Self-regulation refers to the ability to control thoughts and actions to achieve personal goals and respond to environmental demands. It is a term that is broadly applicable and can be used to describe an individual's engagement in any sort of activity.

Socially responsible self-regulation occurs when individuals self-regulate in prosocial and socially competent ways to achieve personal success or foster success in others.

Socially shared regulation occurs during collaborative activities, when two or more individuals engage together in an activity by co-constructing understandings about tasks and pooling their respective resources to achieve goals.

Strategic action is iterative and includes dynamic cycles of interpreting tasks and setting goals, planning, enacting strategies, monitoring, and adjusting.

Chapter 3

Cognitive flexibility refers to executive function processes associated with thinking flexibly and adaptively during learning and performance.

Complex executive functions include higher-level thinking and learning processes, such as critical thinking, problem solving, creativity, and reasoning.

Control processes are executive function processes involved in the top-down control of action, such as prioritizing, goal setting, planning, coordinating thinking and action, and self-monitoring.

Executive functioning is an umbrella term used by many researchers and educators to describe the "cognitive control functions" supported by the brain's prefrontal cortex. These are the processes we rely on to engage in goal-directed thinking and behaviour.

Inhibitory control refers to executive function processes associated with controlling attention, resisting distractions, and inhibiting irrelevant actions.

Social-emotional competence reflects competencies needed to successfully navigate social and emotional aspects of activities and environments. These include self-awareness; social awareness; relationship skills; self-management of one's emotions, thoughts, and behaviours; and responsible decision-making.

Social-emotional learning (SEL) encompasses the processes associated with building social-emotional competence.

Working memory refers to executive function processes associated with holding information in mind and working with that information.

Chapter 4

21st-century learning refers to a constellation of knowledge and competencies required to thrive in today's rapidly evolving, information-rich societies. These include lifelong learning and self-direction, critical thinking and problem solving, communication, creativity and innovation, collaboration, social responsibility, and leadership, as well as technological literacy.

Adaptive expertise involves applying knowledge and skills flexibly and adaptively as needed in any given situation.

Fixed mindsets reflect individuals' beliefs that ability is stable, so there isn't much point in trying hard to improve it.

Growth mindsets reflect individuals' beliefs that ability can grow through effort and persistence.

Mindsets reflect individuals' beliefs about their abilities and whether or not they can grow through experience, effort, or persistence.

Self-determination as a goal defined in the special education literature refers to a combination of skills, knowledge, and beliefs that enable a person to engage in goal-directed, self-regulated behavior. These include capacities to make decisions and solve problems; knowledge skills, and strategies needed to manage one's own performance; self-awareness and self-advocacy; and beliefs in one's capacities to succeed.

Chapter 5

Classroom routines are predictable, routinized ways for participating in learning environments and activities.

Community of learners is created in learning environments when all members are engaged together in working with big ideas; all individuals are valued, recognized, and accepted for their various strengths and challenges, diverse interests and needs are accommodated, and peer-to-peer co-learning is fostered.

Participation structures define expectations and norms of engagement for different kinds of activities; for example, how students should interact and learn with one another, direct their attention, organize their work, ask permission to use the washroom, or ask for help.

Chapter 6

Action learning occurs when students have a hand in deciding goals, planning, and activity organization in partnership with teachers.

Experiential learning affords students the most freedom to set goals and approach learning activities in light of their interests and motivation.

Guided learning occurs when teachers are primarily responsible for defining learning goals, processes, and assessment practices.

Self-efficacy refers to individuals' beliefs in their capacity to achieve particular goals in a particular situation.

Zones of proximal development refer to the space between what students can accomplish on their own and what they can do with guidance or support.

Chapter 7

Activities are coherent sets of experiences assembled by educators to support students' learning. Each requires action on the part of learners.

Complex activities extend over time and include enough depth and variety to enable students to engage in rich forms of SRL.

Fixed mindsets reflect individuals' beliefs that ability is stable, so there isn't much point in trying hard to improve it.

Growth mindsets reflect individuals' beliefs that ability can grow through effort and persistence.

Chapter 8

Procedural facilitators are tools (e.g., graphic organizers) that educators can use to cue particular thinking or learning processes.

Scaffolds are supports that cue and guide learners' engagement in effective forms of SRL (e.g., by instructing, modelling, or guiding).

Social forms of regulation occur when individuals' engagement in activities or environments is socially influenced or interactive. They include *co-regulation*, *socially shared regulation*, and *socially responsible self-regulation*.

Strategic questions direct learners' attention to thinking and learning processes while they are engaged in activities. They compel students to think about how they are learning and why.

Chapter 9

Assessment for learning includes practices that teachers and their students can use to generate information important to guiding both *educators*, in their teaching, and *students*, in their learning.

Feedback is information about performance generated by teachers, peers, or students themselves that is fed back to learners to give them a sense of progress and inform further action and learning.

Chapter 10

Social stories help students learn how to navigate expectations, environments, and activities more successfully. They do this by providing a written or visual guide that helps students interpret important social cues, recognize their own reactions and others' perspectives, engage in action appropriate to a particular situation, and link action to hoped-for-outcomes.

Chapter 11

Autonomous forms of motivation can be intrinsic or extrinsic. In either case, they reflect the extent to which individuals perceive that they have control over their thoughts and actions (i.e., whether they are willingly chosen).

Causal attributions are the causal explanations one gives for outcomes (e.g., success or failure). They can vary in terms of the locus of origin (e.g., internal or external), stability (e.g., changeable or enduring), and control (e.g., within one's control or not).

Epistemological beliefs reflect individuals' assumptions about the nature of knowledge and how it is developed or learned (e.g., learning is "easy" or "hard," knowledge is given or constructed).

Extrinsic motivation is taken up when actions are instrumental to achieving goals. Extrinsic motivations can vary in locus of control (e.g., from compliance with external demands to taking up goals and actions aligned with one's sense of self).

Fixed mindsets reflect individuals' beliefs that ability is stable, so there isn't much point in trying hard to improve it.

Goal orientations reflect the purposes students implicitly pursue in activities.

Growth mindsets reflect individuals' beliefs that ability can grow through effort and persistence.

Interest refers to individuals' disposition to engage or re-engage with different kinds of objects, activities, or ideas.

Intrinsic motivation is grounded in one's interests in and enjoyment of an activity for its own sake.

Learning (or mastery) goals focus on advancing one's development and learning. They focus on personal progress and are associated with an *incremental* view of ability (i.e., as changeable).

Outcome expectations are individuals' perceptions of what are likely outcomes, given their skills, characteristics, and competencies.

Performance goals focus on either gaining positive, or avoiding negative, judgments of one's competence by others. They are associated with *entity views* of ability (i.e., as fixed).

Self-efficacy refers to individuals' beliefs in their capacity to achieve particular goals in a particular situation.

Task value refers to an individual's perceptions of the worth of a task given its intrinsic or personal value, importance, usefulness, and relative cost.

Chapter 12

Agency refers to individuals' capacities to exercise control over their thoughts and actions in a particular situation.

Basic psychological needs, according to self-determination theory, include needs for competence, belonging, and autonomy. Individuals can only be fully self-determining to the extent that these three basic psychological needs are fulfilled.

Index

Page numbers followed by "*b*" and "*f*" indicate boxes and figures respectively; and those followed by "*t*" indicate table.